'An excellent, lucid journey in... ... ...with insight'
Ian Herbert, *Independent*

'A top-class book . . . If you enjoyed *Secret Diary of a Liverpool Scout*, you'll like this one even more' Tony Barrett, *The Times*

'The revelations, insights and tales simply keep coming in *Red Machine* . . . told with wonderful clarity and compassion. It is a joy to read, a masterpiece in nostalgia, and a must for anyone who wants to remember a time when football, and Liverpool Football Club in particular, was littered with people with a story to tell' *The Anfield Wrap*

'Throughout the book there are common themes; threads that link each player with the rest. One of them is the heavy drinking culture which, largely because of the times we now live in, seems quite shocking. Another is the "banter", that in truth verged on bullying, that went on in the dressing room' *Tomkins Times*

'These individual stories are about honesty with a very big capital H. Readers will be thrilled to learn so much more about the life of a professional footballer at a big and successful club' *LFCHistory*

'It was a decade of unprecedented success. During the 1980s Liverpool Football Club won six league titles, two European Cups, two FA Cups and four League Cups. In the excellent new book *Red Machine* author Simon Hughes interviews many of the characters who contributed to those glorious triumphs. The stories told provide a fascinating insight into life at Anfield in the 80s' *Liverpool Echo*

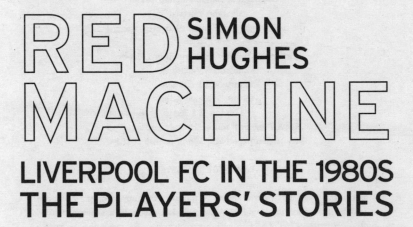

RED MACHINE

SIMON HUGHES

LIVERPOOL FC IN THE 1980S
THE PLAYERS' STORIES

MAINSTREAM PUBLISHING

EDINBURGH AND LONDON

First published in Great Britain in 2013 by
Mainstream Publishing
Transworld Publishers
61–63 Uxbridge Road
London W5 5SA
A Penguin Random House company
Mainstream paperback edition published 2014

ISBN 9781780576916

A catalogue record for this book is available
from the British Library

Printed in Great Britain by
CPI Group (UK) Ltd, Croydon CR0 4YY

1 3 5 7 9 10 8 6 4 2

In memory of Susan Hughes

ACKNOWLEDGEMENTS

THIS BOOK WOULD HAVE BEEN A LOT MORE DIFFICULT TO COMPLETE without the contributions of many good people. They include: Ian Collins (for the title), James Purcell (creative design), Mark Gilbertson (good old friendship), Matthew Keenan (being an Evertonian), Andrew Taylor (also a Blue), Paul Wright (another Blue), Andrew Howie (encouragement), William Le Marinel (machismo), Colin Grogan (humour), John Williams (maturity), John McDermott (spelling and grammar), Peter Hughes (financial support) and, most of all, Rosalind McDermott (understanding, love and beauty).

I would also like to thank some outstanding professionals: David Luxton, Bill Campbell, Graeme Blaikie, Ailsa Bathgate, Tony Barrett, Neil Haines, Mark Platt, Ian Herbert, Chris Bascombe, Ged Rea, David Cottrell, Steven Gerrard and those kind folk at Cult Zeros.

Lastly, I acknowledge the help of the footballers who feature in the pages that follow. Without their efforts and stories, it would have been impossible.

Simon Hughes

CONTENTS

FOREWORD

MY EARLIEST FOOTBALL MEMORIES ARE DOMINATED BY COLOUR. I was born in 1980, and when I think of Liverpool in the decade that followed, reds, whites, yellows and greys enter my mind.

The memories are imprinted indelibly from the kits bought for me, the first of which arrived when I was five years old. My mum returned home from a shopping spree in Huyton village with a special box. It included a replica jersey that sparkled; decorated with Crown Paints across the front. Every year, my main Christmas present from then on would be a Liverpool shirt. I had all of them.

There is also the colour green. My first live game at Anfield was against Coventry City. It was in the League Cup, Liverpool won 3–1 and Jan Mølby scored three penalties – a record at the time. I remember the click of the turnstile, the smell of hotdogs and Bovril, the large groups of people and the claustrophobia attached to that. The roar of the Kop and the movement was scary. I was thinking how fortunate I was sitting in the comfort of the old Kemlyn Road.

Most vividly, though, I remember walking through the bowels of the stand, up the ten or so steps, and then seeing the pitch. Its radiance under the floodlights nearly blinded me. I'd never seen a surface like it before. It was emerald, brighter and bigger than when I'd seen it on the TV – the perfect place to play a football match. I'll never forget the adrenalin still coursing through my body when I got home. It was something I wanted more of.

When I first started playing football in the street, there was an even number of Liverpudlians and Evertonians. My dad was always trying to get the point across that Liverpool were the team to support. There was also the influence of my uncles, who were dying to get one over on my dad by encouraging me to support Everton.

It was a great time to be a Merseysider, with the clubs dominating English football and playing with a style and swagger. Both teams held the top two positions and, reliably, either one would appear in the FA Cup final. In terms of football, it was an era of unparalleled success for the city.

The real clincher for me was the '86 cup final when Liverpool fell behind to Everton. After a goal by Gary Lineker, my allegiance swayed towards Liverpool, and when Ian Rush scored the third to secure a 3–1 win, smashing a BBC camera in the corner of the net because of the ferocity of his shot, that was the moment I knew I was going to be a Liverpudlian for the rest of my life, 100 per cent.

Within 12 months, the club had signed John Barnes, Peter Beardsley and John Aldridge; three totally different players that when brought together were lethal. I often hear people now claim that certain players are 'typical Liverpool players'. There is an element of truth in that conviction but only in the sense that 'a typical Liverpool player' is someone who doesn't take defeat easily. Technical, tactical and physical ability comes into it but what carries you over the line is a tough mental strength. Barnes, Beardsley and Aldridge had all of those assets.

As I was growing up, I didn't know much about the character or backgrounds of the players, nor, indeed, their personal stories. Football didn't really have that kind of coverage back then. My knowledge about a footballer came from watching the matches live at Anfield or on TV. If the games weren't live, my dad would put the radio on. I'd be playing in the house subconsciously; my understanding of these players and their abilities would develop. On the radio, you'd regularly hear the same names: Barnes, Beardsley, Aldridge and latterly, upon his return to the club, Rush.

FOREWORD

I loved Barnes, though. His style summed up Liverpool. The team passed the ball with such speed and precision. They were mesmerising to watch. The thing I now admire most is the way each player grasped the responsibility to try to help the club progress. That's what I've tried to bring into my game and, as captain, instil it in the players around me. When you're a Liverpool player, because of the success that's gone before, you have a duty to carry that history on.

I made my first-team debut for Liverpool in 1998. Having grown up in Liverpool and been through its youth system, I knew what I was letting myself in for. By then, Liverpool hadn't won a league title in eight years. Unfortunately, that record still stands 15 seasons later. There is a pressure attached to that. All of the players coming into the club from elsewhere should know that, despite the lack of league titles, an expectation remains to be right at the very top. It's difficult to deal with, but the players that haven't survived here haven't been able to handle the fact.

When I speak to players from the '80s and before that era, what always strikes me is how a healthy social scene founded strong dressing-rooms. It really used to help Liverpool. Today, we try to get close to that, but it's a lot more difficult for a number of reasons: with the different nationalities and cultures, the size of squads and the number of games in quick succession. There are seldom times throughout a season to genuinely unwind.

Liverpool's success in my eyes, however, was founded very simply on the standard of players mixed with the mentality. It wasn't down to one thing; it was a number of boxes being ticked at the same time. Ian Rush scored more goals than any striker in European football, and when you add that to a steely defence that could play as well, you've got yourself a team. In addition, there was the noise and intimidation of the Kop. Everybody at the club was pulling in the same direction.

When those elements collide, you know you're onto a winner.

Steven Gerrard

INTRODUCTION

It was the most glorious and turbulent decade inside the most successful English football club. These pages are about those on the pitch, who performed the most significant role: the players.

THE IDEA FOR THIS BOOK WAS INITIALLY BORN OUT OF PERSONAL frustration. Few of the active footballers that I have met since starting a career in journalism have anything that is genuinely interesting to say. Steven Gerrard, who contributes a foreword in the passage that precedes this introduction, is one of few exceptions.

There is a perception today that it is only by speaking to or, if you are lucky, getting to know a footballer that you can establish a true picture of the factors that influence the game. Most of the time, though, a player will only say what his employers, or maybe the fans, want to hear. 'Hey, I love the club' or 'We all have to stick together.' Such sound bites are often met with comfortable applause.

Football is now a business. This has a consequence. The schools of excellence that were opened at many clubs at the start of the '90s were superseded by academy systems. At Liverpool, for instance, the intake now begins with children aged five. Such is the focus on reaching the top that youngsters are actively discouraged from developing interests outside the game. As a result, life experiences and the opinions that stem from them are muted.

Retired players, however – those from a different era – have a very different personal landscape. All of the people interviewed in this book were polite and more generous with their time than necessary. Most current footballers, particularly young ones, like to project the image that they can take on the world, as if they are somehow invulnerable. Yet these players were bracingly candid and generally comfortable enough to admit their own weaknesses.

I find it interesting how players are remembered and now perceived by those who were once their contemporaries. Michael Robinson, for example, struggled to fit into the team and social structure at Anfield after joining from Brighton in 1983. Aside from Graeme Souness, he had few allies and left for Queens Park Rangers within 18 months. Yet now, Robinson lives an enriching life just north of Madrid with his long-term wife and two dogs on a luxury golfing retreat, having launched a successful career in Spanish television. Today, he is as recognisable on the street as any of the World Cup winners that have represented the country's national football team.

I later met John Barnes, one of the most revered players in Liverpool's entire history. You would think that his achievements in football would have served him handsomely after retirement. Instead, I found him to be frustrated and unfulfilled in a career sense. His brilliance on the football pitch has not afforded him subsequent opportunities within the game.

In writing this book, there have been some enjoyable occasions: getting half-cut with Bruce Grobbelaar inside a Liverpool watering hole or getting fully cut with Robinson over a late lunch, early evening, late evening and eventually early morning in Madrid.

Listening back to those interviews, the conversation is relaxed and friendly, but the setting helps most. They all took place away from the anterooms that pass for padded cells inside clubs' training grounds, and without the ominous presence of a media officer lurking beyond the door.

The game itself remains fundamentally similar, but what surrounds football has changed beyond recognition since the

1980s. This was long before Rupert Murdoch decided to flog satellite dishes off the back of football coverage; long before red-top newspapers demanded matches to be soap operas, where attractive and controversial figures would secure the emblazonment of their names in the sport as well as the news headlines; and long before Sky Sports saw fit to rant about the awarding of a throw-in as if it was some kind of human-rights atrocity in East Timor.

Football was unpolished and unpackaged. Match-attendance figures would suggest it was also unpopular. There were no all-seater stadiums, no executive boxes filled by suits, canapés and Veuve Clicquot; and no disproportionate number of Louis Vuitton man-bags hanging on the hooks inside dressing-rooms.

At the start of the decade, shirts didn't have a sponsor on them, shorts were hoisted and tight, and wooden advertising hoardings around Anfield were limited to the Ian Skelly car dealership and Wonderfuel Gas. Footballers, meanwhile, often dressed in attire akin to a cast of refugees from a bogus space movie.

As a child of the '80s, I appreciated that, psychologically, Liverpool Football Club had regularly won the title by mid-November. Like Steven Gerrard, my first game at Anfield was against Coventry City not too far into the season. I was aware fully that Liverpool were leading the table and despite the best efforts of those chasing it was a pointless pursuit. When other clubs were in the rear-view mirror, Liverpool were soon out of sight.

Even though they dominated the English game, winning six league titles, two European Cups, two FA Cups and four League Cups, Liverpool were behind the times commercially, and, aside from a kit deal with adidas in 1985, efforts to capitalise on a growing worldwide appeal amounted to the sale at the Heritage Market in Stanley Dock of those grey-and-red replica bench coats made famous by Kenny Dalglish and Ronnie Moran.

Players did not pay agents exorbitant fees to order kitchen fridges for them, and clubs in England offered modest wages.

When Liverpool's all-time leading scorer, Ian Rush, left Anfield for Juventus, he earned a reported basic £900 a week, though this didn't include his goals bonus.

Although outsiders only saw the primary-coloured tracksuit, off the field Merseyside positioned itself as the vanguard of casual culture. Inside Anfield, decent views of its prim surface and team wearing pinstripes (that kit really was the business) were impeded by wrought-iron fences topped with mace-like spikes on the Kop and Annie Road, preventing intrusion onto the pitch or, daringly, the away section, where travelling fans stood expelled like a colony of lepers. Or worse – Mancunians.

Occasionally, attitudes on the terraces were cruel and narrow-minded. Barnes, after becoming the first high-profile black player to sign from another club, took months to win over sections of the crowd. A relative told me the story about an old fella that used to stand in front of him. 'That nigger's not bad after all,' he commented after Barnes scored his second in a 4–0 win over Queens Park Rangers.

Liverpool is the most vibrant and independent of England's provincial cities, a place of legend – apart from the rest. But Liverpool then was not the place of resplendent riverside apartment blocks, fancy restaurants and all-you-can-need shopping centres it is now. The Albert Dock was derelict; industrial factories were inhabited by rodents and dust instead of workers; the parks of Sefton and Princes had more tramps than bohemian types.

The '80s began with a global recession. The upheaval in the British economy brought the highest levels of unemployment since the Great Depression. One in every four adults across Liverpool was without a job and the city was rarely out of the news.

These were Militant years. The Labour Party seized control of Liverpool City Council from a whimsical Liberal–Tory coalition with a narrow majority. Its ruling group was from the hard-line left, led by Derek Hatton. Liverpool became synonymous with political discord. Hatton stood up to Margaret Thatcher's

Conservative government. Yet Liverpool's reputation was acidic. Thousands left the city to look for work but were met in other cities with a barricade of intolerance. All Scousers were charlatans and parasites, leaching off state benefits. Apparently.

That media image of Merseyside was of dilapidation, vandalism and idle, ale-swilling workers controlled by Marxists determined to achieve self-obliteration and total mayhem. More businesses were closing than were opening, and in some areas youth unemployment reached 90 per cent. On returning to the city in 1984, then *Daily Mirror* journalist Anne Robinson produced a report on the decay of the city. 'Talking to ordinary people on the street is like interviewing the recently bereaved,' she wrote.

In the '60s, Liverpool had been the second cultural capital of the country, if not the first. Merseybeat had boomed. American poet Allen Ginsberg said, 'Liverpool is at the present moment the center of modern consciousness of the human universe.' By 1985, its population had fallen by a third. In the Thatcher years alone, 65,000 jobs were lost, the majority of them in the docks and manufacturing as trade turned away from the Atlantic and towards Europe instead. Liverpool wasn't the only city affected, but it became a representation of the deprived north, probably because it had further to fall.

Comedian Arthur Askey once said, 'Liverpool is a city full of comedians . . . you've got to be a comedian to live there.' For long a place that could laugh at itself, now it was the outsiders making fun at Liverpool's expense. 'What do you call a Scouser in a suit?' teased one joke. 'The accused.' Yorkshire-born playwright Alan Bennett referred to Liverpool as 'that sentimental, self-dramatising place'. At football matches, opposing fans sang 'You'll never get a job' to the tune of 'You'll Never Walk Alone'.

Such taunts were partly made out of jealousy: a tribute to the overwhelming achievements of both Liverpool and Everton Football Clubs, who between them won the First Division championship every year from 1982 to 1988. Socially, the '80s may have been a desperate period. But for Liverpool's football clubs, in terms of silverware, it could not have been any better.

RED MACHINE

This book isn't intended to be a comprehensive account of what happened in the decade on or off the pitch at Liverpool. Instead, it focuses on the characters of the players and their stories. Some performed a significant role in the club's history while the contribution of others was comparatively minor. But they all played a part.

Most importantly, this book seeks to answer a question frequently posed when supporters gather for a post-match pint: where have all the characters in football – or more precisely from Liverpool – disappeared to?

CHAPTER ONE

Cult Zeros

BUSH FIGHTER, Bruce Grobbelaar

BRUCE GROBBELAAR NODS EARNESTLY AND BEGINS. 'I CAN TELL YOU this because it's history and we both laugh about it,' says the now 55 year old, who won more medals during his time at Liverpool than any other goalkeeper in the club's history. 'I broke Steve McMahon's nose twice in one night.'

The Reds had eased to a 4–0 friendly win over Dundee in the October of 1987. There was a party at Royal St Andrews, overlooking the golf course. 'We were all having a pint afterwards and Steve got into a disagreement with Barry Venison. All of the Dundee players wanted to get involved, so I pulled the pair of them to one side.'

McMahon's ire turned towards Grobbelaar.

'Steve blew his top and swung a punch at me,' the Zimbabwean continues. 'So I head-butted him and bust his nose. He whinged to Kenny [Dalglish] and the boss tried to blame me. But the receptionist of the hotel confirmed that Steve was the aggressor.'

Grobbelaar roomed with Craig Johnston.

'The attitude from the decision makers was probably "Let's put the two freaks together." Craig was very temperamental and steadfast in his opinion. He was a constant moaner. After the fight, he refused to room with me.

'"You know these Scousers," he said. "Macca will try to get into our room and attack you."

'He must have been desperate because he moved in with Steve Nicol for the night. Nobody ever wanted to room with Stevie because he was a bloody nightmare. All he did was eat crisps and talk.'

At 3.20 a.m. Grobbelaar was awoken by somebody knocking a lampshade outside his door.

'I hid behind the door in the bathroom and watched the person creep in. Craig was right in his prediction – he was canny like that. I tapped Macca on the shoulder and smacked him across the nose for the second time in the night. He never messed with me again.'

Grobbelaar, with his penetrating gaze, earring, handlebar moustache and peculiar accent, bursts into unruly laughter at the story's end with all the intensity of Jack Nicholson's character in *The Shining*. Sitting there with a Peroni and wearing an unprepossessing suit, he contemplates his vertiginous rise from the troubled land of Rhodesia – a rise that is normally the preserve of Hollywood parables. For someone who endures a reputation as a jovial individual, his tale from the start is notably a dark one.

'It is very true that my story is different to a lot of other footballers,' he reflects, reaching for his beer with a right hand that could pass for a hydraulic press. 'You couldn't compare it to a Hollywood story, though. No, no. In Hollywood, when you've made it to the top – you're there for life. In the UK, people look for a way to try to knock you down.'

Speaking to Grobbelaar for just a few minutes would remind any supporter that being a Liverpool player isn't always as wonderful as it is sometimes portrayed. 'When the times are good, it's a bed of roses,' Jamie Carragher once told me. 'But when times are tough, it becomes a bed of thorns.'

'People think that because I was at Liverpool for such a long time – in a period where the club was very successful – that it was bliss all the way through,' Grobbelaar says. 'But at the start, because of poor performances, I received death threats. I played for the club through two stadium disasters then later was falsely accused of fixing matches. I loved my time there, but it would be a lie to say it was always a walk in the park.'

Grobbelaar remains one of football's most distinctive characters. I meet him inside The Monro, a pub that has had more facelifts than Pete Burns and which is close to Liverpool's city centre. In the '80s, it nestled amongst forbidding, abandoned warehouses. Now, the area has been gentrified and renamed The Ropewalks – a district meant for yuppies where in reality there are more empty faceless apartments than people.

After our engagement, Grobbelaar – a natural raconteur – is spending his evening at a charity event being held at a cabaret lounge owned by Ricky Tomlinson. He's been on the after-dinner circuit intermittently since 1983. 'When I started, Bob Paisley told me, "Stop doing them – you're not a legend yet." To be fair to Bob, he was probably right. I took a lot of those kinds of things on at the time because I didn't know when my football career was going to end, so I needed to make money and support my family. Having grown up in Africa, I understood that a working man's life was precarious.'

Grobbelaar was born in Durban, South Africa, in 1957. His father, Hendrick – a Dutch Boer – took a job as a railway engineer and moved the family to rural Rhodesia when Bruce was two.

'My great-grandfathers had fought on opposite sides in the Boer War and my grandfather played the saxophone in a circus band. The surname Grobbelaar is roughly translated in English from original Dutch as "clumsy", so I think I was struggling from the start to rid myself of the clown tag that plagued me throughout my career, especially during the early days at Liverpool.'

The family soon relocated again, this time to the Rhodesian capital of Salisbury (now Harare), where they lived in the comparative luxury of a three-bedroom semi-detached house.

'There was another addition to the family by then,' Grobbelaar remembers. 'My mother, Beryl, decided to take on an African houseboy called Lummick, who acted for us as a poor man's au pair. To British people, this may seem like black slavery, but in Rhodesia it was an accepted way of life. A family's wealth was often judged by the number of houseboys they had living in what would usually be an extension built into the garage at the bottom of the garden. We had no garage in our semi-detached house and a very small garden with just one houseboy. I suppose that tells you where our family stood in terms of wealth.'

Hendrick Grobbelaar eloped with a mistress when Bruce was ten.

'My mum brought us up alone in a duplex flat. She was a single parent with three kids, including my older sister and baby brother. It was tough. She was a good bookkeeper and worked in a shoe shop. She'd often take us with her and we'd act as stock-takers – just to instil how important it was to look after your money. It was an eye opener, because I had no male role model in my childhood. If I look back now, I'd say my mother was my hero.'

In his early teens, Grobbelaar was a rebel.

'My mother was going out with this chap that I didn't like. He was a very dominant person. So one night at 11.30, I decided to escape. I jumped out of my window, climbed down the drainpipe from the third storey of a tenement block with my haversack and headed towards the main road that would take me the 175 miles towards the town where my father was. I was so desperate to get out that I took the bus, which was exclusively used for blacks, at a time when trouble in the bush was starting. I must have been completely crazy, because blacks were killing farmers and I was travelling through a farming area on a black bus. But I didn't think about that.

'I arrived at 4.30 in the morning. My stepmother answered the door and gave me a bed. Then before my dad went to work the next morning, he woke me up, took me outside and tied me to a tree before beating me with a hosepipe. He said, "Never run away from your mother again – you only have one mother." It was a harsh lesson.'

After three months, Grobbelaar returned home and resumed his education.

'I wasn't as conscientious as I should have been,' he concedes. 'My O level equivalents were mediocre, and that is mainly due to the fact that I more interested in chasing girls. It's the oldest thing in the world – men think they're invincible and can go all over the place. My father was one of those said people. I was the same. I saw how my father was with women and I followed. My sister was older and she had good-looking friends. That was when I started the chase.'

Grobbelaar regularly received the strap in school: 'As many times as it was permitted by the teachers' union – sometimes more', and was threatened with expulsion on several occasions, notably for once winking at an attractive-looking female student teacher. Most days, his mind drifted towards the fields outside where he played cricket, rugby and baseball as well as football. Later, he was offered a scholarship in America at the North Adams State College for his baseball skills. By then, though, he had aspirations to forge a career in another sport.

'The first time I touched a football was when I was a baby,' he says. 'My mother put me in a harness with elastic, almost like a bungee cord, and I'd sit down and kick the ball against a wall while she played hockey in goal for her team. I wondered why she spent so much time stopping goals rather than scoring them. I think that's why my instinct was to become a goalkeeper.'

Soon, Grobbelaar's efforts for the school team encouraged an approach from a local boys' club in Salisbury.

'Three thousand would turn up for our home games,' he recalls. 'All of the players were white, and whenever we played the blacks they would bring busloads of people and the attendance would shoot up. When we went out to the townships, there would be more than 30,000 there.'

Racism was on every street corner, but it was something Grobbelaar only began to analyse when he started to play football competitively.

'From an early age we were taught in school that there was a fundamental difference between black people and white people – that we were superior. This view was made even more clear by the way blacks and whites went to separate schools and there were higher standards in the latter. Integration was absolutely not encouraged. This all meant that, eventually, the better jobs went to the whites, because they were educated, and the cycle perpetuated itself. I had no choice in where I was born and brought up, so the sight of Lummick and his children walking around with no possessions was normal to me. It was only later through travel and experience I learnt that this was all wrong.'

Segregation in Rhodesia was made even clearer in social situations.

'Africans were not welcomed in white bars, and though they could stay the night in certain hotels, they could not eat in the same restaurants. In cinemas, a black could show a white man to a seat but not sit in it himself. The rules on public transport followed a similar pattern.'

The biggest social problem Grobbelaar noticed in his younger days was not, however, the black and white issue.

'Most of the problems were with the coloureds,' he insists. 'They were the offspring of black and white parents – what everybody called the "half-caste" kids. There was a team in the league called Arcadia, and they were all mixed-race boys. Whenever we played them, it was a war; and whenever the black teams played them, it was even worse. Whenever the blacks played against the whites, it was a simple game of football.'

Later, Grobbelaar joined a predominantly black side called Highlanders on loan from Salisbury County.

'It made me appreciate who I was and who other people were. Just like when I jumped on the bus to travel to see my dad years before, the creed and colour of skin wasn't something I thought about. I used to ride my bike from school to the townships, and all of my white student friends thought I was nuts. Most of their parents wouldn't allow them anywhere near them, and even my mother wasn't keen at first.'

Upon signing for Highlanders, Grobbelaar was given an interesting signing-on present.

'They offered me a cow, a goat and a sheep,' he smiles. 'Then the second question was whether we wanted them alive or to collect them at the abattoir. We took the goat alive and the other two dead. My mum went with me to pick them up and for the first time genuinely started to talk with the blacks. She realised they were just as normal as us.'

Grobbelaar impressed at Highlanders. So much so that his parent club, Salisbury, decided to cash in on the teenage goalkeeper.

'They sold me to a team called Chibuku for $15,000. The money paid for a new cocktail bar at Salisbury's social club. Chibuku was a brewery side, and they gave me a job as a junior draughtsman and a sheet metal worker. I didn't like the manager of the football team, though, so after six weeks I told my mum I was coming home, with the idea of going back to South Africa to find a football team. It was fate that the day after I made the decision to leave I received a call from the army informing me that I was required for military service.'

With the Bush War raging in the provinces of Rhodesia, Grobbelaar was on patrol on the Mozambican border by the end of that month. The conflict was in its eleventh year by the time Grobbelaar became a part of it, and tensions were as high as ever.

Grobbelaar admits that he found it easier to look on the enemy as 'terrorists'.

'The terrorists hid in border countries like Zambia as well as Mozambique. They were backed by the Soviet Union and trained by North Korea, so they knew what they were doing. The motives were simple – their opposition to Ian Smith and his white government – but the situation was complex because of the sheer number of different terrorist groups. Mugabe and his ZANU PF party was one of the biggest, then there was Nkomo with the PF-ZAPU and Sithole with ZIPRA. To us, they were terrorists, but it was clear they thought of themselves as revolutionaries.'

The next two years would change Grobbelaar's outlook on life.

'How could you forget seeing many of your best friends killed? How can I forget or forgive myself for killing a fellow human being, even if it was in a war? I still have nightmares about it. Everything else in life seems insignificant compared to my years in the forces. When you've had to track terrorists down and kill them, watch people take drugs because they've gone crazy . . . when you've eaten insects because you've run out of rations . . . football is hardly a matter of life and death. If you lose in a cup final, you can still go home to your family and eat a nice meal. If war teaches you anything, it teaches you how to appreciate life and all the good things that come with it.'

At first, the prospect of death seemed a long way off.

'During bayonet training, our superiors tried to make it more serious by making us scream, "I'll kill you, you black bastard," as we stabbed the bag. It made it all feel very surreal and, personally, I thought that the worst thing I'd need a bayonet for would be to open a ration can.'

Everything changed on Christmas Day in 1975. Grobbelaar was 18 years old.

'They started mortaring us, so we had to shell-scrape bunkers for us to live in. From there, we became a mobile unit like the SAS. Some people went away to train as medics, others as snipers, drivers and bomb experts. I was a tracker.

'The war for me became evil. I thought about life. Why couldn't these people sit around a table and sort it out in a civilised way? When a prime minister [Ian Smith] comes out with a statement saying that there will never be black rule in Rhodesia – not in his lifetime or his children's lifetime – it makes you wonder how that can be morally possible. There were only one million whites in the country and more than ten million blacks. If you take the women and children out of the scenario, we were outnumbered one to three in the bush. We were sent out for slaughter. We were cannon fodder.'

Grobbelaar was ordered to kill.

'When you're eyeball to eyeball with the enemy, you know that one of you is going to die. But that doesn't make it any easier in dealing with the guilt. My time came when we were helicoptered into a village on the Mozambican border with the sole instruction of shooting anything that moved. It was a terrible scene. When we landed, the stench of the dead made a lot of guys throw up. There were charred bodies everywhere from the incendiary bombs. Within seconds, the snipers were firing on us and one of my best mates was paralysed from his waist down. One of the enemy came at me and I shot him. I felt nothing but relief at the time.

'I'm not proud of what I did in the army, but when the military tells you to do something, you have to do it. Any military person will tell you that. What I saw on both sides was horrific – the nature of war. What is happening on the borders of Pakistan and Afghanistan is no different to what happened on the borders of Rhodesia and Mozambique. Although I think it would be good for teenagers to go into the military to learn discipline, I wouldn't wish anybody to go into a combat situation when it's not your choice. I lost a lot of friends.'

Grobbelaar witnessed the outcome of a mutilation.

'One of our group was shot and killed, so his best friend lost it and started firing his machine gun up into the trees. Instantly, one of the terrorists fell to the ground, followed by another who was still alive. The episode seemed unreal – as if I wasn't there. Our man chased after the terrorist, and by the time we caught up to him he had already cut off his genitals.'

Death made the prospect of eating Mopane worms, flying beetles and snake steaks seem easy.

'To say it changed my life is an understatement. From then on, I set out to live life to the full.'

Grobbelaar was discharged from the services in 1978, having not played football for two years.

'I soon got engaged to a girl and she gave birth to a boy,' he says. 'They needed provisions and I wanted to support them. An offer came from Durban City to go and train with them with a view to signing, so I took it straight away without thinking about it. For 18 months, I sent half of the money I earned back to Bulawayo where my mum was living then to try to help her out as well.'

Grobbelaar found out the child wasn't his.

'It was my best mate's. They'd got together while I was in the Bush War. That was the end of that.'

After this, Grobbelaar, still waiting to play his first game for Durban, guested for Amazulu in a minor cup competition.

'They were the local black team, and for the tournament I was playing in the authorities encouraged multi-racial teams. Like a lot of these events, it was done for cosmetic reasons as they tried to reduce racial tensions. The chairman at Durban City didn't like me playing for a black side.'

To supplement his modest income, Grobbelaar worked in a clothes shop before becoming a car salesman with Toyota. 'The Durban fans loved me because I gave the biggest discounts in town. It meant they all came to buy their cars off me and the company made a lot of money off it.'

But the military came calling again.

'The South African army said I had six months to make up my mind whether I stayed in the country and did military service with their army in Angola or go elsewhere. They found out my record with the Rhodesian army as a tracker and felt I could be of some use to them. That's when I thought, "I've got to get out of here."'

Problems with visas and work permits meant that trials at West Brom under Ron Atkinson, or 'the Incredible Hulk' as Grobbelaar calls him, and then Derby came to nothing. Instead, he agreed to sign for Vancouver Whitecaps in the North American Soccer League.

'You must understand that after the trials my mother said, "Right – now is the time to get a proper job." She didn't believe that I would go halfway across the world just to play football. But I was helped by my now stepfather, who worked on the railways. He managed to invent a new job for me as a refrigerator mechanic – checking whether all fridges on the rolling stock were working. I did that for a week then a phone call came. I was told to pick up my tickets from the Canadian embassy and fly straight out of there.'

The plane carrying Grobbelaar touched down in Vancouver on a Saturday. After almost 24 hours of travelling, he was asked to make his debut that very evening. He played in the same team as Alan Ball, Johnny Giles and Dutch captain Ruud Krol. Yet his arrival in western Canada coincided with the end of the league season, so before he had even settled, he travelled back to the UK for a holiday with a new girlfriend.

'Her dad owned a small place up near Oban in Scotland. He gave me a job as a jack-of-all-trades. I was a barman by night and a chambermaid by day. I worked there for two months. In the end, the girl didn't become a fiancée or anything like that. I became quite wary of relationships after what happened with the previous woman . . .'

Back in Canada, Grobbelaar acted as a back-up to Phil Parkes during his first season, playing only one game. During the winter break, he was allowed to go on loan to Crewe Alexandra to maintain fitness. It was only when Parkes left Vancouver for Chicago Sting in the summer of 1980 that Grobbelaar, aged 22, became an undisputed number 1 at a professional club for the first time.

'The manager, Tony Waiters [who had a job on Liverpool's coaching staff in the early '70s], wanted players like myself and Carl Valentine [a former Oldham full-back] to stay out there and become naturalised Canadians to try to qualify for some major tournaments. It was as if he could see into the future, because in 1984 he took Canada to the Olympic Games, then two years later they played at the World Cup in Mexico. Maybe if I'd stayed in Canada I would have played in a World Cup, because we never really had a genuine chance with Zimbabwe – one of the biggest regrets in my playing career.'

Six weeks after the end of his loan spell in England, Grobbelaar was back in Canada, resuming the NASL season.

'I was in the bath after a game and Tony popped his head around the door. "Come and join me in my office," he said. "There are two people who have come to see you."

'"Let me guess," I said. "Bob Paisley and Tom Saunders from Liverpool? It's taken them a long time to find me . . ."'

Grobbelaar became aware of Liverpool's interest during his time at Crewe.

'We played a game at Portsmouth and somebody said that I was the man they wanted to see. The next weekend we were at Gresty Road and I was told that two people from Liverpool had come to watch me and left after the warm-up. To me, that indicated they thought I was shite, but as it turned out it was quite the opposite.'

Paisley, so impressed by Grobbelaar's warm-up where he not only saved but also caught every cross and shot that was fired at him, decided there and then to sign him. Instead of telling secretary Peter Robinson to fax an offer straight away, however, he dispatched a special agent from his scouting politburo to follow the goalkeeper's movements.

'For six weeks they sent a guy called Peter Dee to watch me. He was everywhere I went. I was staying at the Royal Hotel and he checked in. I'd go for a pint in the Station Pub and he'd be sitting there with his flat cap watching what I drank. Then I'd go for sausage and egg at a cafe and he'd be there again, sipping tea with his eyes raised over a newspaper. He wanted to see what I ate. Then, on a night before games, whenever I opened my door, he was in the corridor waiting to go out. Sometimes he'd even follow me into a nightclub and start dancing with some of the older ladies just to blend in. It was only after a number of weeks that I realised it was more than a coincidence that this fella seemed to be everywhere I went. Then, before I could do anything about it, because he was worrying me, he'd vanished.'

Paisley made his offer bluntly.

'Bob asked me whether I'd like to play for Liverpool. I said yes and with that he and Tom Saunders walked out of the door, straight to the airport and flew back. It was the shortest but probably the most significant conversation I've ever had.'

Six weeks passed before Grobbelaar was able to fly to England. 'That wasn't the end of the bloody story,' Grobbelaar laughs. 'When I arrived at Heathrow, I grabbed a trolley and looked for a chauffeur holding my name up. Nobody was there. So I called the club and explained the situation. "There must be some mistake." Mr Paisley answered the phone and just said, "Do you know where Manchester Victoria is?" Then he put the phone down. So I got the train from Euston and arrived there. Again, nobody was waiting for me. So I went through the same routine and this time the secretary at Anfield finished with the words, "Do you know where Liverpool is?" So I hired a car and drove. By the time I arrived in Liverpool, I had figured out that nobody was going to be there waiting. I had no idea where Anfield was, so I decided to ask a taxi driver. "Do I know where Anfield is?" he responded. "Of course I do, dickhead. Hop in." I explained that I had a car, so I followed him. By the time we got to Anfield, the gates were shut and everybody had gone home. "That'll be 10 nicker that," the taxi driver shouted. I couldn't say no, could I? I figured that he would be going straight back into town for his next fare, so I followed him again before finding the nearest pub, hoping I could find accommodation for the night. It happened to be the Beehive [on Paradise Street]. They were full up, so the landlord asked me, "Why don't you try Colditz?" He was referring to the Adelphi. So I went there but again the reception told me they were full. I turned round and there was Bob Paisley handing over a pound to Tom Saunders, uttering the words, "I never thought he'd get here."'

When Grobbelaar arrived at Anfield in April 1981, his contract was worth £450 a week, 'pittance by today's standards but decent then', and a signing-on fee of £10,000. Paisley told him that for the remainder of the season he would play in the reserves. He shared duties over the six games with Steve Ogrizovic, who was selected in the three home games. As a test, Grobbelaar was pitched into the away fixtures.

'I made my debut at Goodison Park. We won 1–0. Then in the second game we played at Bolton, and Brian Kidd was their captain. I knew him from my days in Canada, so I started shouting at him, winding him up. "Eh, Kiddy, you're getting too old for this." He was trying like a bear. We won 1–0 again.'

After keeping two clean sheets, Grobbelaar finished the season with a mistake in his third game – a 1–1 draw at Leeds United.

'I didn't panic, though,' he recalls. 'I booked a summer holiday to Hawaii with the lawyer who brokered the deal from Vancouver to Liverpool. It had been a hectic year, so I needed a break – to recharge my batteries and prepare myself for what I thought would be another season in the reserves.'

Grobbelaar was playing golf when his lawyer received a phone call from the UK.

'We were staying in some condominiums right by a golf course and the beach. He [the lawyer] went off to answer the phone, and when he came back he told me that Ray Clemence had been sold to Spurs. I teed off and put the ball in the sea before falling over. I put on a lot of weight that holiday – eating burgers and grilled fish – because I had a bit of money after signing for Liverpool and I was living the good life. It tasted sweeter knowing that I'd have a chance of becoming the club's first choice.'

Grobbelaar's first six months in the first team, however, were especially desperate.

'When I first played, I thought I was invincible. If I'm honest now, the responsibility of being Liverpool's first-choice keeper went to my head and I started to do things that no other keeper in the history of football had dared to try. I sat on the crossbar twice during a game then started walking around the 18-yard box on my hands. I had this misty-eyed idea of Liverpool supporters getting behind you, because they were known as the best supporters in the world – the kind that gave players and managers time to succeed. With me, they didn't.'

Grobbelaar was blamed for Liverpool's early exit from the European Cup in two successive seasons following gaffes against CSKA Sofia and Widzew Lodz.

'I had been at the club barely six months when I started to receive letters through the post. One man wrote to me saying he had been watching top-class football for more than 30 years and that if Tommy Smith were still Liverpool captain, he would have already broken my legs three times for the errors I made. That was one of the pleasant ones. When I arrived at Anfield every morning, there would be dozens of envelopes for me to open. One day there was a blank white piece of paper with a black hole through it. To me, that was an assassination threat.'

Grobbelaar admits that he became paranoid about the negative media comment he was receiving, particularly from the local press.

'The *Liverpool Echo* and *Daily Post* really had it in for me,' he says. 'No matter how many saves I made, they'd constantly refer to Ray Clemence and how my predecessor was much better. I became convinced that the Merseyside press didn't like me because I wasn't English.'

Two people he confided in were Phil Neal and Harry Gregg – the former Manchester United goalkeeper and his former manager during that loan spell at Crewe.

'Phil had taken a lot of criticism through playing for England during a time when results were particularly shit in the late '70s. He had won everything for Liverpool, but the press barracked him for the national team – they argued his form wasn't quite the same. Phil advised me not to read the back pages until Thursday afternoons, when the column inches were taken up by league tables and fixtures for the weekend. It got to the stage where I was buying every single newspaper to find out which journalists liked me and which didn't.'

While Neal tried to help Grobbelaar, other players in the squad distanced themselves from him.

'Souness, Hansen and Dalglish were very harsh. They'd be your best friend if you were playing well and winning. But if you made a mistake, they never spoke to you. I don't think it was a personal thing; it was just a device by the older players to sort out the stronger-minded players from the weaker ones.

If you were weak, you didn't last long. It meant that for newcomers, if they didn't start well, Melwood became a lonely place. Until I got married, there was nobody to talk to about it, so I found myself confiding in strangers while drinking at the pub. Maybe I did that too much.'

Matters reached a head after the 3–1 home defeat to Manchester City on Boxing Day.

'I blamed Phil Thompson for the first. It was my mistake for the second, which went in off the post, but I didn't know who to blame for the third. Bob dragged me in and asked me how I felt about my first few months as a Liverpool player. "It could have been better," I said. Then Bob pointed at me and replied, "Yerp y'right. And if y'don't get better, you'll find y'self back at Crewe Alexandra."'

Paisley kept faith in his goalkeeper when others probably wouldn't have.

'Bob could look at a player while he was running and tell what part of his body was injured. It meant that during games, he'd tell our wingers to take on their marker in a certain way. "The right back has a sore left leg. Take him on the outside and come in on the inside – you'll kill him." Nine times out of ten, he was right. He was a genius. The only problem with him was that nobody could understand what he said. He wasn't the clearest when it came to instructions. But I loved the man so much. Had another manager signed me, I probably would have been packed off back to where I came from after my first few months.'

Joe Fagan was different, but another person who helped Grobbelaar through the hard times.

'We called him "Smoking Joe" – he'd make everything clear. With the team around both Bob and, later, Joe, they had quite an equilibrium. Roy Evans was the peacemaker; Ronnie Moran was the tough bastard – the barking dog. You didn't want to get involved in an argument with a Rottweiler.'

Form aside, Grobbelaar was suffering from a series of personal travails. He received another letter through the post, this time from Wormwood Scrubs, the prison in London.

'It was from a fella asking me to pay his bail,' he recalls. 'He used to work on the local radio in Rhodesia and had fallen on hard times before being caught smuggling cannabis into the UK. Customs and the drug squad had vetted the letter and figured that I was Mr Big, so my house phones were tapped. They were made more suspicious when I got a call off a friend who'd moved to England from South Africa. He called and said, "Bruce, I'm not going to be over to pay my subs at the golf club – could you pay them for me?"

'I asked him which golf club. "Don't be daft, Bruce, we played at the same golf club together." So I went down to the club and there was a message to call him from there. My friend had found out that there was a police investigation and I was a part of it. "Next time you answer the phone, listen for the pause when you pick it up."

'So I did that, and as I looked out of the window I could see a suspicious-looking van waiting just down the road. I went and knocked on the window and there were two coppers sitting there.

'I went over and said to them, "If you want to listen to my phone conversations, come into my house and I'll make you a cup of tea." I had nothing to hide, and with that it all stopped. The whole experience was an eye opener towards becoming a professional at a top club.'

Life didn't get any easier. In December 1981, he was on the losing side in a 3–0 defeat to Flamengo in the Intercontinental Cup while playing for Liverpool when he found out his father, Hendrick, had died.

'I'd literally just walked off the pitch when Bob told me. He'd passed away a few days earlier, but my mother insisted that the club not tell me until after the match – it was an important match. It was very thoughtful of her. The club said that I should try to relax because they had made all of the arrangements for me to return to Africa for the funeral. Again, it was typical of the club's kind nature – they tried to help one of its people when he was down. I didn't, however, realise they were going to take the airfare out of my wages the next month.'

Grobbelaar travelled with the team as far as Paris.

'I had a lot on my mind, so I thought the best thing to do would be to take a couple of sleeping pills to send me on my way. Half an hour in, an Indian bloke shook me and asked me to move. Maybe I was blocking his view of the TV or snoring? But he wouldn't tell me why, so I told him to fuck off. An hour later, a Japanese air stewardess woke me up again and told me there had been a complaint and asked me to move. I became very angry and walked to the back of the plane cursing the Indian gentleman because I thought he'd grassed on me. Terry Mc [Dermott] was there and he'd had a few to drink. I told him my story and he was all for going back to sort the Indian fella out.'

The Indian 'fella' then turned up at the back of the plane.

'He was very apologetic and explained that he was upset because of the way I was lying – with my feet pointing at a locker above his seat which contained the figure of a Buddha. Terry didn't see his point and again he wanted to throw the fella and his Buddha off the plane and over Alaska.'

Despite experiencing so many problems during his first season, Grobbelaar finished the campaign with a set of League Cup and First Division winners' medals.

'For a long time, the defence and myself just weren't bonding on or off the pitch. There was a settled back four of Neal, Kennedy, Hansen and Lawrenson – they knew each other's job inside out. But I was the black sheep and felt responsible pretty much every time a goal went in. Eventually, our understanding together improved naturally – it wasn't forced by management or anything like that. They just gave it time.'

The title was secured ahead of Liverpool's final game of the season at Middlesbrough.

'We travelled up to Ayresome Park on a high. Terry Mc knew somebody in Middlesbrough who owned a wine bar. Bob said, "Listen, lads, have a few drinks, but be professional about it."

One drink turned into five or six, and a few hours later all the lads were bouncing about on a raised floor. Unfortunately, the floor fell in and Terry tumbled through it, injuring himself. Bob wasn't too annoyed, though. He was on the bench during the game with a tot of whisky. It wasn't even that cold. It was May.'

The summer afforded Grobbelaar time to look for a new home.

'Before I signed for Liverpool, my captain from Crewe, Bob Scott, gave me some invaluable advice. He said that if I went into digs or bought a house in Liverpool's city centre, I'd end up drinking more than George Best. He probably would have been right. So, instead, I bought a little cottage just outside Wrexham, overlooking the Minera Mountain. I installed a jacuzzi. It meant that at the start of my Liverpool career I could restrain myself if we were having a few beers because I knew that I had to drive home.'

On more than one occasion, the decision nearly backfired.

'We were due to travel abroad. There was heavy snowfall across the north-west of England and Wales. Naturally, living miles away from urban civilisation meant that I was snowed in – because people always shit themselves whenever it snows in the UK. Everything stops. I was lucky that I had a Suzuki Jeep and managed to make it to Speke Airport. By the time I got there, the weather was so bad that everywhere shut and the flight was rescheduled to go from Manchester instead. I was lucky, because just as I arrived in the car park, the Liverpool team bus was pulling away without me. Bob Paisley asked where I lived and when I told me, he said, "Get y'self a place in near the training ground. If that happens again, you're out." Liverpool were big on punctuality.'

Grobbelaar bought a house in West Derby village. Later, he moved over to Heswall.

'When Kenny was manager, he wanted us to all go and live in Southport, but I wasn't willing for the manager to come around and find that my car wasn't there before he started asking questions about what I was doing in my spare time. The Wirral was a good option because there was a spate of robberies on the houses of Liverpool and Everton players, and I figured they'd wouldn't bother going to the Wirral because they'd have to pay to get through the tunnel.'

Grobbelaar drank in the Queen Victoria pub in Heswall.

'I wouldn't say I had one particular tipple,' he says. 'I drank everything. It didn't bother me. Before I signed for Liverpool, I drank regularly, but once at the club you had to drink more to become a part of the social scene, otherwise you could easily become an outcast.

'Everybody started to believe in me by the second season and this in no small part was down to taking part in the spirit-building exercises in the pub. Everybody had different party tricks and mine was opening bottle tops with my eyebrow. You've got to know which bottles to use, though; otherwise you're fucked. I arrived at training loads of times with cuts across my head.'

One morning, Grobbelaar woke up after a night out with a deep wound to his chin.

'We were out in town and we bumped into an ex-con who was a bit of a fitness fanatic. He was slightly pissed and so were we, so we started testing each other – how far we'd go to outdo one another. One of his dares was to put our hands behind our backs and fall face forward, only using our hands in the last split second. I was exceptional at it, but the ex-con called me a chicken for using my hands too early. In the second attempt, I fell all the way to the ground just to prove a point. Unfortunately there was some glass on the floor and I cut my chin so bad that I could put my whole thumb right through it the next morning.'

Another time, after a Christmas party, he turned up at Melwood with the 'hangover from hell'.

'We were warming up and I was leading the group with Roy Evans just behind me. I let rip with the biggest silent fart ever and, unfortunately for Roy, he was the first to run into it. The smell was so bad that Roy started vomiting, because he was a bit worse for wear as well. All of the players behind him either keeled over or ran away to escape the poisonous gas. I was pissing myself.'

Sometimes, the tomfoolery would go too far.

'I liked to wind people up and Liverpool was the kind of place where you thrived if you were quick-witted. But you had to earn the respect of everyone first by playing well on the pitch, and that didn't happen with me. So I had to earn my stripes. Everybody had arguments. I fell out with probably every member of the team throughout my time at the club over various spats.'

One teammate Grobbelaar struggled to get along with was Howard Gayle.

'A lot of the first-team players liked to call me "Jungle Man" because of my military background. But Howard was of West African descent and did not appreciate the context. Instead of laughing it off, he became tetchy.'

Their relationship worsened when Olympic decathlon champion Daley Thompson visited Melwood for a training session.

'Daley was a decent footballer as well as a brilliant all-round athlete. Howie, though, reckoned he could out-sprint him in the 100m. Terry Mc was on the finishing line and I was the starter. Everybody was acting very seriously until I said, "Ready, steady . . . pick up your lips . . . go!" Daley fell on the floor, pissing himself with laughter, but Howie didn't see the funny side. I realise now that the reactions of both Daley and Howard were different because of their upbringings. It was a lot tougher for Howard than Daley.'

For the next few weeks, Gayle stalked Melwood in search of revenge.

'I knew he was going to come for me straight away in the training session, so in the next tackle I slid 15 yards to win the ball off him – just to prove I wasn't scared. He started swearing at me and wouldn't let it go.

'We get along fine now, but it was a shame that Howie went around with a great big chip on his shoulder, because it probably held him back at that time. He could have become a Liverpool regular and an England international – he had that much ability – but on a lot of occasions he went around with a scowl on his face.'

Liverpool and Grobbelaar completed 1982–83 with another league and cup double, cantering towards the First Division title by 11 points. Such was their domination, the Reds could afford to lose five of their last six games.

Grobbelaar married new girlfriend Debbie in the summer of 1983, a sign that he was beginning to finally settle down both on and off the pitch. The team travelled to the Far East for a pre-season tour and spirits were high – 'Sammy Lee thought we were in Hong Cock and Bangkong' – but the lax form from the end of the campaign before continued with defeats to Manchester United (twice if you include the Charity Shield) and Atletico Madrid, along with draws against Hamburg and Feyenoord, concerning Bob Paisley and his staff.

'The reason why Liverpool got it right so often was because the management saw problems early on and eradicated them,' Grobbelaar says. 'Bob let us all know he wasn't happy and bombed certain individuals out of the team. That scared a few and results soon changed.'

And change they did. Although Liverpool only won the title by three points that season, with Southampton their closest challengers, they clinched a cup double for a third year on the run by beating Everton in a League Cup final replay.

Better was to follow. Grobbelaar's performances were outstanding in Europe – where he had failed previously – particularly in tough ties against Athletic Bilbao and Benfica. A 3–1 aggregate victory over Dinamo Bucharest cleared the way to a European Cup final in Rome against the city hosts and Italian Serie A champions Roma. The game finished 1–1 and this was Grobbelaar's moment.

'When it went to penalties, I was probably the most relaxed person in the stadium,' he recalls. 'Before the shoot-out, [Bruno] Conti cheekily started dancing around with the ball – he looked over-confident. So I said to the lads, "If he's going to be cheeky and cocky, then so am I." So I said to him as he walked up, "Let's dance, Bruno." I don't think he understood what I said, but he ran up and scuffed it over the bar. I just started laughing my head off.'

Next up was Ubaldo Righetti, who scored. 'I thought that I dived the right way, but then I remembered that I was watching him in practice from the other side. So I fucked up.'

Then came Francesco Graziani.

'He had his arm around the referee, and I didn't like that. I decided that the net looked like a bowl of spaghetti and started to bite it. Then I turned around and started wobbling my legs. Graziani bottled it.'

Grobbelaar was supposed to take the fifth, and possibly deciding, Liverpool penalty.

'When Graziani missed, I went crazy, running about everywhere, celebrating. The boss thought my mind had gone, so by the time I realised it was my turn to take a kick Alan Kennedy had grabbed the ball and started walking with it towards the penalty spot. It dawned on me that if Alan scored, we were going to win. I think I speak for everybody when I say that nobody truly believed Alan would beat their goalkeeper.'

Kennedy did score. The European Cup was Grobbelaar's seventh major medal in just three seasons at the club.

'When I think about the shit I had to put up with at the start, it was definitely worth it,' he says.. 'There is usually one player in every team that the fans look to blame when it all goes wrong, even if the team is successful. That person was me. But on that night, everything went my way.'

By the following September, though, the crowd were once again voicing their concern following a mistake against Sheffield Wednesday – a mistake that the goalkeeper concedes was his worst in the Liverpool shirt.

'It's the one that I look back and think, "My goodness gracious." Peter Shirtliff [the wardrobe-jawed Wednesday defender] cleared a long aimless ball from the back and I came out to meet it about 35 yards from goal. I tried to pass it to

Barney [Alan Kennedy] but Imre Varadi intercepted it, ran around me and scored.

'The worst thing about the whole experience was that the boss [Joe Fagan] sussed that my mind wasn't on the game and I got bollocked. Ronnie Moran was incandescent. They didn't like me flying off for international duty because they thought it was a distraction. On that day, I'd already organised a private car to take me straight from Anfield to Speke Airport, then a private plane from Speke to Gatwick, where I could catch an Air Zimbabwe flight at nine o'clock that evening for an international match. This was on my mind all the time.

'Before the kick-off earlier that day, Joe comes up to me and asks me who plays in goal for Zimbabwe when I don't. I thought, "That's a funny question." We were flying over Birmingham when the pilot called me up to the cockpit to inform me that the onward plane to Zimbabwe had blown its engine and there wasn't going to be a replacement. I asked the charter pilot to return to Speke and because it was only six o'clock when I got back I thought I might as well go back to Anfield, as I knew most of the lads would still be in the players' lounge. I was walking down the tunnel inside the Main Stand and Joe was the only one waiting for me there. He said, "Why didn't you ask me about the Air Zimbabwe plane that blew an engine this morning? If you'd gone there, you'd have been dropped." Uncle Joe knew everything. At Liverpool, the manager always knew more than he let on.'

Fagan would soon announce his retirement from football ahead of Liverpool's fifth European Cup final in eight seasons. The Reds were due in Brussels to play Juventus. It was 29 May 1985.

One hour before the match was due to start, with more than 60,000 fans assembling inside the Heysel stadium, a riot started, resulting in the collapse of an already crumbling wall and the deaths of 39 Juventus supporters. Liverpool fans were cited as the aggressors, and a five-year blanket ban on English sides playing in Europe followed. Liverpool received an additional ban of 'indeterminate plus three years' or, more precisely, three further years in which the club would be banned if they qualified for European competition. If they didn't, the ban would roll on until they did. Eventually, it became 'plus one year'.

The shame attached to being associated with Liverpool at the time was razor-edged. For the perpetrators of the violence, it was deserved. When the 27 names to be charged with manslaughter were released, most had Merseyside addresses. Yet hooliganism was endemic across English football in the '80s.

'Heysel was almost certainly going to occur somewhere, because no one anywhere seemed capable of stopping the violence,' said Peter Robinson, Liverpool's club secretary, who wrote to UEFA before the tie to complain about the stadium's capability of hosting a match of such magnitude, not only because of its fragile preservation but also because of absurd ticketing arrangements.

Robinson's main concern was that there was to be a neutral section of the ground set aside for Belgians right next to the two pens that would entertain Liverpool supporters. He disputed that this neutral area would only lead to both sets of fans being able to buy tickets from Belgian touts, thus creating a vacuum that potentially could be filled by troublemakers. Given that Brussels had a large Italian population, it was likely that the part of the stadium now infamously known as sector 'Z' would be filled with Juventus supporters. They would only be separated from Liverpool fans by chicken-wire fences. 'I looked at the ground and hoped to God that there would be a sufficient police force near those fences,' Robinson said. 'On the day, my prayers were fruitless. UEFA and the Belgian authorities ignored my letter, and even as late as an hour before the kick-off there were only a handful of policemen on patrol inside the entire stadium with a few dogs.'

'Some people see all of these reasons and all they see are the same old excuses,' Grobbelaar says. 'What happened that day was a disgrace to football. I felt like quitting afterwards. I am a man of impulse – I wanted to go back to South Africa. But a lot of people around me said that by doing that I'd let the scum survive.'

The Liverpool team arrived at the stadium 90 minutes before kick-off as usual. Grobbelaar followed Alan Kennedy onto the pitch to breathe in the atmosphere while the kit was being laid out.

'I remember remarking to Barney about the number of Italians in section "Z". It was so obvious to me that surely the authorities could see the same thing? Me and Steve Nicol went for a walk around the ground to pass time, and it was a mistake. Rather than the jeering we expected from Juventus supporters, they showered us with concrete blocks and flash bombs. I started to get concerned for my wife and family in the stands, so after I got my shorts and socks on I returned to the side of the running track, topless, to see if I could spot them.'

It was then that he saw a group of around 50 supporters in Liverpool colours surge across the terraces behind the goal.

'It was clear to me that the group they were running towards didn't want to stop and fight. They backed off and backed off before they became crushed against a wall like sardines. All I could think was, "Where are the fucking police?" The wall went like a crack of thunder and all I could see was a mass of arms and legs.'

Grobbelaar's nightmares of old returned.

'It was worse than witnessing what I saw in the Bush. You expect death in wars but not at a football match. These were grown men behaving like savages.'

He is adamant, though, that the instigators of Heysel were not from Liverpool.

'People are still free now with blood on their hands,' he insists. 'My then mother-in-law came over for the final on the ferry, and she was one of many who were handed pamphlets by the National Front, which basically said, "Liverpool will not be in Europe again." The NF saw Scousers as scroungers and envied Liverpool's success on a football field. My mother-in-law said that a lot of the people handing out pamphlets had Chelsea and Millwall tattoos on their arms.'

In an interview that Peter Robinson gave to the *Liverpool*

Echo on the eve of the 25th anniversary of Heysel, he also intimated that the National Front were involved, 'At 9 p.m., I made my way to the area where the disaster occurred. I tried to speak to a group of Liverpool fans. Some explained the problems – the total lack of control . . . people had tickets that hadn't been torn off. Then a group of men descended on me and said their tickets were from the black market but they wouldn't show me them. They had strong southern accents and they suddenly turned aggressive and started shouting, "Shankly". It was well documented that members of the National Front went to matches. And it was very odd to me that this group should be here.'

Grobbelaar was so 'depressed' and 'obsessed' by what had happened in Belgium, he later decided to try to find out for sure whether the NF were really implicated in Heysel.

'I travelled to one of their headquarters just outside Slough for a group meeting. They recognised me straight away and because I was a white guy from Rhodesia, they assumed that I was racist. So they welcomed me. I had a drink and tried to relax. One of the heads approached me and we got talking. I asked whether they knew anybody who was involved in Heysel and all of a sudden he went cold, said no, then walked off. He sussed me and I decided it was best I leave for my own safety.'

A few days after the disaster, British Prime Minister Margaret Thatcher pressured the FA to ban all English clubs from Europe indefinitely. The English Football Association had pre-empted warnings by withdrawing all clubs from the following season's European tournaments pending UEFA's announcements. Given Thatcher's previously stated aversion towards the city of Liverpool – because of its left-wing politics and strong opposition to her government and philosophy, not to mention the negative image created by the Toxteth Riots a few years earlier – it is unsurprising that Thatcher was granted her wish when UEFA banned all English sides for 'an indeterminate period of time'.

'I don't think the ban for that length was necessary,' says Grobbelaar. 'OK, they felt that Liverpool fans were instigators.

Therefore, they should have made Liverpool play behind closed doors in Europe for a couple of seasons. But as players, we were not responsible for what happened. When it comes to blame, it's easier to blame groups rather than individuals. Criminals are deemed innocent until proven guilty, but here everybody associated with Liverpool was found guilty by implication.

'Thatcher was quick to make a decision on the miners and she was quick to make a decision on the football supporters. Personally, my quality of life in England improved under her governance. When I first arrived here, the tax on foreign workers was 85 per cent, but she brought it down to 40 per cent. It meant that people like me and Craig Johnston benefited. But I could also see that for most working-class people, she didn't do a lot of good things.'

Critics argued that Heysel and the European ban that followed would see an end to Liverpool's dominance of English football. But they didn't count on Kenny Dalglish's ability as a player-manager after he succeeded Fagan.

'The result of the match at Heysel didn't matter to me, and when we were in the changing-rooms waiting for somebody to make a decision whether we should play, I just wanted to go home. I knew I couldn't, because the stadium was a powder keg waiting to go off. Had the game been cancelled, the death toll might have been even worse.

'My mind wasn't on the game and I wasn't even bothered that we lost to a dubious penalty . . . I think a lot of the lads felt that way. We all wanted to get away, and because it was the last game of the season we could forget about football for a while. But even when we returned for pre-season, I can definitely say that my appetite for the game had gone. Fortunately, Kenny recovered it.'

Dalglish's relationship with the players changed when he became manager.

'He opened up more and communicated with people,' Grobbelaar says. 'I suppose he had to. He moved so easily into management, when before he was the piss-taker. He was ruthless with the younger boys, especially; but when he was manager, he realised that he had to change. Before him, there were a few cliques in the dressing-room, but he sorted it out and brought the family back together. Sometimes he could have protected me more from the continued criticism that came my way, but after a while I realised that he left me alone because he thought I had the mental strength to deal with it myself. That gave me a lot of confidence.'

Under Dalglish, Grobbelaar rediscovered his passion for the game as well as his form. By August 1986, with another set of League championship and FA Cup-winner medals in his cabinet at home, the goalkeeper made his 310th consecutive appearance for the club. He hadn't missed a game since his debut five years earlier – a remarkable feat.

'I don't think any player will break that record. I also know that I am still the most-decorated goalkeeper that has played in the English league. Although I didn't think about them too much at the time when I achieved them, landmarks like that are things I look back on now with a lot of pride. I'm not the kind of person to want to keep those records, though. I'm a Liverpool supporter and I'd love to see someone else surpass everything I've achieved, because it would mean that the club is doing well.'

There were still mistakes, however: like the one in the 2–0 derby defeat of February '86 when he let a hopeful Kevin Ratcliffe effort from 35 yards creep under his body. But by now Grobbelaar was changing attitudes towards goalkeeping. Before him, it was rare for a player in his position to go for a high ball beyond 12 yards from his goal or to sweep up behind his defence. Yet the Zimbabwean, who had such a torrid start to life in England, redefined the boundaries of what was acceptable for goalkeepers to do.

'It gave me a real buzz to charge off my line and grab a high ball – just as much as a point-blank save when the centre-forward was clean through. I thought that you had the privilege of being able to use your hands being a goalkeeper, so you should bloody well use them. I couldn't see the point of letting somebody have a free header at your goal when it was easier to catch it. Catching from well off my line was something I had always done – my father encouraged me to do it.'

He learnt to 'sweep' while in Canada.

'Tony [Waiters] was a big help with that. He taught me to narrow the forward's angle of goal by coming well out of your box. If he had the whole goal to aim at, he had a better chance of scoring, so by coming off the line it sometimes also helped stop the play developing before it was too late. Playing in the NASL was a breeding ground for adventurous goalkeepers because of the shoot-out that was devised to decide matches. If the score was a draw at full-time, the teams would take turns with the ball placed on a 35-yard line and the forward would have five seconds to score. As a goalkeeper, the best way of stopping them was to come off the line and either smother it or boot it clear before the forward could get his shot away.'

Grobbelaar says that the most complete keeper in England during the '80s was Peter Shilton.

'Although the boldest I've ever seen was John Burridge, who would have thrown himself under a bus to save a goal, Shilts was the ideal build. It was the way he trained that set him apart. When I was at Crewe, I was allowed to go over to Nottingham Forest for a few weeks to try to learn from him. Brian Clough was there when I arrived; he was sitting there dressed in squash gear. "Mr Grobbelaar, I understand you aspire to be a goalkeeper in the English First Division," he said. "If you really want it, you should pack in that Mickey Mouse stuff over the other side of the Atlantic." Shilton was as obsessive as Clough about the game. His intensity just during training was frightening. It was like he didn't concede a goal.'

Grobbelaar also rated Rinat Dasayev, the Soviet Union's captain, and Spain's Luis Arconada, although his hero as a child was Brazil's maligned stopper, Félix. 'He was the complete athlete and didn't get the credit he deserved.'

Outfield, he counts Graeme Sharp his fiercest opponent but says Pat Van Den Hauwe, also of Everton, was the craziest.

'There was always a banter between the Everton boys and us, but we never socialised. Kenny wouldn't allow it. I was driving up to Southport with my then wife and first-born child in the back of the car. I stopped at the lights on Lord Street and this fellow was walking across the road with his family, pushing a pram. He gave the pram to his wife, looked at my car and jumped on my bonnet. That was Pat Van Den Hauwe. You get nutters in football, but they're not all goalkeepers.'

There were other brilliant players. 'I've faced a few: Hugo Sánchez, Johan Cruyff and Pelé, all greats. But I regarded anybody with the ball as the most dangerous person. It didn't matter who he was – a Fourth Division player or an international – whoever had the ball in front of me was the best player in the world because he could score. The best player I played with was undoubtedly Graeme Souness. He had everything in every position except goalkeeper and was a phenomenal leader.'

Souness had long left Liverpool by the late '80s, but the medals kept on coming. Out of Europe, Liverpool played arguably their best football in the latter part of the decade under Dalglish. Again, triumph would be met with disaster.

On 15 April 1989, Liverpool were drawn to play Nottingham Forest in the FA Cup semi-final at Hillsborough. The match was abandoned six minutes in. Ninety-six people were crushed to death. As a goalkeeper in front of the Leppings Lane end, Grobbelaar saw and heard everything.

'I knew exactly what was happening from the pitch, so why couldn't the people who had the power to make the right decisions change things? I told a policewoman to open the gates, but it seemed to take a long time for it to register with her the desperation of the situation.

'On the 15th of April every year, I feel uneasy with myself wherever I am in the world. Mostly, I think about why nothing has been done for the 96 families. That's what hurts most. It has taken so long for successive governments to even look at the police files. There are people still alive today who were in charge of safety that day that should have been made responsible in court for what happened. The simplest decisions would have changed everything. When *The Sun* newspaper took control of the story, it was the worst case of victims being made to feel the perpetrators.'

The *Sun* claimed that Liverpool supporters 'pissed on the dead' and 'stole their wallets'.

'If the people who were writing those headlines or writing the stories genuinely believed what they were saying, they really have a lack of common sense. Anybody who is savvy will understand that if you just have one or two [drinks] en route to the match like you always do, then arrive at the ground before getting crushed to death, you are going to piss yourself because of shock and fear. I have seen grown men in the army piss themselves in times of desperation, so when there are thousands of people around you and you can't breathe, it happens.

'As for people going into wallets, how can you identify somebody without looking for identification? Some of the dead people had drivers' licences, so the good people of Liverpool, naturally trying to help their own, left the ID of the dead on their chest. Instead, *The Sun* said they were trying to rob. It was a disgusting reaction.'

Even after everything else that Grobbelaar had witnessed in his life, Hillsborough was the most difficult to deal with.

'What Kenny and Marina [Dalglish's wife] did should never be forgotten. They were incredible. I was shattered as a human being, but Kenny insisted that we try to help counsel the victims' families. By doing that, we counselled ourselves.'

Grobbelaar remained at Liverpool for another five seasons, winning another League title and a couple of FA Cups, but the appointment of Souness as manager and the arrival of David James from Watford in 1992 signalled the beginning of the end.

'Graeme called me into his office and he said that the new guy [James] was going to take over first-team responsibilities from me in the medium to long term. He wanted me to teach him what it was like to be Liverpool's number 1 goalkeeper. I understood because I was getting older and I think it's important to help youngsters progress in the game if you are one of the old heads.'

Grobbelaar's understanding with Souness – the player he admired so much – deteriorated quickly. At this point in our conversation, he refrains from calling him 'Graeme' and instead uses the surname 'Souness'.

'Our first game of the following season was originally scheduled for 15 August 1992 away at Nottingham Forest. On the 16th, I was due to play for Zimbabwe in a World Cup qualifier against South Africa. The game was obviously very important to me because I was born in South Africa and had grown up in Zimbabwe. It was also South Africa's first World Cup qualifying game after the end of apartheid. I told Souness that I was going to play for my national team, so I went over and we won the game 4–1. Liverpool unfortunately lost and Souness took the hump.'

Relations between the pair got worse.

'A few months later, having hardly played, I was in Lomé, Togo, for another international with Zimbabwe. The following weekend, we had another crucial game against Guinea. Souness called me and asked me to get myself back to the UK because Liverpool had a game midweek against Bolton Wanderers in the FA Cup. I flew from Lomé to Accra [Ghana], Accra to London and London to Manchester to make sure I was there for Monday, which would give me two days to prepare. I trained like a beast, but when it came to Wednesday night and the team was announced, Mike Hooper was in goal and David James was first reserve. It seemed like he did it in spite.'

Even though they have since reconciled their differences, Grobbelaar believes Souness failed as a Liverpool manager.

'Souness was the best player I've ever played with – the best in the world for a time. For that, I admired him. But his skills as a manager and his judgement were questionable. For a long time, we didn't see eye to eye because of it. Maybe if he managed today, he'd be the best manager in the world as well, because now I can see that a lot of his ideas were visionary. He could see what way football was going, but the problem was he tried to change too much too soon. He always demanded instant success as a player and was intolerant of people who didn't feel the same. As a manager, when you come in, it takes patience and time to change things, but Souness was impatient. Now, we get on well. He's the nicest person you could meet. He's been through his bad times and I've been through my bad times, so we have something in common.'

With Roy Evans in charge, Grobbelaar was injured in a game against Leeds and never appeared again.

'I would have liked a better finale. I read in a newspaper that I was going to be released on a free transfer. Roy had taken over by then and he is a great person, but he didn't have the opportunity to tell me face to face what was going on. It disappointed me at the time, but my move to Southampton came about very quickly, so I didn't have a chance to dwell on being upset.'

Grobbelaar's contract at the Dell meant that he earned more there than he did at any time during his 14 years at Liverpool. If he thought life would be easier from now on, though, he was wrong. In November 1994, he was accused of match fixing by *The Sun* newspaper during his final years at Anfield.

'When it broke and the picture [of Grobbelaar in a meeting with the supposed fixers] was shown to me, I knew I was innocent,' he says. 'So I kept quiet, went to my lawyers here in Liverpool and sued the newspaper that very night. The police questioned me for days and days, but there was no evidence. They advised me to maintain a silence and allow the newspaper time to prove that I was guilty of wrongdoing. Because I knew I was innocent, that's exactly what I did.'

The saga eventually left him bankrupt.

'Had the newspaper come to me with the story before it went to print, the whole business would never have gone to court. People ask me all the time whether the allegations affected my relationship with Liverpool supporters. But my answer is always the same – I had made mistakes since my first match as a goalkeeper. It made me an easy target. Do you think I threw every match?'

Grobbelaar signed forms with eight different clubs following the court case. Like so many footballers on the verge of retirement, he struggled to deal with the fact that the training ground would no longer be his place of work.

'A lot of ex-footballers go off the rails because they don't know how to deal with the real world,' he says. 'I struggled for a time, especially around the time of the allegations and afterwards. The first game after the story broke, Blackburn supporters threw money at me. So I put it in my cap and gave it to the nearest steward. I could laugh at stuff like that. You have to have a sense of humour.

'Life has got to go on. You can't worry too much about the past, because you have the rest of your life to live. My mother was a huge influence on me, and she has always told me that life is full of disappointments and that it's how you get over those disappointments that makes you a better person. Without her, I might have cracked.'

Grobbelaar tried management with four different clubs in South Africa but now lives in Canada and supplements his income by doing motivational speeches for factory workers throughout Africa. 'They are mainly very poor people – minimum wage. As a foreign player in England, I learnt what it was like to work for what was essentially a foreign company. A lot of the people I speak to don't have the skills to communicate with their bosses and therefore get into conflicts. I was once a bit like them.'

He seems to have found solace in his life.

'I've got a beautiful wife, who works as a lawyer, and daughter, and it feels like I've got a second chance. This time around, everything is geared towards my wife's career and I just do as she says. For so long it was about me. It was unfair on everyone else.'

CHAPTER TWO

Cult Zeros

ORIGINAL TOXTETH TERROR,
Howard Gayle

'I'VE JUMPED IN STOLEN CARS, BEATEN UP POLICEMEN AND FOUGHT on the Annie Road terraces as a latter-day football hooligan,' Howard Gayle reflects with a hint of remorse. 'Then I made the first team.'

Gayle, better known as the first black footballer to play for Liverpool, was born in Toxteth and spent many of his teenage years knocking round on Granby Street – a gritty melting pot of a community south of Liverpool's city centre.

Gayle played just five times for the Reds in half a decade between 1978 and 1983, yet he's included in this book at the expense of more decorated Liverpool stars because he was a local lad whose upbringing and career path is unique and worth writing about.

When I meet him at a school adjacent to Granby – the name given to it by people familiar with the area – the neighbourhood is deserted. Once a busy but underprivileged working-class bazaar of Muslim-, Hindu-, Rastafarian- and Christian-owned food stores, it is now your quintessential inner-city nightmare of steel-shuttered shops, wire grilles and boarded-up terraces. Many of the buildings look like crack dens.

The district expanded to cope with the post-war influx of Afro-Caribbeans and West Africans, but today Toxteth has been taken over by refugees rather than immigrants. The modern Al Rahma mosque sits nervously nearby, and although some of the people outside are like second-generation Scousers with their adidas Spezials on foot, there is a resigned apprehension overpowering the scent of garam masala from a run-down restaurant. Looming in the distance is Britain's largest Anglican cathedral – a brooding, enigmatic presence.

Nestled amidst a hard-to-police low-rise enclave of maisonettes and bleak backstreets, this part of Liverpool is notorious because of what happened halfway down Selbourne Street on the evening of 3 July 1981, when an angry crowd watched Leroy Alphonse Cooper's arrest.

What followed was more than a week of rioting, with pitched battles between police officers and youths armed with petrol bombs and paving stones. It became a place of anarchy and has suffered since. Toxteth is now twinned in people's minds with the Lebanon.

Robbie Fowler, a future Liverpool great who grew up on Windsor Street, parallel with Princes Avenue slightly to the west, once observed that every top-flight footballer came from an inner-city council estate. 'But Toxteth is somehow portrayed as being much worse than all the rest,' he said. 'Toxteth is the bogey-man of the inner cities.'

Gayle can't disagree. 'Granby Street is gone – it's dead,' he sighs. 'It has a negative reputation because of the riots. There's only Danny Fife's on the corner – a place that has served the community for generations – that has survived. That's the only original shop. There's currently a cafe and a place that sells halal meat. That's it.'

Gayle, who now lives a few miles further to the south, close to Sefton Park, is clad in a black leather jacket and black jeans – the colour broken only by a green badge that promotes the end of racism in football. He has razor-cropped hair, a head like a bullet, the shoulders of a boxer and fists that could be a pair of wrecking balls on two bulldozers. His accent is nasally soft and classically Scouse, unlike the rapid-fire impenetrable twang you are likely to hear from some urban dwellers today.

Gayle is back here because he runs a social-inclusion project, encouraging kids back into education with the promise of football coaching from an ex-pro. He is articulate and rarely swears, almost whispering most of the recollections from his playing days.

'I don't pre-judge kids,' he says. 'I treat them on the merit of what they do with me. I try to speak to kids on a level. I know where many of them are coming from because I've been there myself.'

Gayle was born in May 1958 and spent his formative years close to the docks on Carter Street. Liverpool is a place where all roads feel like they head to the banks of the Mersey: the brownish trail of water that is the city's lifeblood. From the waterfront, Merseyside's historic dockland stretches north for eight miles, eventually gulped by the haze above Seaforth and Waterloo. It is no surprise that the river which shaped a city should also mould its relationship with colonial Britain, encouraging, amongst many others, Gayle's parents to these shores.

Liverpool is a city whose capitalists originally grew rich on the blood of slaves. No other port in Europe could compete with Liverpool's geographical location as one point in the triangle linking Africa, England and the Americas.

'Me dad was from Freetown in Sierra Leone and moved here at the end of the war as a seaman,' he continues. 'Me mam's roots were in Ghana, but she was born and brought up in the south end of Liverpool. Her mum was a daughter of the Ethel Austin family. She ended up with a black guy, and once they had children she was excommunicated. Mixed relationships just weren't accepted then, so she ended up in Toxteth.'

Less than 12 months after his birth, the Gayle family were forced out of Toxteth and across town to Norris Green.

'We were informed by the council that we were being shifted so the house could be refurbished. Six weeks later, one of me mam's friends called us up and said that they'd pulled the house down. They were containerising the port. For years, she tried to get us a transfer back to the south end, but it never happened. She was up at the housing office on Storrington Avenue every other week. We never got an honest answer from the council.'

His brothers Abdul and Alan were back in Toxteth within a year, living with a grandparent, but together with his sister Janice, Gayle, as the youngest sibling, stayed in Norris Green until he signed terms with Liverpool as a 19 year old. 'Noggzy, as it is now commonly known, was then in effect a self-governing estate where problems were sorted out internally. Outsiders and authority were distrusted. Families of ethnicity were scarce.

'I went to St Theresa's School and I suffered a lot through racism,' he explains. 'I was the only black kid and I became a target. I was constantly coming home with my clothes ripped and with grazes all over my body. I was fighting most nights of the week. I didn't pass my 11-plus.

'All me mates in Norris Green were white – great mates and still lads I socialise with now . . . Peter McNamara, Carl Howard, Keith Foster, Tony Kinnear, Jimmy Wilson, Phil Cannon [who now works for Blackburn Rovers as a youth-development officer]. But I had to establish myself first. There was a time when I was bullied and I let the bullies know that I was prepared to take a good hiding and try to give it back so it didn't happen again. By the time I got into my mid-teens, it stopped because I had a reputation. I had no fear at all. I didn't care about school; I cared about looking after myself.'

After physical force prompted little response, Gayle's father used football as a tool to motivate his son in education.

'Me dad would batter me if I got into trouble,' he says. 'Sometimes it would be with his fist, other times it would be with whatever implement was close by, maybe a shoe. But the beatings didn't do much to change my behaviour. I'd still hang around with the same crowd and get into the same trouble. But he knew that I couldn't live without football. When he kept me inside the house and stopped me playing, it killed me, especially in the summer months when I could see kids making their way to Ellergreen School field for a 20-a-side game. Me dad wasn't the kind of person who you could go to and reason with. You couldn't get around him by doing jobs around the house. He was old-school.'

Gayle's father worked at the Ford car plant in Halewood, while his mother was an auxiliary nurse at a children's mental-health hospital. All he wanted, though, was to become a footballer and play for Liverpool.

'Me mam once bought me a Liverpool kit for Christmas, the one with the old round collar and big white badge,' Gayle recalls. 'I had it on every single day for about six months. Roger Hunt was my hero, and I tried to replicate his goals out on the street. Every single night when I went to bed I'd dream about playing for Liverpool. It seemed like a distant dream and maybe unrealistic because there was hardly any black players in this country during the late '60s, early '70s – in sport generally. Soon John Conteh came along at the same time as Muhammad Ali. Then there was Pelé and Eusébio. Clyde Best played for West Ham as well.'

When Gayle wasn't playing football, he was in a gang. The sink estates of Norris Green are notorious today for their association with the murder of 11-year-old Rhys Jones, who in 2007 was gunned down on his way home from football practice after being caught in the crossfire of a feud between dark-hooded scallies trying to work their way up the local criminal food chain.

'I was an original member of the Strand Gang,' Gayle says regretfully. 'The press makes out that they're a recent phenomenon, but I can tell you there has been rivalry between Norris Green [the Strand Gang] and the Crocky lads [the Croxteth Crew] for generations. Admittedly, at first it was just fist fighting and there was some kind of respect, but now guns are involved. These lads have limited social skills and sort their problems out by pulling a knife or a machine gun.

'The first time I got into trouble, it was for something I didn't do. A pack of us had gone up to Formby [an affluent town in between Liverpool and Southport] with the sole intention of getting into trouble. We ended up in Freshfield, and one of the lads robbed a ball from a garden. We went and had a game on a bowling green. Playing on grass like that was like Wembley.

'You couldn't get away with it round our way because all the bowling greens had cocky watchmen looking over them. One of the lads decided to break into the park keepers' hut and a few of the others started breaking windows. Next thing, two police vans slammed up beside us and fifteen to twenty of us got locked up. They lined us all up in a long corridor and the first lad denied responsibility. The policeman pulled out a leather glove and started slapping him really hard. Eventually, the lad admitted smashing two of the windows, thinking that would be the end of it. The police started the same process with me until I was forced into admitting that I'd smashed one, even though on this occasion I was only guilty of playing footy on the bowling green. If it was a choice between mischief and footy, I'd always choose footy.

'It took six months to go to court and in the end I was found guilty of criminal damage. I was 14 and me dad went mad. He told me that I was staying in the house till I was 16. I thought he'd relent after two or three months, but every night I'd have to be home from school by quarter past four, otherwise he'd wanna know why. Sometimes if he was working on shifts, there was a bit of leeway with me mam. Eventually by the January of the year I was going to turn 16, he started to loosen his grip on me.'

Soon, Gayle's mother died.

'It wrecked me head,' he continues. 'I went to live with me brother in Toxteth, and I got into all kinds of trouble. I was robbing cars, breaking into factories, stealing from shops. The police were knocking round all the time, and my brother couldn't handle me. So they sent me back with me dad. I'd lost my mother, and there was nobody to talk to. I was devastated, but me dad wasn't the approachable kind and all the kids on the street weren't the kind of lads you could talk to about deep feelings. The only person I could speak to was my cousin Barry. He took me out for an hour around Norris Green at about two o'clock one morning. He tried to help me understand about life and death. To some extent it was comforting, but the next day I knew I'd be back to normal, acting unruly.'

Gayle began travelling regularly to Liverpool away matches and started to immerse himself in all the culture that went with it.

'I was a hooligan,' he admits. 'It was the culture. When teams came to Anfield, there was us always waiting for them and it was the same when we went away. It was accepted. Skinheads and hooliganism was part and parcel of football. I gave out a fair share of digs and I took one or two as well.'

The worst beating he received was at Highbury.

'As we got older and more experienced, we learnt not to get on the football specials [a bus that took supporters directly to the stadium]. Instead, we'd travel on the service trains and get there early. It was a game of cat and mouse. They'd be catching us by surprise and riot, then we'd do the same when the Cockneys came up to Liverpool.

'Whenever we went to London, we'd get the midnight special from Lime Street. It was like a milk float – it'd stop bloody everywhere . . . Stafford, Birmingham, Nottingham, Northampton, Oxford . . . then we'd get into Euston by half-six in the morning. This one day, all the Arsenal boys came into Euston unaware that we were already there, and we rounded up behind them and gave them a kicking despite the efforts of the British Transport Police. When we got to the game, we all managed to get into the Clock End where all the home supporters used to be. Alan Ball scored two and we were well beaten, so I thought about getting off home. When I turned round, I saw this boy that I'd just given a kicking to back at Euston. All of a sudden, I was on my own. I didn't have a clue where the rest of the lads had gone, and I was surrounded by loads of Arsenal. Most of my mates had spewed it, and I must have fell asleep, so to speak. This boy went, "Do you remember me?" I did. Then, within a split-second, they were all on me. The only thing I could do was curl up in a ball and hope for the best. That was the thing to do if you were caught – curl up in a ball. I was praying that none of these lads had any knives on them. I was waiting for that sharp prod in my body. But all I could feel was kicks.

'I was fortunate that all this happened in the ground, because the police came. When they got hold of me, though, all they did was fling me outside the ground and leave me to fend for myself. All I knew was that I needed to get back to Euston quick. Because if I got caught on the street when it was dark, that was it.

'I don't know how I did it, but I got back to the station. It was a lucky escape. It went with the territory, and you knew that sometime you were going to get a kicking. You always tried to make sure the odds were stacked in your favour, but if it came you had to accept it.'

When the Liverpool hooligans fought, they did it with an eye on fashion. Gayle was a young casual who wore the right clothes and listened to the right music.

'We used to wear Oxford bags and tank tops. Budgie jackets were also popular. They were like bomber jackets with two different colours. Later it went into the adidas Samba trainers. Personally, I had patchwork jeans. Liverpool fans and Evertonians both used to love it when the Cockneys came up to Liverpool because they'd turn up at the match in leather jackets. They'd end up getting twatted and they'd have the jackets robbed off them. It was a frenzy when you knew a match against Arsenal or particularly Chelsea was coming up because you knew they weren't as streetwise as us.

'People would be down Lime Street early to check that none of the Cockneys came in early. There'd be someone there keeping lookout when the first train came in from London on a Saturday morning. If anyone was on that train, well . . . news travels fast in Liverpool, doesn't it?

'It was like a territorial game. Later, amongst hooligans from other clubs, it became properly arranged, with heads calling people up on mobiles, but originally in Liverpool it was instinctive. The only arrangement was to meet all the lads in the American Bar [over the road from Lime Street Station], and one person would be on watch. Even if a train came in from Birmingham we'd be suspicious, because sometimes the Cockneys would try to deceive us by travelling to the Midlands first and hoping they wouldn't bump into us. But the head [of the group] always stood out.'

Gayle's wayward behaviour continued, and he ended up in a detention centre for young offenders at Wellington House in Stoke-on-Trent.

'I was there for four months,' he reflects. 'It was the best thing that ever happened to me, because it straightened me out. It was a short, sharp shock. One of the lads had stolen some chequebooks, and we went into town kiting it. We went into one shop, and it turned out these plain-clothed police had been following us. They grabbed us, so I assaulted one of them by thumping him around the head. It was one of a catalogue of minor offences that I'd committed. But when those doors at Wellington House slammed shut, I realised things had to change.'

After doing time, Gayle found solace in the south end of Liverpool – a place he'd yearned to return to since he was in nappies.

'I worked as an apprentice plasterer at first, but it was a sham,' he laughs. 'Then I started playing football regularly again. It was for my brother's team, and he ran it from a nightclub in town called The TimePiece on Fleet Street. Eventually, I joined a pub side called The Bedford, and from there the manager Eric Dunlop got me a trial at Liverpool because I was scoring so many goals. Eric was a fantastic fella. He knew John Bennison [one of the original Bootroom] at Liverpool.

'There still wasn't many black players about. There was a lad called Lawrence Iro and another one, Stevie Cole, who were known around the city and they'd had trials at Liverpool as well. Stevie got murdered a few years ago in Fazakerley when some lads bounced into a pub. Stevie never made it at Liverpool and fell out with football. He went the way that I didn't want to go.'

Gayle remembers his first trial at Melwood vividly.

'It was on a Tuesday night in August. It was really nerve-wracking. To be going into an institution like that and somewhere where I'd been on the outside of the walls for so many years, trying to get Kevin Keegan and Bill Shankly's autographs, and now I was finally in there. The trial game went really well for me – I was excellent and I knew it.

'I got the ball on the halfway line, beat three or four players and hit a shot on the run that's come back off the crossbar. Before it's bounced, I've hit it again and it has gone straight in. I've turned and as I'm walking back for the kick-off I can see Ronnie Moran, Joe Fagan, Reuben Bennett and the gaffer Bob Paisley all talking and smiling. A few minutes later, I went over on my ankle and I was clearly in pain, but I carried on. There was a perception, probably at every football club, that black players went missing when they got kicked, but at that moment I think they could see that I had the potential to be different to that perception.'

Two nights later, Gayle was invited back for another trial where he scored four goals. Within a week, he was offered amateur terms.

'It was a short-term contract over three months,' he explains. 'Kenny Dalglish signed at roughly the same time. Sammy Lee had played in the same Sunday league as me and quickly became my best mate. He had two lovely, lovely parents. Every Saturday before a game with the reserves, I'd go to his house on Brownlow Hill and his mum would offer us a "pre-match", meaning steak and mushrooms with a bit of brown sauce. She was the nicest, most welcoming person I'd ever met. Sammy is exactly the same – you'll never hear anybody say a bad word about Sammy.

'I worked hard in the three months and didn't want to give the club an easy excuse to let me go. It got to the November time and we were sitting in the lounge at Anfield after training and Phil Thompson goes, "What's happening with you – are you signing 'ere or what?" I told him that I was still on the amateur contract. "Go in and confront the gaffer," he told me. I was thinking that there was no way I could do that. "Tell the gaffer that you think you've done well in the reserves and deserve a full-time contract," he continued. "And before you leave, tell him that there are other clubs sniffing around."

'I was like, "There's no way I can do that. What happens if he calls my bluff?"

'"Do it," Tommo said.

'I had to wait a week to pluck up the courage to carry it out. We were at Melwood and I went up to the gaffer before we got on the bus back to Anfield. "Yeah, course. Have your lunch and come and see me." It was almost as if he'd been waiting. I thought Tommo might have said something. I goes in and gives him the spiel that Tommo told me, but stalling on the bit about other clubs being interested. Bob told me that he was pleased with my progress and felt I could eventually make a contribution to the first team if I continued to work hard.

'Bob said they were going to give me a year's full-time contract but to remember that the really hard work starts now. He asked me how I felt about it and I said that I was proud for my family because I knew they'd be delighted. "Anything else?" Bob asked. "Well, you know that I told you I was 18 . . . well, I'm actually 19 . . ." Bob started laughing, then asked me again whether there was anything else. So I told him that other clubs had asked about me. I didn't even need to say it. There was a wry smile on Bob's face. "Yep . . . we'll see you in the morning." I hadn't been so nervous since I was standing in front of the judge and he sentenced me to four months.'

The people at Liverpool were unaware of Gayle's previous misdemeanours off the field. As a product of a tough neighbourhood where fighting and sticking up for yourself was as natural as breathing or sex, he had to react differently now. For the first time in an aimless life of unemployment, petty crime, street thuggery and prison, Gayle had found his vocation.

'If they knew about me being in jail, I don't think I'd have been taken on,' he insists. 'The club knew that there was an edge to me even within that short period of time because I had to deal with racism from some people inside the club. I wasn't having it, and there were a lot of things that I wasn't prepared to accept. Anybody who crossed me like that would be confronted. I didn't care how big, old or how high-profile they were, because if you let people get an advantage over you in any workplace it's only going to affect your own progression in the long run. So I kicked off when I had to.'

In signing a professional contract with Liverpool, Gayle knew that with black players progressing at other teams across the country, there was an added pressure on him to either confirm or contradict perceptions by either succeeding or failing at what was becoming the most pressured club in England.

But Gayle was also entering a sporting dressing-room with a culture of mockery. Many players believed it accounted for Liverpool's success. Even new signings arriving with fees and reputations to match were swiftly repressed. Players like Graeme Souness and Ian Rush were not immune from that process.

In the name of comradeship, a perverse equality was strived for. Through ritual ribbing, newcomers were subconsciously asked the same questions: Are you one of the boys? Can you mix? The theory goes that if a player could deal appropriately with the relentless levels of banter from teammates, he could set foot inside Anfield on a Saturday and perform in front of a crowd, no problem.

Gayle insists that racism wasn't institutionalised at Liverpool. But some at Melwood were from the 'old school'.

'There were those that had pre-conceived ideas about black footballers,' he says. 'There would be little jibes. There would be racist jokes. But one of the worst things you can do to a black person is say, "Oh, I don't mean you . . . you're all right." I'd been brought up in a way that confronting people on such issues had become second nature to me. My brothers used to tell me if you needed to pick up a brick or a rock to defend yourself, then do it – whatever you do, never let anybody bully you. At Melwood, clearly I couldn't start scrapping, so I needed to respond to it in a different way. I soon realised that I could only change opinions by what I did on the football pitch.'

Gayle did not find the transition to full-time football particularly challenging.

'It was two hours a day, sometimes three on a Tuesday and a Thursday. If you're playing with better players, you learn quicker and become a better player yourself. The ethos was five-a-side on most days, but they were played at such a high tempo and the pass-and-move game was so extensive that when it came to three o'clock on a Saturday afternoon, the actual games seemed easy. Most clubs just couldn't live with it.

'When I went to Birmingham, Sunderland and Newcastle, the first thing that the manager at each of those clubs asked me was "What's Liverpool's secret – what do they do in training?" I always told them that it was five-a-side. At Birmingham, they tried it for three or four weeks, but it didn't change results, so we just went back to the tried-and-tested method of running, running and more running. What Birmingham didn't understand was that the tempo was so high at Liverpool because they had good players who could deal with it. Because the whole club from the first team to the B team trained in the same way, it made Liverpool virtually invincible because every single player was ready to make the step up.'

Roy Evans was Gayle's coach in the reserve team. The pair shared a 'special understanding'.

'We had a banter between each other that perhaps nobody else would have. He'd call me a black so and so and I'd call him a white so and so. From my experiences in life, I know whether somebody means something when they say it. We respected each other and both knew that the other one meant no harm.

'Evo had a great way of getting the best out of me. He made me want to win just for him. While I was at Liverpool, we won five Central League titles in succession. He was such a good man-manager because he could get the best out of players on the way up as well as players on their way down.

'One day we were playing at Goodison Park against Everton in the derby and I was having an atrocious game. Everything that I did went wrong. Then I heard this voice on the touchline, "Right, he's fucking coming off. I've had enough of this." I looked across at him and he shouted something like, "You're coming off, you black bastard." I was fuming and I wanted to kill him. The next minute, the ball falls to me in the box: 1–0. Within three minutes we were 2–0 up and we won the game. At the final whistle I've gone down the tunnel because I wanted to confront Evo. I can see him vanishing towards the dressing-rooms as quickly as possible because he knew that I was coming. When I caught up with him, he was putting the kit away and there was this uneasy silence. We'd just beaten Everton 2–0 away from home and the manager wasn't saying anything at all. I waited for everybody to leave, then just as I went to say something, he goes, "Bloody hell, that woke you up, didn't it?"

'The penny dropped. He did it deliberately to wind me up, and it worked. He went, "You know what, Howard, you've got so much ability that you should be playing at a higher level. But you've got to concentrate." It was genuinely a fantastic moment because he knew that I'd have beef with him after the game but he got the best out of me.'

One person Gayle found difficult to please was Ronnie Moran.

'Ronnie had his set ways in what he thought constituted a good footballer. He preferred grafters over carefree players with a skill base to them. I had that. He didn't seem to recognise that I was quite good with two feet, adaptable in the air and I could tackle as hard as I got tackled. Ronnie didn't like that I stood up for myself. He thought I was a young player who should have known his place. I was a young player who wanted to play for my club and wasn't going to accept any sort of crap from somebody who might stop me achieving that because I wanted to be judged on my ability with a football rather than by the colour of my skin. At times it seemed like I couldn't do anything to please Ronnie. There were times when he'd watch me play for the reserves and he'd pick the bones of everything I did, always focusing on the bad points. He was like that with a lot of players, though – always trying to push you further by design to keep two feet on the ground. In the end, I had to learn to adapt to Ronnie rather than Ronnie adapting to me.'

In October 1980, Gayle made his debut in the Liverpool first team, arriving as a 68th-minute substitute for David Fairclough at Manchester City.

'It was a beautiful sunny day for once at Maine Road,' he recalls. 'We were 2–0 up, and the gaffer put us on. I had a small part to play in the third goal, but for me that was the start of living the dream of putting on a Liverpool shirt and playing in the first team in a first-class match. Even though I was on the pitch for 20-odd minutes, it seemed like hours.

'I had indifferent memories of Maine Road because we'd lost the Central League there the year before after winning it three or four years on the bounce. City beat us with two games to go and did us by six points. There were 10,000 at Maine Road on an April night in 1980. It was a sad occasion. We'd been brought up on winning. Not to win the league was a heavy burden.

'Making my debut at City banished those memories, because City were a very good side and had spent a lot of money to catch up to Liverpool. So for us to be beating them 3–0 on their own ground and me making my debut, the day couldn't have gone any better.'

If Gayle thought he'd made it into the first team, he was wrong. He was only used once again over the next five months, appearing on the bench during a 1–0 win over an Aberdeen team managed by Alex Ferguson at Pittodrie. After Christmas, he was sent on loan to Fulham, then in the Second Division.

'It was a valuable experience in terms of my development as a person rather than as a footballer. It was my first time out of Liverpool on my own. London is a big and exciting city, but it made me realise how unique Liverpool is. The people are different, the culture is different, there's a different way of thinking and socialising. Especially now, I think there's so much going on and so much for younger people to do and aspire to be, the expectation levels and the achievement levels are a lot higher as well. In the '70s and the '80s, that wasn't the case. The only major employers in the city were Ford, the docks and Jacobs. For a city of bright, creative people, that wasn't enough.

'Going from playing in front of 3,000 to 15–20,000 was a big step. It was a different level. It took me two or three weeks to adapt to it. But Fulham was a lovely, lovely football club. They were a family club and the type of people that ran it tried to help you in any way they could. I remember meeting Johnny Haynes, an England international, and he was like Cally or Yeatsy – a figurehead who'd give you the shirt off his back.

'Bobby Campbell was the Fulham manager, a Scouser. He was a great character. He could have been at the London Palladium – he was that funny. He had a lot of charisma and was a grafter. I guess you had to be at that level because it was a hard time for the club. They were struggling to stave off relegation. Fortunately, that season they managed to do it.'

Gayle was recalled to Anfield a month before the European Cup semi-final against Bayern Munich. After not even appearing on the bench in a goalless first leg at Anfield, Gayle was thrust into the limelight after only nine minutes in the return at the Olympic Stadium following an injury to Kenny Dalglish. Ian Rush, meanwhile, yet to score in nearly twelve months after signing from Chester City, was left on the bench – a mark of how the two were regarded at the time.

'There were 70,000 people and I was the only black person inside the stadium,' he half chuckles. 'So I became the target for all the abuse. I honestly didn't give a shit. It spurred me on. I was thinking, "I've come here with Liverpool." We were never going to get beaten. I kept on thinking about "You'll Never Walk Alone". We were never beaten and there's always hope. No matter how bad things get, we can always get a result anywhere in the world because we're Liverpool Football Club.

'Every time I got the ball, the German supporters were doing the Sieg Heil sign. They had banners up with the swastika, and every time I looked into the crowd there was hatred and anger. They made monkey noises at me every time I touched the ball. I was relieved that there was a running track around the pitch, because it would have been even more hairy if the fans were closer.

'Bob brought the pamphlet that was issued to all the Germans inside the stadium with directions to Paris for the final. It was very arrogant of them. We didn't need a team talk. That's why we won.'

Gayle accepts that the game is fondly remembered for his impact, although the performance of fellow reserve-team player Colin Irwin should be appreciated as well.

'Colin and Hansen were up against Dieter Hoeness and Rummenigge – world-class internationals – but they were kept quiet all the way through the night. Colin was really unfortunate that he didn't become a regular Liverpool first-team player. Hansen, Thompson, Lawrenson and Emlyn Hughes had been knocking around when he was coming through, and they were all seasoned internationals. He was like the Hansen of the reserves – great touch, comfortable on the ball and prepared to join the midfield. In my opinion, at a different time he could have been an international player. I likened him to Bobby Moore because he was that composed on the ball. I'd grown up in the same area of Norris Green and was roughly the same age. Everybody knew about him and suspected that he'd become an England captain one day because he was that good. He also had that Scouse factor – a fighter.'

A goal from Ray Kennedy with seven minutes to go sent Liverpool through on away goals – but only after Gayle had been substituted by Jimmy Case.

'I was gutted and I think Bob acted too hastily,' he says. 'The gaffer subbed me because I made a foul, but it wasn't malicious. He reckoned I was getting wound up by all the stuff going on in the terraces and the way the German defenders were trying to scythe me down every time I touched the ball. But I wasn't.

I was loving the atmosphere and the fact that these German players reckoned I was a handful. I was buzzing. But Bob got the wrong impression. He thought I was going to get sent off, and he didn't want us going into extra time with ten men. Usually, I've kept my composure on the pitch. I was only sent off twice in my career, so the gaffer's decision was really, really harsh.'

Gayle recalls the first time he was sent off.

'It was at Anfield in a reserve-team match against Bury. I'd gone in for a 50–50 with a defender, and as I've got up he's spat on me and gone to say the word nigger, but before he'd got to "ger" I'd battered him. As soon as I'd finished, I walked, because I knew what the consequences were going to be. The other lad got sent off as well. It was in the first half, but fortunately we were already 3–0 up. As I sat in the bath, I was thinking, "I shouldn't 'ave done that." But there was one thing that got my goat and that was spitting. It's a horrible habit, and I reacted the way I thought was right. Even if it happened today, I'd do the same. That's my reaction.

'Evo was fuming, but because the game was won he came in and went, "I'm gonna promote you in the boxing ring, Howie – I've never seen such a left-and-right combination." When I went into Anfield on the Monday, the gaffer [Bob Paisley] wanted to see me straight away. He was waiting and I knew I was in trouble. But to be fair, he was brilliant. I explained what had happened and he said that I'd been stupid. "People are going to do whatever they can to stop you from playing because of the club that you play for and because of who you are. Being quick, strong and skilful, the only way they can stop you is by doing stuff like that. Eventually you'll get sent off and you'll be the one that suffers from it." He was right. In fact, that talking-to from Bob was going through my mind around the time he substituted me in Munich.'

Gayle's post-Liverpool career might prove the club were right in letting him go. Yet with a little faith and appreciation of his background, his performance inside the Olympic Stadium is a clue of what he could have been. Gayle was quicker and more powerful than anyone else in the squad – a ball player who liked to dribble and excite the crowd.

It is clear from interviewing other players who knew him that Gayle was perceived as having a 'chip on his shoulder'. Although he now understands the difference between a friend's joke and an enemy's jibe, all he could do back then when entering an unfamiliar environment was revert to instinct. 'People would say they were having a bit of a laugh. But, initially, I didn't know whether they were, so the easiest way to deal with it was by attempting to put a swift end to it.'

Gayle was also entering Anfield formed by experiences from Norris Green and bearing beliefs that he was neither willing nor understandably able to overlook. He confronted racism regularly throughout his career. It happened out of public earshot as well: inside the dressing-room, on the training pitch, at the players' canteen, everywhere. On one occasion, Gayle admits threatening Tommy Smith – the former Liverpool captain – with a baseball bat after one too many 'bad' comments. 'Tommy Smith upset me a lot because he'd been a hero of mine growing up.'

All through his childhood and teenage life, Gayle had contested antagonistic behaviour towards him with hostility. To let something pass would be to reject his upbringing. He was not prepared to concede that for the benefit of the club or, indeed, his own career, even if it meant his superiors questioning his 'character' or 'temperament'. But why should he have to? Gayle, a lone black teenager doing something that nobody had done before – even if it was in his hometown – really had no chance of being a long-term success at Liverpool.

Ahead of the European Cup final of 1981 in Paris, though, his future seemed rosy. And that was despite the dark cloak of Thatcher's despotism beginning to castrate Liverpool as a city barely two years into her reign. The People's March for Jobs from Liverpool to London to highlight the escalating unemployment rates would take the whole of May to descend on the capital. Some Liverpool supporters who walked it carried on over the Channel and landed in Paris for 27 May.

'Laurie Cunningham was playing for Madrid, and he was somebody I looked up to,' Gayle recalls. 'He was brilliant for West Brom. Like me, he was black, good with both feet, played down either flank or up front. He'd been out injured for most of the season, but the Real medical staff rushed him back into the team because he was that important to them.

'The game itself was a non-event. The Parc des Princes was like a cow field because they'd played a rugby international there the Saturday before without cutting the grass afterwards. When we trained the night before the final, everybody was saying about how shite the pitch was.

'Nothing was really happening, and with ten to go the gaffer told me I was going on because Kenny was struggling with his Achilles. He hadn't trained for ages and was just trying to get through games because he was so important to the team. If we could get 60 or 70 minutes out of Kenny Dalglish, it was wiser than putting someone else in with less experience from the start. As I grew older, it was something I began to understand.

'So I went to warm up, charging down the touchline, looking all prepared. Then we got a throw-in and Ray [Kennedy] threw it quickly into space for Alan Kennedy. I honestly didn't expect to see what happened. Alan controlled it with his belly, took it past the first man and hit it. I was right behind the flight of the ball and I thought, "This is in." The ball took its course and hit the net. I looked at the referee to make sure, then everything went off.

'I knew it was all over, because Madrid had nothing in them to come back from a late goal. Then it dawned on me that I wasn't going to go and replace Kenny. Bob brought Jimmy Case on instead and left Jonno up front on his own. That was that.

'I was disappointed not to be going on, but I'm a Liverpool fan so that disappointment quickly turned to elation because the team was more important to me than any personal achievements. I was running round the pitch with the European Cup and a bobble hat on singing "You'll Never Walk Alone" in a foreign country where 90 per cent of the supporters inside the stadium were Liverpool fans. There were people on the terraces who I'd fought and there's me on the pitch. It was surreal.'

Afterwards, the squad celebrated in the Moulin Rouge – the famous show house in Paris's seedy Pigalle district.

'They got us up with the can-can girls and we were dancing on the stage. The champagne was flowing and there were lots of women with limited clothes on prancing about and we'd just won the European Cup. All the wives were there as well. Nothing untoward went on.'

Gayle looked forward to a summer of celebrating with the Liverpool squad as well as his mates from Norris Green and Toxteth. On an average weekend, Gayle's drinking buddies were Sammy Lee, Kevin Sheedy, Ronnie Whelan and Ian Rush, as well as reserve-team players Robbie Savage, Alan Harper, Robbie Ditchburn and Alex Cribley (now the Wigan Athletic physio).

'We used to go to Kirklands on Hope Street then the Continental, or "Snobs" as we called it. Ugly's on Duke Street was another one. There was a regular routine: out on the Saturday night, sleep for a few hours, back up again and out on the lash for the whole Sunday. That would happen every week. Terry McDermott had hollow legs – he could drink all day and night. There was another lad at Birmingham just the same called Robert Hopkins. With Terry, though, if he'd been out, he'd still be right at the front of a running session the following morning, while everybody else would be throwing up on the side of the pitch. That would happen a lot – lads being sick – but if it ever affected your performance, even in training, you'd be out of the team quickly. In that sense, we were all aware of the limits our bodies could take, because there was a queue of people waiting to take your place.'

Gayle believes that some of the funniest people in football were at Liverpool towards the beginning of the '80s. There was one game called 'Ricks'.

'If you mispronounced something, the whole squad would be on you. Hansen was ruthless for it. We were away in Marbella and having a five-a-side. The ball got kicked behind the goal and into the bushes. The common shout, of course, is "Don't beat about the bush." But I've shouted, "Don't bush about the beat." Hansen got on it straight away and I got slaughtered for months.

'If someone said something stupid during a game, it would start straight away, and if you dropped one, there would be a kangaroo court at Melwood the next day where everybody would have the opportunity to laugh at you. There was a hierarchy as well – players you couldn't touch – Alan Hansen, Terry McDermott, Tommo and Graeme Souness. If you went against one of them, the four of them would jump on your case and that was something you didn't want.'

Some couldn't handle the baiting. On one occasion at an end-of-season party, a comedian targeted a number of players in his stand-up routine. For Ian Rush, there was his nose and fashion sense; for Steve Nicol, there was his ginger hair; and for Bruce Grobbelaar, his accent was enough. Then he came to Gayle. The comedian dispensed a bag of white flour over his head. "Now walk through Toxteth," he is alleged to have said. The room roared with laughter, and on this occasion Gayle is said to have not reacted.

'The rigour of the banter was relentless and it hindered some of the lads' progress,' Gayle admits. 'Maybe they took it to heart. Rush was one of them. People question why he didn't score a goal for Liverpool in 12 to 18 months when he first signed, but a lot of it was down to confidence off the field. He let the banter get to him and nearly went down because of it. He'd get slaughtered because of his clothes and his hair. I remember speaking to him one day and he was really down. Because he was from Flint in Wales, he'd never mucked about with a group of lads who had generally grown up in the inner city. Everybody thought they were style icons, wearing the best gear and being quick about the tongue.

'I wore whatever I wanted and turned up at Melwood with flared bottoms. I come in one day and Evo said, "What the fuck are they?" I didn't give a damn. I had an Afro comb that I used to keep in my hair on the drive into training and the lads would rib me about it. Souey would say, "Ere comes the satellite dish." Again, I could take it because I could give it. Rushy, for a time, couldn't.'

Nearly 23 years old and already a member of a European Cup-winning squad, Gayle should have had ample opportunities to enjoy the company of the city's young women.

'We'd be in the TimePiece five or six nights a week. It was a predominantly black club and people would come from all over the place for a night out. There would be a lot of black males with black females or white females – not a lot of white fellas. So there was plenty of women to go about in theory. Yet Liverpool women are some of the hardest women on the planet to pull on a night out. They're so wised up to what goes on around them. It has always been that way. Being a footballer didn't really matter to girls in Liverpool. Most of the time they thought you were pulling their leg. When I went to other clubs in other cities after Liverpool, like Birmingham and Sunderland, they'd be all over you because they weren't switched on like the Liverpool birds.'

After meeting a girl on a night out in town, Gayle had previously moved in to her family abode off Parkfield Road, close to Sefton Park and the bohemian Lark Lane. Later, after signing an improved contract, he bought an apartment in Mossley Hill. Despite settling down, living in the south end of Liverpool became an issue for Bob Paisley and the club.

'It was constantly thrown at me. The gaffer was desperate for me to move, because he wanted all of his players to live in suburbia, where it was a bit quieter. He had his opinions about Toxteth and I had mine.'

Toxteth did not always hold such a dubious reputation. It was once countryside until Liverpool expanded with sea captains and rich merchants as well as bankers and judges building resplendent Georgian and Victorian houses around Canning Street. Even up until the Second World War, it was an upmarket suburb. Then, at the start of the '50s, it started to change when the people with the money moved out as Liverpool rebuilt its port that had been reduced to rubble by Hitler's Luftwaffe. The servants lost their jobs and, gradually, the grand homes in Toxteth were split into flats and, together with the construction of terraced houses, the area gradually took on a more working-class identity. Despite the wrecking balls, it still retained much of its ebullience. In the Granby ward, 'swarms of spidery- limbed brown-skinned children were running everywhere, their ample mommas sitting on the steps of the towering, dilapidated old houses, chatting idly in the sun' (John Cornelius, *Liverpool 8*). It was a close-knit community where everybody knew everybody else. Yet by the '70s, as unemployment began to rise, Toxteth was particularly hard hit. Jobs vanished and even casual work on the docks dried up. Alehouses that once flowed closed down. Few white employers wanted workers from the place some labelled 'Jungle Town'. Toxteth became inward-looking and understandably resentful.

By early July 1981, Paisley's concerns about Gayle and the area he came from appeared vindicated. A month after Phil Thompson lifted the European Cup in Paris, the residents of Toxteth and thousands more who came to support them, lifted up paving stones and threw them at Thatcher's stooges, the police, following months of tension. The stop-and-search law, 'SUS', had created a stand-off between many black residents of Toxteth, and the arrest of Lee Cooper proved a catalyst. The rioting was the most brutal case of civil unrest in Britain in the twentieth century, worse than Brixton and worse than the miners' strike. More than 500 people were arrested, 100 policeman injured and 150 buildings burnt down across a period of just nine days.

Battles were fought with every weapon imaginable; there were lootings, cars overturned and set fire to, and historical buildings like the Rialto destroyed. (The Rialto was an old cinema and dance hall where The Beatles once played.) The Racquets Club, a private establishment where the circuit judges used to stay when they were sitting in Liverpool, was stormed and all of its old paintings stolen before the building was torched.

Ironically, Gayle went on holiday the day it all began.

'Sammy Lee had booked a trip to Portugal with his girlfriend, and he was going to take Davie Fairclough with his missus as well,' Gayle explains. 'But Davie couldn't go in the end, so I went instead. As it transpired, on the evening when it all started back home I was in the air somewhere above France with Sammy.'

Gayle knows a lot of people who witnessed what kicked it all off.

'In the afternoon before, the lad who got caught, Lee Cooper, was riding up and down Granby on a motorbike. I'd gone to see my brother on Beaconsfield Street before I went, and I knew Lee. By the time I got up on the Sunday morning in Portugal, Sammy came rushing up to me with a newspaper saying, "Eh, lad, look at this." I thought it was going to be a story about football. Instead, it was Toxteth with a load of buildings on fire. Lee had been dragged off his bike by the bizzies and people stood up for Lee.

'I went and bought every newspaper. I couldn't believe it because I'd been telling Sammy on the plane about what had been going on in Toxteth. People had just had enough; it was a tinderbox waiting to go up. It's called the Toxteth Riots, but people were coming from all over the city – from Bootle, Speke, Kirkby, from everywhere. There were people getting the bus down there to take part in the social unrest because a lot of people were fed up with the police state and Thatcherism.

'Two weeks later when I came home, it was still happening. It was like an event. The police were bussing in officers from Wales and Yorkshire – fellas that had just been policing the miners' strikes. I was told that the police took a real hammering on the first night and they underestimated the ferocity of the reaction from the locals. The army were ready and waiting to go in and, allegedly, Thatcher said that if the riots spread into the city centre [less than a mile and a half away], then they'd be called in. If that had happened, I am sure that more people would have lost their lives.'

Had Gayle been at home rather than on holiday when the riots started, he dreads to imagine what he might have done.

'It affected everybody in my family. It was such a huge statement of how people were thinking about the country and its governance. Coming from the streets and the background I had, I probably would have started fighting as well.'

Thatcher sent Michael Heseltine, then the Conservative environment secretary, to Liverpool on a PR and charm offensive when the rioting had stopped.

'Heseltine didn't change anything,' Gayle says. 'He devised the garden centre that cost £11 million of taxpayers' money. One of the things that people had been rioting over was the lack of work and jobs. This garden centre [situated on the fringes of Otterspool], which wasn't in our community and didn't employ any of the people looking for work in the community and cost so much money, was a quango, because 12 months later it was gone.

'There were some great organisations that were formed like the Liverpool Eight Law Centre [which closed in 2007] that stood the test of time. But from a social side, Heseltine and Thatcher did nothing for Toxteth. What they were good at was throwing crumbs on the floor and making people fight over the crumbs. Thatcher was an expert at dividing a community.

'I'm very sceptical of all politicians. They're all as bad as one another. They promise you the world, and as soon as they get into power they deliver nothing. People say to me, "Ah, if you don't vote, you can't change things." But people do vote – lots of people – and they still don't change things. There were millions of people who protested on the streets of London telling the country's leaders not to go to war in Iraq. But what did we do? We went to war in Iraq. People go into politics with the best intentions, but as soon as they get power they're corrupted by it and they forget the people that they're serving.'

When Gayle returned for pre-season training towards the end of July, teammates within the Liverpool squad were talking about what had happened in Toxteth.

'The Liverpool fans were vociferous in their support of the rioters as well, because they're working-class people and understood what people were going through. It changed the perception of black people within the club. Fellas who used to maybe look down on me because I was black began to understand who I was and where I'd come from and the struggles I had to face on a daily basis. They appreciated that I wasn't going to put up with any crap from within the club.'

But elsewhere, it got worse through the middle of the '80s before it got better.

'I remember turning up to Chelsea, and the BNP were handing out leaflets outside the ground. How the fuck could that happen? Chelsea were renowned for promoting racism and the BNP. Burnley was another one and to a certain extent Blackburn. Political racists were using those clubs as a tool to promote evil.

'At Chelsea, they caned Paul Canoville – one of their own [black] players. It sickened me. In the middle of the game I said, "How can you play 'ere, lad, when those bastards are giving that to you?" He said, "You know what, la', I get it everywhere I go. It's normal now." I told him to look for another club, but he loved Chelsea.

'I later played at Chelsea for Sunderland in a Milk Cup semi-final second leg and they had to bring horses onto the pitch during the game because it got that bad. The government and the FA were talking about electrifying the fences on the terraces at that time and, although I fundamentally disagreed with that idea, maybe it would have been a good thing for some of those Chelsea BNP supporters. They were horrific that night. We were 2–0 up from the first leg at Roker Park and we went down there for the second leg. I got the impression that the Chelsea fans were trying to get the game postponed because they knew their team was going to lose. Stamford Bridge was a bad place to be.'

Like John Barnes after him, Gayle suffered at Goodison Park.

'I only played there at reserve level for Liverpool, but when I later went to Birmingham I scored there and you got the usual monkey chanting aimed at you. Personally, I loved it because I knew I was pissing the Evertonians off. It was the best way to get back at them by scoring and playing well. I couldn't jump in the crowd and start taking them all on, could I? Having said that, it was always a minority at Everton and not en masse like it was at Chelsea. I think Everton need a pat on the back, because that club has turned itself around.'

Opponents on the pitch also abused Gayle.

'The old-school, experienced pros used to give it to me personally when I first started. I learnt quickly not to have a go back directly, but next time we came together in a challenge I'd just leave my foot in there. If a centre-half had a go at me, I'd do my best to make sure he had a bad night. And if I got the better of him, I'd torment him by letting him know that he had a shit game. Often they'd get wound up and end up getting sent off. I think that's what made me a better player by the fact that I didn't go under and instead said, "Bring it on." I'd be going, "There you go – megged you again. There's another goal."'

Gayle believes the government and the FA did little to stop racism.

'Their efforts were non-existent. Margaret Thatcher and the Conservatives blamed many of the country's social issues on football, so she didn't care whether players or fans were being abused racially. She banned all English clubs from Europe even before UEFA did after Heysel. What happened there was terrible, but a large part of it was a reaction to what was happening within the country – problems caused by Thatcher and her government.

'Throughout the late '70s and early '80s there were that many factories closed down that people had no work and couldn't live with themselves. So it created social problems. Thatcher moved those social problems onto football. Dog dirt had a better reputation than football, so she wasn't going to bother herself dealing with issues within it like racism.

'It wasn't until the late '90s that black players really started coming through different clubs' academy systems. In my opinion, that's how you mark whether there is racism in football. You saw more at the southern clubs than the ones in the north. I know there were exceptions like Remi Moses at Man United and Roger Palmer at Man City, but throughout the '80s especially there were very few black players emerging through youth systems at football clubs in the north.'

When the 1981–82 season began, Gayle expected to feature within the first-team squad on a regular basis during the league season. Instead, he and the club suffered frustration. While Gayle was kept in the reserves, Liverpool struggled to maintain form. After a Boxing Day home defeat to Manchester City, the Reds were nine points off the leaders.

'People sometimes overestimate the difficulties clubs face. Every season, we'd always make a slow start. On *Match of the Day*, Jimmy Hill would love saying, "Ah, that's Liverpool finished now." The warmongers were out. But the one thing about Liverpool was we'd always finish strong. You could never write us off. People overlooked the fact that we'd suffered a lot of injuries at the same time and there were lots of youngsters like myself and Rushy breaking through into the side.'

Bob Paisley stripped Phil Thompson of the captaincy after the loss to City and replaced him with Graeme Souness. The decision started a feud between the pair that has continued for nearly 30 years. Gayle says that the pair clashed frequently at Melwood.

'Until you'd played 250 games for Liverpool, you could never call yourself a regular. Everybody felt threatened. Tommo had been at the club for more than a decade but had the captaincy taken away from him because things weren't right on the pitch. It caused problems between the two of them because they're both proud men. If you look at Souey's background and the single-mindedness he had as a leader, then if you look at Tommo's background and understand the proud man that he is – a Scouser from Kirkby who'd led Liverpool to championships and European successes – there was always going to be a personality clash. Ultimately, the club benefited from that because it shook everyone up and made the players realise that nobody was infallible. At one point Tommo came down to the reserves and we were playing at Preston one night. Tommo wasn't having the best of games and maybe inside his head he was feeling a bit sorry for himself. At half-time, Evo tore into him. Then Robbie Savage, who'd never played a first-team game, kicked his backside as well. Tommo was told that he was still playing for Liverpool – even though it wasn't at first-team level. Robbie went, "If you come down 'ere, you work your fucking tripe off like everyone else." Then Evo went, "The only way you're gonna get back in the first team is if you do it 'ere." It was all very surreal. Second half, Tommo was brilliant and we went from 2–1 down to 5–2 winners. He came up to everyone and apologised for his first-half performance. The following weekend he was back in the first team.'

Gayle explains why he similarly holds an enduring respect for Souness.

'Souey symbolised what the club is all about and why it achieved so much success. He understood that leadership isn't just about what you do in matches; it's about how you conduct yourself with the rest of the players and interact with people. Particularly Graeme's attention to detail with helping younger players was fantastic. He couldn't do enough for us and although some people say he was a bit big-time, he wasn't. Big-time characters weren't allowed at Liverpool in the '70s or the '80s. Everybody was humble and knew their place within the club. Graeme was a born leader. A lot of Liverpool fans caned him for that article with *The Sun*, but I think as Liverpool fans we have to think a bit beyond that. [In 1992, Souness sold the story of his heart bypass ordeal to the newspaper three years after it printed lies about the role of Liverpool supporters during the Hillsborough Disaster.] What Souey did for our club as a captain, he cemented us as the one of the greatest sides in modern-day football. Some people don't realise how sick he was at the time when the article went to print, so maybe he wasn't thinking straight. He managed to get off his sickbed and get to Wembley to oversee the victory over Sunderland, and for me that epitomises what the guy is about.

'A lot of people also try to lay blame for the changes in fortunes for the club over the last 20 years. He came back from Italy with some great ideas and probably tried to change it too quickly. I reckon he had the foresight to see where football was going by making Melwood the daily base for the club and introducing fresh dietary regimes. A lot of people pooh-poohed the ideas, but now every club has adopted it. His biggest mistake was to sell some of the club's most-experienced players a year too early. The same people that say the club didn't change quickly enough over the last two decades also blame Graeme. That's contradictory in my opinion.'

Gayle likens Souness's coaching methods to those of Tony Waiters, a coach who arrived at Liverpool in the early '70s after studying in America.

'Liverpool's methods were tried and trusted, but they weren't ready for changes in football. Waiters came into Melwood, but other people on the coaching staff didn't accept him. Ronnie [Moran] once joked in front of all the lads that he couldn't do a training session without a clipboard. "In the end, we just chased him." Now, I'm not saying that Waiters was a great coach, but the club should have been more open-minded to change. I've played in America, and there are some skills that can be transferred. They're so meticulous: everything is written down and planned. Because Liverpool was so successful with no qualified coaches or even physio – Bob Paisley was the only person with a medical certificate – maybe they rested on their laurels.'

Gayle admits himself that after the European Cup final in '81, maybe he too 'rested on his laurels'. After only being an unused substitute against AZ Alkmaar the following November, he disappeared back into the reserve side and never played in the first team again.

'Sometimes, I still go to bed at night and dream about scoring in front of the Kop for the first team when there's 25,000 standing there. Unfortunately, my only goal came in an away match against Tottenham. But I still have that memory. Sometimes, I still can't believe that I fulfilled what hundreds of thousands of kids grow up dreaming about. There are days, even now, when I miss training. There were days at other clubs when I thought, "Nah – I can't be arsed going in today." But it was never like that at Liverpool. Every single day was brilliant. When you went to bed of a night, you couldn't wait for the next morning.

'It was a personal tragedy that it all had to come to an end. Maybe I jumped off the ship too early and took a calculated risk that didn't quite work out. But once you've played in the reserves and gone into the first team, it's very hard to adjust to reserve-team football again and be motivated in the same way, because you crave that atmosphere.'

Gayle spent another 18 months frustrated in the reserve team before agreeing to sign in 1983 for Ron Saunders and Birmingham City. Saunders, born in Birkenhead, was not to every player's taste because of his rudimentary tactics. In an interview with John Gidman, a fellow Scouser who played under him previously at Aston Villa, the mere mention of the manager's name provoked the response 'that cunt'. Gayle, however, has fonder memories.

'I've got a lot of time for that man,' he says. 'He'd be great in modern-day football. I'd liken Ron to José Mourinho – that's how he turned everything round. It was always them against us. Anybody outside of the club was considered the enemy. You'd get journalists following us around at Birmingham, sniffing round for front-page news rather than sports stories. Ron would create this siege mentality. He kept all the focus off us and heaped it all on himself.

'Ron was a disciplinarian, and all the players would know where the line was. If you stepped over it, you suffered the consequences – it should be that way in any walk of life. He wasn't regimental with it, but he didn't like players who didn't put in a shift. He wanted commitment and that's why I got on so well with him, because I needed a manager like that.'

The atmosphere at Birmingham was different to Liverpool.

'When I went to Birmingham, Noel Blake was already there, so it was different sharing a dressing-room with other black players. That made it easier for me to settle, although the banter wasn't quite as instinctive amongst the players as it was at Liverpool. Birmingham was and still is a big club, and I don't think people across the country appreciate just how big they are. If they won the Premier League, I'd imagine that Birmingham is the type of club and place where they could sustain success. They're a bigger club than Aston Villa.'

Gayle's performances at St Andrews earned him a call-up to the England Under-21 side as an overage player, despite the opportunity to represent both Sierra Leona and Ghana.

'We won the European Championship in Italy, which was great, and I enjoyed the experience of playing with some top-class players. But I'm not one of those people who goes round singing "Three Lions on my chest". For me, the pride always came playing for the club, because they're the people you share the day-to-day affinity with, whereas England was once every couple of months. As a fan, it always miffed me how one week people can be kicking shite out of each other on the terraces and the next week be singing "Two World Wars and one World Cup".'

Despite enjoying life living in Solihull and scoring nine times in his debut season at St Andrews, Gayle joined Sunderland when Birmingham were relegated from the First Division.

'I signed for Len Ashurst shortly after Gary Bennett from Cardiff,' he remembers. 'Unfortunately for Lennie, he only lasted a season. It was a funny situation, because initially Len was only on a trial contract. After we beat Chelsea in the Milk Cup semi-final, they offered him a three-year contract and we were buzzing. The following Saturday, he came in the dressing-room and he was a changed man. It was his downfall. He was in the comfort zone. Previously, everybody in that dressing-room had been playing for him. As a manager, that's what you dream of. But against Leicester, he pinned the team up on the wall and said, "If anyone doesn't agree with it, come and see me on Monday morning." Then he walked out.

'Gordon Chisholm had scored in the midweek and he'd been dropped for no apparent reason. The whole room went quiet.

Leicester had Alan Smith and Gary Lineker in their side. They scored two each and Leicester beat us 4–0, and we couldn't put two passes together. It deflated the whole team and we ended up getting relegated. We got beaten by Norwich in the Milk Cup final as well, but they eventually went down too.'

Ashurst was replaced by Lawrie McMenemy. Quickly, Gayle's future became clear.

'In my first game for Sunderland, we'd played Southampton and I'd ripped Reuben Agboola to bits. The Sunderland fans loved it and McMenemy [then Southampton manager] was fuming. He was going to Steve Williams [the Southampton midfielder], "Isn't somebody going to deal with that fucking Gayle?" I went over to the touchline and said, "Not today, mate." He didn't like that.

'When he arrived at Sunderland, we played Norwich, got a good result, then stayed down south for a game against Wimbledon midweek. They were beatable, and I assumed the manager would keep the same team because we'd played well at Carrow Road.

'I went to put my shirt on and McMenemy marches over, "Oh, oh, oh, oh. What are you doing? You're on the bench." He got his assistant Lew Chatterley to explain why, but it was bullshit. I was close to walking out of Plough Lane there and then. We lost the game 2–0, but the next week we beat Stoke to stay up and he started me. With ten minutes to go, he took me off and it seemed like a statement to me. So I walked towards the bench, threw my shirt at him and walked down the tunnel.'

Gayle walked out of Sunderland and moved to America, where he played indoor football with Dallas Sidekicks for a season.

'Dallas was brilliant. The decision to come home was one of my biggest mistakes. I remember listing to BBC World Service on the radio when we had a game in New York with Keith Weller [the former Leicester City playmaker], and Watford were beating Arsenal 4–1 at Highbury in the FA Cup. Barnesy and Luther Blissett were ripping them to bits. I thought, "I've gotta go back home and start playing proper football again." It was all indoors in America and that was a bit weird. I spoke to the coach, Gordon Jago [a Londoner who played for Charlton in the '50s], and he agreed to let me go. But when I stepped off the plane at Heathrow on a miserable day in March I just thought, "You've just made the biggest mistake of your life." There were so many opportunities out there away from football, and Dallas was a great place to live. I loved the show – the glitz and the glamour.'

Gayle spent time on loan at Stoke before signing for Blackburn.

'When Jack Walker came in as the owner, it all changed. We started bringing in players like Ossie Ardiles, Steve Archibald, Frank Stapleton and Kevin Moran. These were the big names that the club needed. They went for Teddy Sheringham at Millwall as well for £2 million. Then there was a big offer for Brett Angell at Southend. But they didn't come because there wasn't a figurehead as a manager. Don Mackay had done a great job previously on a shoestring, but I got the impression that people at the top of the club wanted a high-profile person in charge who would attract expensive players.

'We were on our way back from Ipswich on the bus, and we all knew Don was on his way out. The players were talking and I said, "Kenny Dalglish you know, he'd fancy it." He was on gardening leave from Liverpool. Jack Walker wouldn't have a problem paying the compensation, which was something like £500k. By the Monday, it was in the newspapers in Blackburn and I was thinking, "What have I started here?" By the end of the week, Kenny was in place.'

Gayle retired from football after short spells with Halifax and Accrington Stanley. He was offered a deal by Michael Knighton (a businessman who had earlier failed to buy Man United) for £150 a week to play for Carlisle. '"Fuck that," I thought. My enthusiasm had gone so I spewed it.'

Gayle has been working back in Toxteth for two decades.

'It's an area that's close to my heart,' he says. 'I've spent a large portion of my life here, and it's where my family have spent most of theirs as well. Toxteth is populated mainly by black people, and it's the black kids in the main that have been underachieving.

'A lot of kids have got themselves into something through peer pressure, but when you look behind the mask they're genuine young kids who can change. Society tends to bar its youngsters at this moment in time. They're told that they're lazy and bad constantly by the government through ASBOs and heavy-handed police work. In the end, if you tell somebody they are something often enough, they become it.

'The kids here have problems at home and they bring all that baggage with them into school or, even worse, don't attend school at all. It means they fall behind in their education, and by the time they reach secondary school they're way behind a lot of the other students. Some of them stop going to school altogether and that creates a problem for us as a community because kids are out hustling on the streets.'

You get the impression if anyone can straighten a youngster out, Howard Gayle is the man to do it.

CHAPTER THREE

Cult Zeros

GUARDIAN READER, Michael Robinson

'THATCHER BORE THE SAME CHARM AS THE BUBONIC PLAGUE,' declares Michael Robinson, Liverpool striker turned Spanish television presenter. 'Because of that woman,' he pauses, pointing a Marlboro Red in my direction, leaning forward with a plume of smoke spiralling skyward, 'we live in a society where you have to save up to get ill. That is not an absolute truth, of course. But it is a part of her legacy. I believe in a capitalism that I can embrace with a social conscience, remembering that there's a great difference between having a shit and tearing your arse.'

Robinson, or Robín, as he is affectionately known in Spain, became the country's most popular sporting pundit and arguably the most famous TV star by pioneering the Canal Plus magazine show *El Día Después* (The Day After). Even the old litmus test has him way out in front of other public figures – his rubber double fronts the Spanish equivalent of *Spitting Image*.

He is also your original version of a term that has now become a cliché, 'the thinking man's footballer'. Like Graeme Le Saux, he would read *The Guardian* or the *Financial Times* on buses or train rides while travelling to away matches. Unlike Le Saux, there is something incredibly endearing about him. Robinson is fabulously good company.

When I meet him in Madrid at his office on Calle de Almagro, a street parallel to the regal Castellana and just a few blocks down from the Santiago Bernabéu Stadium, he has already booked a table at a restaurant. 'We'll do the interview over a long lunch and a few G&Ts,' he informs me on arrival, rubbing his hands and grinning before carefully arranging a neat-looking briefcase. The office is very Zen, with whitewashed walls only broken by a desk, a laptop and two quilted chairs. Robinson moved into this space in 2008 to deal with the extra business and entertainment opportunities that have been afforded to him since becoming Spain's answer to Gary Lineker. I am aware, however, that this comparison annoys him.

'The BBC get Lineker because he's Julie Andrews,' he told me in a previous interview. 'Sling him on and throw in Hansen and Lawrenson, and that'll do. There's no recognition of the cultural elements that envelop football in British broadcasting. Period.'

Wearing a grey suit and fitted light-blue shirt minus the tie, Robinson adjusts a pair of thick-rimmed black glasses that have seemingly been modelled on Nana Mouskouri, before revealing a little bit about his life at the moment. It's hectic. Only in the last fortnight he has played at a charity golf tournament in Augusta in honour of his old friend Seve Ballesteros, flown back to Spain for a live interview with Morgan Freeman on his television show *Informe Robinson* (The Robinson Report), before enjoying lunch with the former vice president of Spain, Roberto Figaredo. They ate in the same restaurant we are dining at today.

En route to La Parra (The Grill), on the fringes of Madrid's prosperous Salamanca district, I am reminded why Robinson is the football equivalent of the Kings of Leon – underappreciated, if completely anonymous at home yet hugely popular in a foreign land. He enjoys cult status in Spain. 'Robín,' chortles one of a hat-trick of admirers on the street. 'You're a genius.'

'Thank you,' he responds, in a mix of smooth Spanish and nasally fading Lancastrian, stretching a toothy almost goofy smile, his broad shoulders bobbing up and down with contentment. Robinson is taller and heavier than one remembers. His physique reveals that he is a former centre-forward.

Underneath La Parra's restaurant sign on a tree-lined street it reads 'Londres, Paris, Madrid, Seville'. We are in Madrid's equivalent of Mayfair. Inside there is a mosaic of green, yellow and brown Moorish tiles, a reminder of Spain's Islamic past. There are leather seats, the finest linen tablecloths and a wine list the length of the nearby Manzanares River.

Robinson's face beams underneath the lampshade that hangs above. A pianist sporting a tuxedo and a pencil-thin moustache tickles the ivories. The scene could be fresh out of a *Poirot* episode in some mysterious Arabic shisha den. I almost expect a shady character with an ominous silhouette to appear at our table, opening a copy of *El País* before commenting assertively that the eagle will fly north from Moscow this autumn. And everybody knows Robinson. The hurried waiters can't do enough for their esteemed guest.

Speaking to a number of ex-Reds who played with Robín during an 18-month spell at Anfield between 1983 and 1984, they say that he was the most likely to carve an alternative career upon retirement. They also half-joke that he is probably a better TV presenter than he was a footballer.

'I can't disagree with that,' he laughs, reflecting on the 13 goals he scored in 52 appearances in a Liverpool shirt. 'One of my best moments came when I got three away at West Ham. After the game, all the lads signed the match ball. Kenny Dalglish left a message. It read, "I don't believe it."'

Robinson was a closet intellectual amongst his teammates at Melwood, reluctant to let it all come out. Not that he spoke in a voice somewhere between Quentin Crisp and the Duke of Edinburgh. He was just brighter than most and thought deeply about life, a side of his character that he later tells me affected his performances.

Here, almost 26 years after he left Anfield, we enjoy an outstanding three-course meal washed down with an '02 Rioja, four pints of *cerveza* each and a G&T like he promised. Considering there's a saying in Spain, 'We eat everything in the pig except the walk', and that the night before I'd eaten sautéed pig's ear in a tiny Galician tapas bar on a scruffy side street in the rundown immigrant barrio of Lavapiés, Robinson's enriching choice for the two of us of asparagus and prawns followed by langoustine risotto is welcome. As the freshest seeded batch of restaurant-baked bread arrives on the table from the furnace in the busy kitchen behind, thoughts of Robinson's upbringing in the South Shore area of Blackpool must seem very far away.

'I was still an egg when my mum and dad decided to leave Leicester to run a boarding house in Blackpool,' he explains. 'They'd been publicans beforehand. For a shy boy like me, it was quite an experience growing up in what was really a small hotel. I became sociable.

'I lived my childhood on the beach. For a kid, living in Blackpool was like being in a giant playground. It was fantastic: slot machines, roller coasters. It was nice to grow up in a place where everybody was reasonably happy because they were on their holidays. People of a working-class background went on an annual pilgrimage to the seaside: the Scots, Welsh, Brummies and Geordies were everywhere. I remember thinking I didn't want to live anywhere else. The rest of the country seemed normal, whereas Blackpool was exciting for a young boy.'

Robinson's parents were working class.

'But they had aspirations to be middle,' he interrupts. 'I was ten when I went on my first holiday – a cruise around the Iberian Peninsula. Cruising was a holiday that boarding-house owners in South Shore tended to do.

'I was never really influenced by my parents in terms of ideologies, because they weren't deep thinkers on such issues. Blackpool was a Conservative oasis or a dark corner depending where you come from politically. But I had more empathy with the left. My dad was a devout capitalist – a businessman with a 90 per cent mortgage. The family needed capitalism to survive. But it also needed the money from working-class people, many of whom came to Blackpool as socialists. There seemed to be a lot of geography teachers wearing brown corduroy trousers.'

Robinson went to Palatine High School, an institution that in 2002 was targeted as a hotspot of teenage pregnancy by the local council. He says not much has changed since his time there.

'Whereas kids from most secondary schools in the area would go on to further education or industry, the primary destination from my school was jail. It was an extremely violent place. We used to win the local schools football league every season for the main reason that three of the other schools wouldn't turn up to play us. That was the Blackpool way. On the surface it was a cheery place, but beneath that there was an undercurrent of local thuggery. Most of it probably started at Palatine.'

The football bug caught Robinson earlier than an Ian Rush opening goal at Goodison Park.

'It was in my blood. My dad [Arthur Robinson] had played professionally with Brighton, Aston Villa and Wrexham before the Second World War came along, where he fought in Holland. He spent most of his six years behind enemy lines and was later decorated by Queen Wilhelmina. My brother was a fine player too.

'Coming from the north-west meant there was always lots of teams to watch. Dad supported Villa, but they were too far away, so on a Friday night I'd go and watch Southport, who were in the Football League. Then Saturdays it'd be either Blackpool or Liverpool. I worked as a bagging boy at Blackpool train and bus stations to finance my trips to Bloomfield Road. It meant wheeling a trolley halfway across town with holidaymakers' luggage to B&Bs and hotels. I was like a poor taxi driver with no wheels. Because I was a lot cuter than my older brother, he pushed me forward: "Carry your bags, miss?" It worked.'

Robinson went to Anfield for the first time as a six year old.

'It was 1963 and Liverpool played Burnley,' he recalls instantly. 'I remember a near-post header from St John, which flew into the net. It sounds romantic, but my dad tells me that I'd fallen in love with football before the teams came out. We stood on the Kop and the crowd were singing, "We love you, yeah, yeah, yeah – with a team like that, you know you can't be bad." My dad says I was totally enveloped by the atmosphere and ten minutes before the kick-off I told him I wanted to be a footballer.'

The journey to Merseyside became a regular thing.

'Every fortnight seemed like Christmas Eve. I always insisted to my dad or brother that we be there at least an hour and a half before the game so I could get my place on the Kop. Half of the time, I didn't know what was going on. But the noise and the sound made my hairs stand on end. I'm not religious, but Anfield was my cathedral. I was a devotee to something and that was the red shirt.

'I used to show off my experiences when I went to school. All of my inspiration for games on the yard or the beach came from Anfield. I was desperate to one day be one of those protagonists that walked out of the tunnel and received the adulation of the supporters who pledged their lives to the greatness of the club. Again, I know it sounds romantic, but when it later happened it was no less romantic than I ever envisaged it to be.'

Robinson started playing competitively when he was seven.

'I was a striker but for some reason given the number 6 shirt and that disappointed me greatly. It wasn't very glamorous. I wanted 9 or 8. But Dad said it was a number of responsibility. "Look at Bobby Moore," he told me. It felt like some kind of consolation, because in the playground I was the kid that scored all the goals. Although any Liverpool fan reading this interview may struggle to believe it, I was by far the best player of my age in the junior leagues around Blackpool, so I became the number 6 that went everywhere and did everything. A lot of managers at every level now want to control everything a player does on the pitch. Luckily, I was blessed by not having a tactical schoolmaster like the guy from *Kes*. We were allowed to develop naturally and enjoy ourselves.'

At the age of 12, Robinson had a few clubs asking him to sign schoolboy forms. He went on trial to Chelsea.

'I played in the same team as Ray Wilkins and Steve Wicks. I stayed in a really posh hotel on Gloucester Road in Kensington, and they really made an effort. But I missed home an awful lot and soon had a go with Man City and Coventry. But on both occasions I had problems with homesickness. I was a bit of a tart.'

Robinson has 'romantic' memories of the moment he agreed to sign for Preston.

'*Coronation Street* was my barometer of time in the evening because I had to go to bed at eight o'clock. By 7.30 I had to have my pyjamas on. *Corrie* was in the advert break and the doorbell rings. I went to answer it and there was a small guy who introduced himself as Jimmy Scott. Then there was another guy who looked just like Bobby Charlton. "Are you Michael?" they asked.

'"Yep."

'"We'd like to speak to your dad."

'So I shut the door on them and told him that there was a guy who looks just like Bobby Charlton who was after him.

'As it turned out, Jimmy Scott was the chief scout of Preston North End and the baldy guy *was* Bobby Charlton – the club's player-manager. They immediately offered my dad a contract. I was sent upstairs and my dad, looking all embarrassed because Bobby Charlton was inside his house, followed me up to get a tie on. In all the commotion, I missed the end of *Corrie* and it was well past eight when I was called back down.

'My dad said, "Mr Charlton thinks you might have a future in football and wants to know whether you'd like to become an apprentice professional with North End." Being a diligent son, I said, "But, Dad, aren't I going to St Anne's College of Further Education?" He said, "You're not listening to me, son.

Bobby Charlton thinks you've got a future in the game," then looking at Bobby, he added, "Sorry, Mr Charlton. My son can be a bit thick at times."'

Robinson played under three different managers at Preston, then in the old Second Division.

'Preston treated Mr Charlton rather shoddily. He took over in the Third Division and brought through great players like Mel Holden, Mike Elwiss, and Tony Morley before having the carpet swept from beneath him. Newcastle came in with a bid for our centre-half, John Byrne, and Mr Charlton said that if the club accepted the offer he would leave, because he was trying to build a team. Until then he had an immaculate if all-too-brief managerial career, and he had no option but to resign. He was a very human character.'

In Charlton's place, Harry Catterick was appointed and soon gave Robinson his first-team debut.

'Catterick was a very dour, hard man and I didn't get on with him at all,' Robinson recalls. 'I rubbed him up the wrong way and he did the same to me. It was a shock after Mr Charlton, because they were completely different people. Harry treated me badly and didn't really know how to manage youngsters. He was a bit out of touch, and it was no wonder he gained a reputation as a completely miserable human being – even amongst the Evertonians that were supposed to revere him. Harry put me in the first team but dropped me back down quickly, and it didn't seem like I was going to get another chance because of the way he kept himself distant. I suppose that wasn't just me, it was everybody. But as a young professional, it was hard to understand.'

Eventually, the lugubrious Catterick was sacked.

'Nobby Stiles was the reserve-team manager and got a promotion. All I can say for Nobby was that he was a players' manager and got the best out of me. He decided to throw me back up into the first team. I repaid his faith by scoring a dozen or so goals, and at the end of that season Man City came in with a huge offer.'

Robinson's first contract at Preston was a modest one, but the move to Maine Road reportedly made him the game's wealthiest teenager.

'I was 19 when City offered £750,000. Trevor Francis, an experienced player and a great player, had moved shortly before from Birmingham to Forest for a world-record £1 million fee. I became the most expensive teenager. I'd started out at £6 a week with a pound a point bonus at Preston, then moved up to £8 when I reached the first team. I finished there on £30 per week, but the City contract blew everything away. They gave me £330.

'I was built up to be a wonder boy. The season opened with a game against Arsenal, and I was playing Alan Ball – a Blackpool legend. He was a World Cup winner and had moved for a fraction of what I'd gone for when he left Everton for Highbury. He was a great player and I was a nobody.'

Robinson had a rough time at Maine Road.

'It was an absolute fucking nightmare,' he reflects, chugging on the butt end of what is already his third cigarette. 'There was such a divide between the older players and the younger players, and there seemed to be a lot of jealousy from the older ones towards me because of the figures involved in my transfer. I was young and did not know how to deal with it.

'I've always aligned myself with a certain cause. With the greatest respect to Manchester United, I grew up loathing their arrogance. The option of signing for City was an attractive one because it gave me the opportunity to beat United – I identified their downfall with a social vindication. I later enjoyed playing for Osasuna because it was pseudo-Basque and the supporters had a way about them that identified them as separate from others. I chose City after Preston even though half of the clubs in England wanted to sign me. But it was most unfortunate that I never got around this log rhythm that was playing football for Manchester City. Because that's what it was – a bloody log rhythm, a fucking nightmare. I lived in Wilmslow in a house that was upside down. I spent my afternoons upstairs and slept downstairs because people would come looking through my window by day. I was frightened to go into supermarkets. I couldn't handle the pressure. It sent me round the bend.'

Robinson didn't get on with boss Malcolm Allison.

'Big Mal was round the fucking bend too. I couldn't understand him and neither could anybody else. Some of the tactics that he tried to apply were most certainly strange. He used to cut the pitch up into zones, bring in ballroom dancers to teach us about movement, use basketball coaches for jumping and even an East German swimming instructor for lessons on how to limber up our muscles. He brought a sweeper in from Serbia called Dragoslav Stepanovic from a strange German club called Wormatia Worms that nobody had heard of before. Malcolm wanted him to break forward from the back and play forward and wide in order to leave space for other players to move into. I couldn't relate to him and my relationship with him was the worst I've shared with any manager.'

In 1985, Robinson made his peace with Allison at a PFA convention.

'In my first season at Brighton, we played Manchester City in the league and there was a war of words before the game. I scored, and maybe it's not very bashful from me, but it was a wonderful goal. I ran towards the dugout and slid on my knees right in front of Malcolm. I was a young, stupid boy and it was very disrespectful, but it felt right because he did nothing to help me at City.

'He was a sworn enemy, but I went up and shook his hand at the awards ceremony. I realised that a lot of the stuff he'd told me only slotted into place later in my career. Malcolm made the mistake of not realising that many of his footballers were really adolescents and incapable of grasping something new. When you're judged by an immediate result, it is judged by black and white, wrong and right. Unfortunately, it didn't work for him.

'It was only years later that I realised some of the stuff he told us was quite correct. Some of his ideas were pooh-poohed by the players – including me – but I was a teenager who hadn't accrued any information about football. The senior ones like

Willie Donachie, Mick Channon, Paul Power and Joe Corrigan all hated him too. They all laughed at his methods. But bugger me, as the years have passed, I've realised he was ahead of his time and it was the senior players that were wrong. Only now I realise that in some ways Malcolm Allison was a visionary – it was us players that were the idiots.'

Having scored eight times in thirty league games in a season where City finished six points above the relegation zone, Robinson signed for Brighton in the summer of 1980. On the south coast, he found solace.

'It was my rehabilitation,' he says. 'At City, I'd fallen out of love with football and seriously contemplated what I was going to do with my life.' He met Alan Mullery. 'Alan realised I was a bit of a softie at heart and knew how to manage me. Alan was a real gentleman and he saved my career. Brighton was the right place to go for me at the time, because I was fed up with the pressure. Brighton had and still has no real great football criteria. People used to go the Goldstone Ground and fill it every week as if they were going to the cinema or the theatre. There was no long tradition down there and it just seemed to be happy people rolling up every Saturday afternoon to watch a dose of First Division football.'

Waiting for Robinson on the south coast was Mark Lawrenson. 'I played with Mark for Preston North End, Brighton, Liverpool and Ireland. We grew up in the same area – in the same age group, roughly – but we never really became friends. We had nothing in common. I think he didn't get me. Mark used to play Sunday-league football for Bispham Juniors when I played for their main rivals. He was a timid left-winger and nine times out of ten would be the sub. Mark was the sub that never got a game. Mark's stepfather, Tom Gore, was a director at North End, and when I was an apprentice at the club he'd come down in the school holidays to get cones out, arrange bibs and set pitches out for five-a-side.

'In the Central League, we opened one season with an away game at Villa. We stopped off at the Post House on the way there and ate egg on toast. Nobby Stiles was the player-manager of the reserves, but the food gave him the squits and he couldn't play. There was only one sub and Mark was in the travelling party, sitting next to his stepdad on the bus. Because we had nobody else, Mark had to take his [Stiles's] place on the bench.

'Within minutes of the kick-off, one of our players got injured. Nobby encouraged him to carry on, but it was clear he had to come off. Remembering that Mark was a timid left-winger that couldn't get a game for Bispham Juniors, Nobby brought Mark on and tried to hide him at left-back. Immediately, the Villa tried to get at him. But Mark was absolutely fucking superb.

'The next week, there was a match against Bury. Again, superb. A couple of months went by and David Sadler had arthritis and couldn't play for the first team. Throughout the week, they tried different people at centre-half to play alongside John Byrne. But nobody convinced. By the Thursday, they tried Mark. He was told not to go back to school and, immediately, they gave him a professional contract at 17. That was unheard of. But to be fair, he was superb again.

'Mark started the year as this willowy winger that couldn't get a game for Bispham Juniors, who was only at Preston's training ground because his director stepdad knew he was a football fan who wanted a kick-about in his school holidays. Nobody would have imagined he would become a top defender. At the end of the season, he went to Brighton for £100,000.'

For the first time in his career, Robinson became part of a drinking culture at Brighton.

'I was too young to really go out at Preston, although I could see the older fellas drank,' he continues, gulping on a large glass of Estrella Damm. 'Then at City, there was no team spirit, no dressing-room banter and no drinking culture because everybody was miserable. I had no friends there. At Brighton, there was a lot of fooling around with drink, and when I think back now I wonder how sometimes we ever got on the pitch. Because it wasn't a town obsessed by football, we could go out a lot more and not get hassled.

'Alan Mullery liked the players to relax and trusted their ability in knowing when to draw the line. It changed slightly when he was replaced by Mike Bailey, who was a wonderful man but slightly more reserved. I wouldn't say I was thrilled about his football ideals either, because I was a centre-forward and wanted to score goals. All he cared about was keeping a clean sheet. It showed, because in his season in charge we drew a lot of games 0–0 and it infuriated the crowd. The entertainment value that the Brighton crowd enjoyed seemed to disappear, while the novelty of being in the First Division also ran out. Fewer people went to watch the matches, whereas underneath Alan we played gung-ho and the supporters loved it.

'Brighton were the only club where the players and management were on a crowd bonus. For every 1,000 people through the turnstiles, we'd get a few quid in our back pocket. We were on fortunes. It was wise in some ways, because it made everybody happy. We scored lots of goals, won games and we entertained the crowd, who were in it for the showbiz element of football, and the club and its staff made a lot of cash in the process. It was perfect. Then under Mike we became a proper team – more diligent – and we did what we had to in order to survive. Yet we became slightly boring and the crowds fell and the board worried themselves about how they'd pay the players. So they fired him.'

Jimmy Melia, a former Liverpool midfielder under Bill Shankly, took over.

'Jimmy was an avuncular character, a jovial man – good fun to be around, and a Scouser. The players loved him even though he was not so conventional. Things went reasonably well. It was true that we got to the FA Cup final, but it's also true that we got relegated. It was a dreamy period and it was very different. We played a relaxed style of football, and because of the way we were off the pitch you could say that we were the first pub team to play a major final at Wembley.

'Because of our FA Cup run, we went losing silly games in the league, but nobody seemed to care. Everybody thought we had far too good a team to get relegated, and the FA Cup run vindicated that. We'd walk around the streets and fans would congratulate us on our performances in the Cup. In the meantime, we were spiralling towards relegation. They were romantic times set amidst not necessarily the most professional environment. We drew 2–2 with United in the final and lost the replay 4–1. Gordon Smith should have won the game for us, but he missed a sitter after I set him up. He still blames me for it.

'Jimmy rested me in two of the last four games of the season ahead of the final, and it proved to be crucial. It was a bizarre decision to make. But I complied with it. Maybe I should have been more opinionated. We finished bottom of the league, but if it wasn't for the cup final I think we'd have stayed up.'

After relegation in 1983, Brighton couldn't afford to keep their star players and big earners. Robinson was on a bumper contract at Brighton. Whoever wanted to sign him would have to pay handsomely.

'It was £1,400 a week with an automatic 15 per cent a year inflation over ten years. Brighton was a very wealthy club. Bryan Robson had gone from West Brom to Manchester United and at the same time Peter Shilton had left Forest for Southampton. They were reportedly the biggest earners in English football, on £800 a week. But I knew at least four lads, including myself, already on more than £1,000 a week at Brighton: Peter Ward, Steve Foster and Mark Lawrenson were the others.

'I had no previous notion that Liverpool were after me. I knew Seville in Spain had made enquiries, as well as Everton and Newcastle. I'd spoken to Howard Kendall over the phone and he was very endearing. But I never wanted to sign for them because I'd grown up as a Liverpool fan and Everton were the enemy – the monied elite. It's funny now how they portray themselves as paupers, when back in the '60s they were known as the Bank of England Club, with the lovely Harry Catterick throwing money at anything that moved.

'Anyway, I went away on holiday and came back for pre-season at Brighton. I'd just bought a Golden Labrador called Paddy for my girlfriend, later to become wife, then a call came from Mike Bamber [the Brighton chairman]. I got round to his house and he said, "There has been an offer, we've accepted it, and you'll never guess who it is . . ."'

Robinson's new contract would break Liverpool's wage structure. To avoid the press breaking the story and alerting other clubs, he met officials at Amsterdam's Schiphol Airport.

'When Peter Robinson asked me how much I was on, he couldn't believe it. He rang up the Brighton secretary to check I wasn't pulling his leg. I told him that I'd sign for nothing. It seriously didn't matter. "Pay me what the fuck you want – give me the pen," I said to him.

'In the end, John Smith, the chairman, insisted on giving me a rise and agreed with Peter that all the other senior players should get a rise as well. I remember saying to Peter that it was going to be an honour to play with such wonderful players. "We don't sign players," Peter told me. "We sign people that play good at football."

'Joe Fagan and Bob Paisley were there when I went to sign the contract and I asked them whether I could have a coffee or some fizzy water. "Here's a beer, lad," Joe told me. "Get that down your neck."

'Later, Joe asked me whether I had any other questions. "How do you want me to play?" Bob and Joe looked at each other, smiled, then Joe took charge. "We rather hope that you know how to play, otherwise we're going to lose a lot of money here."

'"According to the system, I meant."

'Joe put his hand around my shoulder, sat me down and said, "Listen, lad, we play 11 players here – just to make sure we aren't disadvantaged. In midfield, when we get the ball we try to kick it to somebody dressed the same colour as us. As a forward, Michael, kick it in the net, and if you can't, kick it to somebody who can. Then at the back, we're gonna break our balls to make sure the oppo don't score."

'"There's no more to it than that?" I asked.

'"You'll find, Michael, that we leave players to figure it out for themselves. But we'll help along the way. This isn't a major science . . . you'll work it out.'

'It was the greatest example of man-management I'd ever come across.'

Robinson moved to Merseyside on a three-year deal but he failed to score in his first nine games. In covering one early match, a former leading BBC Radio commentator described him on air as a 'dyspeptic water buffalo grazing with a herd of gazelle – clumsy, awkward, a yard behind the play and a thousand yards from Dalglish's analytical, surgical football'.

'I had a terrible start,' he says. 'Christ, another fucking nightmare . . . seriously couldn't hit a barn door, and I could tell the crowd and media hadn't really taken to me. I remember waking up the morning before we played Odense in the first round of the European Cup and the papers were saying I was going to be dropped. Craig Johnston was coming in and the goal seemed like the eye of a needle to me. But I wasn't a pretty player and I knew it.

'I used to be the first person into training. Like everybody knows, we changed at Anfield and got the bus up to Melwood. When I arrived, Ronnie Moran comes up and goes, "Boss wants to see you." So I walked the longest walk down the corridor to his office. I goes in and Joe asks Sheila [the former secretary to the manager] if she can get an official teamsheet.

'He proceeds to tell me that that morning his wife Maisy had given him two sugars in his tea instead of three, without handing him a copy of the *Racing Post*. He could sense something was up. "Are you not going to play Michael?" she asks. "He has such a nice face . . . give him a break."

'Joe told me that he hadn't said a word to his missus and hadn't even considered dropping me. "I want to put the record straight, lad. Look at this teamsheet: you're the first one on the list."

'He explained that he thought I'd given Kenny a new lease of life and he was really pleased with me. "Bloody Maisy," he finished. "Lovely woman, but she don't know much about footy, does she, lad? Can I give her a call and tell her you're all right?"

'The whole story may have been a load of bollocks, but it made me feel the greatest man on earth. I scored two goals that night then went away to West Ham soon after and scored a hat-trick. It was genius from Joe.'

The gentle approach with Fagan was a departure from Paisley's regime, where he preferred to distance himself. Robinson, clearly in his element telling this story, believes that directions from those in the dugout made everything seem easy for the players.

'The attitude throughout the club was that if we didn't do well, anybody could beat us. If we did do well, nobody could beat us. It was a humble attitude. I remember once before a game against Brentford in the League Cup, Graeme Souness had the dressing-room buzzing like we were playing against Manchester United. There was no complacency – ever.

'I used to have this recurring nightmare of Ronnie Moran's voice: "Give it, get it, go . . . give it, get it, go." It was a drone. He was the mouthpiece for the coaching staff, the taskmaster. We'd played Tottenham one day, and on the way back Joe Fagan asked me to go and sit next to him on the bus. "Y'all right, Michael . . . happy? We're delighted with you, lad . . . God bless ye."

'"Thank you, boss," I replied.

'"Got any questions . . . any goss?"

'I immediately thought I was doing something wrong. I joked that some nights I went to bed hearing the words, "Give it, get it, go . . ."

'"There's always a reason behind things, Michael," Joe responded. "Do you like shooting – shooting guns? Well, imagine we went shooting hare or rabbits – I bet you I'd kill it straight away if it was standing still. Do you reckon you could?"

'"Suppose so."

'"Well, if it starts to run about all over the place, nobody can kill it. The ball's the fucking same. If it stays still in one fucking place for a short period of time, the other team will capture it and keep it. If the ball or the fucking hare starts moving quickly, the ball or the hare doesn't get fucked, does it?"

'Again, I thought this was genius.'

Robinson speaks almost lustfully about Graeme Souness.

'He was my best mate – a wonderful man. Friendship apart, he was the greatest footballer I've ever played with. Graeme was also a misunderstood soul. There was a varnish around him – an aura. But once you chipped off that varnish, I found him a very personal, cuddly chap who was actually quite vulnerable about being a human being with emotions. To this day, he still tries very hard not to be this lovely cuddly person, when really he is.

'We were bosom buddies. He saw me as a reasonably well-spoken kid, and I think that he viewed that as different and interesting, whereas I was completely in awe of him as a person and a footballer. We became extremely close friends, and he looked after me when the times were hard at Liverpool. I love Graeme dearly. He has to be the greatest leader I've ever come across in my life. When he left to go to Sampdoria, it was like losing five players all at once.

'Graeme was fundamentally a slow footballer, like Kenneth [Dalglish]. But as Bob Paisley once coined the phrase, "They both played the first five yards in their head." Dalglish was already there before you'd started thinking about it, and Souness was the same. While also being an immaculate passer of the ball, he was a great tackler and tactically so astute. Souness was greater than Hansen, Kenneth, Ian Rush and Liam Brady.

'Everybody knows that Graeme was rather partial to a glass of champagne, but he wasn't a drinker. He was a dresser. I'd irritate him by calling him a posh Jock – but he liked my use of language. He also liked my thought process. In some ways, I think I entertained him.'

Not all the players related to Robinson like Souness, however.

'A lot of stick came my way, but it was never vindictive. The only genuinely hurtful thing that somebody said to me was when Graeme left for Italy. Ronnie Whelan saunters up and goes, "Well, now your buddy's gone . . . let's see how you do." That really hurt me. Although I get on with Ronnie and respect him – he's a friend of mine now – what he said that day was nasty.

It may seem a bit pathetic in some ways. But it bothered me.

'One of the things players thought strange about me was the fact that I bought newspapers – the broadsheets. They struggled to *get* me, and Graeme was probably the only one that truly understood what I was about. But on the whole, they were a very humble and non-pretentious group of lads. Nobody was too big to get ripped.

'Joe Fagan and Ronnie [Moran] wouldn't allow any dickheads in the squad. Whenever one of us was going away on international duty, we'd shout across to Ronnie, "Who are we playing in a fortnight when we get back?"

'"Fortnight? Who gives a fuck? We might all be on the dole by then."'

In the 1983–84 season, Ian Rush plundered 47 goals, his best tally in any campaign. Dalglish, meanwhile, scored 12 times – the lowest total in a season since joining Liverpool. Robinson, like Souness, also netted twelve – yet the forward was dropped from the squad for the final ten league games and only appeared on the bench at the European Cup final in Rome because five substitutes were permitted. Robinson admits that he struggled during 18 months at the club and never truly felt comfortable wearing a Liverpool shirt – despite being a supporter.

'It felt like I always scored against Liverpool whoever I was playing for – City, Brighton, QPR. When I walked outside the left-hand dressing-room and down the stairs and past the imposing "This is Anfield" sign before hearing "You'll Never Walk Alone", you'd wait for the Liverpool team to run out. They seemed like giants, and as opposition it felt like being a lamb led to the slaughter. That seemed to be the role of the opposition player.

'When I had the experience of being in the right-hand dressing-room, it was very different. I remember looking at the red shirt, and the jersey weighed so heavy. I'd walk out and touch the sign, and "You'll Never Walk Alone" was now for you. I remember in some games half-wishing that I was that lamb again being led to the slaughter, because there was no responsibility in that.

Instead, I had to be at the level of Liverpool Football Club. And I wasn't too sure that I could be. Anfield was far more imposing to me as a Liverpool player than as a visiting player. That played on my mind and I thought about it far too much.'

One player who didn't *think* was Ian Rush.

'On the pitch, Ian could smell fear in the opposition,' Robinson says, dilating his nostrils. 'He was a beast, an animal – purely instinctive. He may have had some problems with reading the text of certain newspapers. He wasn't blessed with an intellect, yet he was a genius of football. Ian was somebody that made me look a great player in the air. Whenever Bruce knocked it long from a goal-kick, I'd look to lay it off, and Rushy would always be one step ahead by reading my corporeal language. He could taste football and was incredibly intelligent on the field. He was unconscious and had no fear of failure – something that perhaps more intellectual folk suffer from. Ian was unaware but an unbelievable footballer and undoubtedly the most lethal striker that has ever played for Liverpool. I had little in common with him, but he was a kind soul.'

Kenny Dalglish, or 'Kenneth' as Robinson uniquely and regularly calls him, was somebody with whom he shared a rapport.

'Kenneth has a heart the size of a lion. He was the first person when I arrived to invite me to his house. He was adorable. Of course, he was an absolute genius. King Kenny – I can't argue with that. I found him a lovely man and he still is today. So many years later when I went to Liverpool to film for *Informe Robinson* on a piece with Fernando Torres, I asked him to come along. He was due to go to Glasgow that same night, but he still insisted on having dinner with us before he left. He always has been generous with his time, and I love him to bits.'

Robinson also respected Alan Hansen.

'As a footballer, there was no finer defender of his time. When you talk about Franz Beckenbauer or Bobby Moore, Hansen was in that category. He read the game unbelievably and his distribution was superb. In the blood and thunder of English football, he was the progressive centre-back that was the next stage of Beckenbauer. People often ask me to compare Mark Lawrenson and Jocky. I always say the same. Mark used to fly into slide tackles, everyone would applaud and he'd be a hero. But Hansen would have seen it long before. Lawrenson was never on his feet; Hansen never needed to be on his bum. Lawrenson was brilliant, but Hansen was a genius.'

Hansen was also the joker in the squad.

'Sarcasm was Hansen. There was more of a clown element amongst the squad – a collective banter. Brucie was somebody we'd all make fun of, and he'd always take it wonderfully, along with Stevie Nic. There are some legendary tales about Steve – one where a couple of the lads asked him to check the boot of the car while they were driving through Scotland before driving off and leaving him in the snow. There was another I was told much later when he was made captain for a match at Old Trafford. He charged out the tunnel but all the lads waited. He'd made it to the halfway line by the time he realised he was on the pitch on his own surrounded by 40,000 Mancs.'

Nicol, like Robinson, was a staunch Labour voter. Although the players rarely discussed politics at a time when it seemed like Liverpool's economy was being strangled, castrated and bathed in acid all at the same time by Thatcher, Robinson was aware of other players' views on issues of governance.

'Paul Jewell, who was trying to forge a place in the first team, once said that he was the only Labour voter at Melwood. Well, I don't think he ever asked anybody about what they believe in. But I can understand why he might have thought that. We were all very well-paid soccer players and he wasn't. Sometimes you can add two and two and make seven. I respect Paul as a soccer manager and I read his comments, but I don't think he should necessarily share those opinions without asking people. He certainly never spoke to me about my views.

'I was a teenager when Edward Heath came to power, and I didn't like him. The Liberal Party looked like a stab in the dark and nobody really knew what they stood for. When I think back, I was a great believer in the third way, something that didn't really exist in our democracy. You had to be Conservative – the establishment – or Labour – the unions. There had to be space for something else.

'I remember my dad asking me at a dinner party what I believed in. I explained that I believed in a socialist democracy – a society that embraced capitalism with a socialist awareness. Politics was very much at the forefront when I was young because of the problems in the United Kingdom. For a lad of 14 like me, it was difficult because the government only tried to inspire insecurities amongst its people.

'I'm Labour now, but even that is not a clear definition of my beliefs. Mr Blair was one of the people I most detested on planet Earth, for one simple reason: I couldn't expect any more from Mr Bush, I couldn't expect any more from Mr Aznar [the former Prime Minister of Spain], but Mr Blair deceived me. When you have a few pounds in your arse pocket, you think you don't need anybody. A nation is only as strong as its weakest link, but Brits are too busy loving themselves. There was amnesia and Blair targeted that. I waited years for Blair to come and tell me, "Santa's actually your dad." I'll never forgive the bastard. But I bet you Paul Jewell didn't know I felt like that.'

In 1984, all Robinson cared about was getting into the Liverpool team on a regular basis. Despite featuring mainly as a substitute, his memories from the period are fond.

'Being a part of it was just brilliant,' he says. 'When we got through the semi-final, our options in the final were either Dundee United or Roma. I asked Graeme who he wanted, thinking with the greatest respect to Dundee that we'd batter them. It was potentially, and as it turned out to be, my only European final, so I hoped Dundee won. I wanted the easiest opposition. But Liverpool were in the business of collecting trophies, and Graeme had seen it all before. When I told Graeme about this, he looked at me like I'd just fallen out a fucking tree.

'My nickname was Cat, because I always went in goal before training in the kickabout. "What are you going on about, Cat?" he replied, staring at me. "We're the best team in the world.

Nobody can fucking beat us; it's impossible that we'll go to Rome and get beaten."'

In the meantime, Liverpool won the league, three points ahead of surprise runners-up Southampton. In between the final game of the season, a 1–1 draw against Norwich at Anfield, and the trip to Rome, the squad flew to Israel.

'We played a friendly against the Israeli national team by arrangement of the famous Jewish super-agent Pini Zahavi and it was sponsored by Budweiser. It was supposed to help us acclimatise to the more humid weather in Rome. Instead, the trip was in essence a major piss-up, and Joe gave Graeme a wad of money to take us all out to forget about the final that was looming. By the time of the kick-off against the Israelis, everyone was steaming. I had a bottle of lager ten minutes before the start of the match – hair of the dog 'n all. [It worked, as Robinson scored the first in a 4–1 victory.] *La Stampa*, the Italian tabloid newspaper, was outraged by the way we were acting and followed us everywhere, taking pictures of the lads getting pissed up. We were out every night, swimming in the sea after a few. It was great. They wrote a lot of stories about us and compared us to the Italians, who were stuck in the Dolomites contemplating the game and getting wound up. I don't think the Israelis saw the funny side either, because we were meant to be the great *professional* Liverpool, but instead we were acting like a gang of British holidaymakers.'

When the team boarded the flight to Rome, it was time to get back to work. For the fans, though, trouble was waiting on the streets of the Italian capital. Fewer than 15,000 Liverpudlians made the journey to Rome. In 1977, when Liverpool lifted their first European Cup in the Eternal City, double the number had travelled. Given that the previous victory over Borussia Mönchengladbach is widely accepted as the greatest night in the club's history – and a night played out against the backdrop of the most historic city in the world – the dwindling number of travellers reflects how Thatcher stripped income levels on Merseyside during the '80s. Given what happened, though, perhaps it was a blessing there weren't 30,000 Scousers there this time around.

Upon arrival at Termini, the main train station in central Rome, Liverpool supporters were greeted by riot police laden with machine guns and CS gas. Roma were champions of Italy and, having not won a European trophy before, were expecting to lift their first on their own front lawn. Liverpool fans had questioned the logic of how necessary it was to hold a European Cup final on the home ground of one of the finalists, but UEFA didn't care. 'The canapés were ordered, the Pinot Grigio was on ice, the five-star hotel suites had been assigned and the club-class suites booked,' as Brian Reade, a respected columnist for the *Daily Mirror*, noted.

While the Roma Ultras waited inside the Stadio Olympico burning Union Jack flags, Liverpool supporters were herded onto buses that headed straight to the stadium. Following on Vespas were hooligans with scarves across their faces, making slitting gestures across their throats. The entire city seethed with vitriol and hostility.

The players felt the wrath too.

'The Italians tried to destroy our hotel from the ground,' Robinson recalls. 'On the morning of the game, there were bricks and glass all over the streets that had been thrown overnight, but we were well protected deep inside the complex in central Rome. It was like the Christians being fed to the lions. There were banners outside specially welcoming the English infidels. But it never crossed my mind that we'd lose. And we weren't frightened of playing in front of their own crowd. We were brainwashed into believing we'd win.'

And Liverpool did win – on penalties. Souness was magnificent, and Robinson appeared as a substitute in extra time when a leg-weary Dalglish was taken off.

'Graeme was a Trojan that night,' Robinson remembers. 'Every player on the pitch was in awe of him. He was brave and magnificent, and led the team like a warrior. Roma had Falcao and Cerezo – two fantastic Brazilian players in midfield. But I forgot they were playing, because of Graeme's performance.'

While the Liverpool players celebrated inside and long into the night, Liverpool supporters struggled back towards the station for the long journey home. Again, they were greeted by hooligans outside the ground. On a Radio City press bus, one journalist helped a stabbed and bleeding supporter to a nearby hospital.

'We had to wait for a few hours inside the dressing-rooms for the frenzy to die down,' Robinson says. 'It didn't bother us because we'd just won the European Cup. But the Romans, it is fair to say, were not the most welcoming hosts.'

Winning the European Cup should have represented the zenith of Robinson's Liverpool career. But there was a nagging doubt festering at the back of his mind.

'I didn't want to become cynical about the game or my passion for Liverpool. My dreams had come true when I signed for them, and I didn't want it all to end. After winning in Rome, I sat with my wife next to Graeme and his missus, sipping champagne, thinking, "I'm finished." I felt I'd lost something – even though we'd beaten Roma in their own back yard. It couldn't get any better than this for me. In some ways it felt like the only way was down from here. I didn't want to become an also-ran. I kept thinking that I needed to leave Liverpool before I became surplus to requirements. OK, we'd done the treble [the League Cup was collected in March over Everton, with Robinson looking on from the stands in a Maine Road replay] but, personally, I had an average season after a really dodgy start. I realised Liverpool never stood still and they were always considering how to improve. Maybe I'd be sacrificed.'

Six months later, after only another ten appearances, Robinson's fears became a reality.

'I had to live up to greatness, and I thought about that too much. I thought back about when I was a boy watching games from the Kop and idolising the players. Now, people were idolising the team I played for, and I struggled to deal with that. Was I worthy? It was impossible to strike a deal with Liverpool. Be there and be the best or go. The alternative was to rot in the reserves and pick up my money, but I'm not a businessman and football shouldn't be a business.

'Paul Walsh was coming in, and I figured that it was principally to replace me. Their criterion in signings was always spot-on. I thought I'd be condemned to be the reserve team. So I went and told Joe that I was uncertain of the future and he immediately offered me a two-year contract. I told Joe that it really wasn't about that, and I spoke to him like he was my dad. He thanked me for being so honest but didn't understand why I felt that way, although he respected it as well.'

Robinson received a call from his old boss, Alan Mullery – now at QPR.

'The day before I went to speak to him, he got sacked, but I went down nonetheless and agreed the first deal I'd ever done in my life because of the money. It was my biggest mistake. I was unfair to QPR because I compared everything unjustly to Liverpool, when really I should have gone abroad. Before everything was completed, I called Joe Fagan to tell him about my plans. I was due to sign for them on the 27th of December and Joe said, "Well, you're in the first-team squad on Boxing Day, and don't forget I'll give you another two years . . ."

'So I went to Anfield and picked my boots up in the Bootroom, because I wasn't in the team. I walked away from the ground as all the fans were leaving, and I must have looked like a kid that had lost his first dog. I wept like a baby. It was so fucking painful. But I knew if I'd stayed I'd have become cynical about the team I'd loved, and it would have ended up breaking my heart in a different way. I just knew that I was never a great enough footballer or supremely professional enough footballer to become a Liverpool regular.'

Robinson lived on a Hyde Park estate during his time at QPR. But the move did not work out, prompting his retirement from international football also. He'd made his debut for Ireland in 1980 at Brighton under Eoin Hand. But with Jack Charlton now in charge, he stopped enjoying it.

'Jack Flinstone [referring to Charlton] came along and had

wonderful success born out of a prehistoric anarchy,' he says. 'He gave joy to all sorts of people, but I fell out with him. Basically, I disagreed with everything he ever said. He was a tad rustic. When you compare him to Bobby Charlton, all I can say is that it seems strange that someone from the same family could be so different in their approach to football and humanism.'

Robinson needed a fresh start, so he accepted an offer from Osasuna – a club he knew nothing about.

'I had a frivolous image of Spain that included summer holidays, *costas*, drinking lots of cheap alcohol and chasing girls. But I also knew they were passionate about their football and they had these great teams called Real Madrid and Barcelona. When I first moved, it wasn't a cultural choice. I only moved because I wanted to play football.'

Recalling the exact date he first landed at Bilbao Airport, Robinson continues after ordering a steaming espresso coffee.

'I came over on 7 January 1987. I didn't know whether I was going to be here forever. What I did know was that I was going to receive an education – an education that I wanted. But something strange happened. I enjoyed more or less everything about Spain and the way the Spanish interpreted life. I finished up realising that I had loads in common with the Spaniards. We laughed about the same things, cried about the same things, so much so that when I was 36 or 37 I said to my mum, "About 36 years ago, you didn't bump into a Spaniard, did you?" She slapped me for that.'

Osasuna were second from bottom in La Liga when he arrived, and they lost 4–1 at Athletic Bilbao on his debut.

'We were so bad that I said to my dad that they shouldn't be signing me, they should be signing David Copperfield. What made it even stranger to me was that the club was run by Opus Dei, and when the bell rang before we went out to play everyone prayed to God. I didn't realise this, and I said to my dad, "I tell you how bad we are – before we go out, we have to pray we don't lose." They still do that to this day. Pamplona is the most religious city in Spain.'

Despite initial fears, Osasuna managed to avoid relegation and finished respectably at the end of his first season. That summer, the club's president then asked Robinson to do a special deed by recommending an English player they should recruit. Robinson suggested Sammy Lee.

'He came on 13 July – the day before the end of the Fiesta de San Fermin, also known as the running of the bulls. The festival runs for around ten days, and most of the residents in Pamplona don't go to sleep during that time. You get architects, lawyers and doctors – the pillars of society and mainly upright people – day in day out getting paralytic on booze. There are fireworks every day, and I remember as I drove Sammy into the city off the motorway we could see rockets exploding. Sammy couldn't believe it. His first experience of Pamplona was 1.2 million people going bonkers. In fairness, it wasn't a true representation of what Pamplona was really like. Sammy must have thought it was a really crazy place.'

The way Robinson talks about Pamplona, you would think he was an agent of the city's tourist board.

'Pamplona is a great city when you don't know what is going on. I am very grateful to it because it was my port of entrance to Spain. It's a difficult place because half of them feel Basque and the other half certainly don't feel Basque, so you can't speak about politics at all. That means you can't really talk about football as well, because Real Madrid are the most popular team in Spain and are considered nationalist. It's beautifully complex, because when you don't understand what's going on you don't realise its quirky ways. But when you know what it's about it becomes prohibitive. Then it becomes less of an easy place to live.'

Settled, Robinson began to genuinely enjoy his football for the first time in his career.

'The autumn of my career all of a sudden became spring,' he says. 'It made me realise how unlucky I was as a footballer in England. All of a sudden, someone would have a shot and it would ricochet off my head and go in the top corner. This was strange for me. In my whole career, I was never under delusions of grandeur. When I was at Liverpool and I went in that dressing-room, I didn't know whether to treat them as teammates or ask them for autographs. I don't have any videos of me playing football because I didn't like the way I played. I would never have paid to watch me play. Then, all of a sudden, I was a star.'

By the end of the summer of 1988, Robinson decided to play one final season before retiring. On a Good Friday fixture against Las Palmas, he scored both goals in a 2–0 win.

'After the game, I walked out of the dressing-rooms and people were laying down palms for me to walk on. I couldn't believe it.' Better was to follow. Osasuna travelled to the Bernabéu to play Real Madrid on Bernd Schuster's debut. Robín, as he had been christened by his teammates by now, was asked to room with a teenager who was due to make his debut. 'The manager just wanted me to tuck him in and make sure he didn't get panicked.' During the night, the youngster suggested that Robinson should perform a special celebration, as it was likely to be his last game at the Bernabéu.

'Whenever we were in the showers after training, I always used to pretend to be a bullfighter and use my towel as a prop. The whole squad used to shout "Olé, olé" when I moved from side to side. It was a bit homoerotic.'

After ten minutes, Robinson volleyed his side into an unexpected lead. Recreating the celebration in full view of a now half-empty restaurant, he performs the groove.

By the end of the game, the visitors had settled for a draw and with time to waste time the Osasuna manager, Pedro Mari Zabalza, decided to substitute the furthest player away from the dugout. It happened to be Robinson.

'My number came up, number 9. Everyone was telling me to walk slowly, so I did, with my head down because my knee was hurting. All of a sudden, the whole of the Bernabéu started to clap. I felt embarrassed and started to trot. I reached the centre circle and the referee went, "Michael . . . *saludo*." Then I realised they were applauding me. It was a standing ovation and I walked off the pitch crying my eyes out. They did it because of the celebration. The Spanish media couldn't get their head around the fact that an Englishman had come and played for an unfashionable team, then scored a goal and in the centre of the Bernabéu done this celebration of a traditional bullfighter.'

Robinson never considered management, although he was approached in the mid '90s by Atletico Madrid's rabble-rousing former president Jesús Gil y Gil. After Robinson rejected his offer to be Radomir Antic's assistant, Gil concluded the conversation by calling him a 'fucking tart'. Instead, important breaks followed after his retirement: Robinson commentated on the 1990 World Cup in Italy.

'For the first time I saw football and it had nowt to do with the pitch,' he says. 'It was about people arriving in Italy from all over the world with painted faces, sleeping on pavements, jumping in fountains. I'd never really seen fans – as a footballer you are isolated – and it was like opening Pandora's box. But there weren't snakes and reptiles in there; it was beautiful. If I had been aware when I played of what football meant to people, I wouldn't have been able to tie my fucking boots up because of the responsibility.'

It was an education that underpinned the show Robinson was asked to present on Spanish television, *El Día Después*.

'I couldn't believe it when they asked me,' he says. 'I only had 100 words in Spanish and most were expletives. They told me that was the least of their worries.'

El Día Después was written, directed and presented by Robinson. 'It was as if I had been given a blank canvas to play with all the paints and all the brushes that I wanted and create something completely out of my own imagination. I felt like I was a kid and been locked in Toys R Us and everybody had gone out.'

The show was a universe away from the way football is covered in Britain. Despite being a former player, Robinson had told me in the past that he considers himself to be a journalist who wants to 'invade living rooms'. He resents the way sports broadcasting, and that of football in particular, has been 'hijacked by ex-pros' in other countries, mainly England.

'There is a screaming necessity for journalists to challenge the ex-footballers. They chat with a certain vernacular, whereby they all relax: Lineker, Hansen, Lawro and the rest. Alan thinks every goal is a defensive error because you can stop a tape anywhere and find a mistake. Then Lineker and Lawrenson just agree. It's all happy families. Alan and Lawro know I think that because I've said it before and I'll say it again. It's nothing personal, but it's quite sad that they're not challenged.'

Robinson, who has been the player most generous with his time in the production of this book, could genuinely talk all day and all night about football, politics and social issues. By now, the pianist is looking at us as the only people left in the restaurant while playing a tune that sounds like music to the closing credits of *Custer's Last Stand*.

While I am due at the Calderón for Atletico Madrid v Osasuna later this evening, where I will still be suitably oiled following this predominantly liquid-based lunch, Robinson heads back to his villa just outside Madrid on a road that leads to the distant northern barrack town of Burgos. I've been there before on a past press trip and it's an elegant piece of land, resting on the edge of an exclusive golfing resort.

'Destiny brought me to Spain,' he concludes, shaking my hand as we stand outside in the early-evening shade. 'Destiny has been kind to me. I've never had a real plan. I remember when I signed for Liverpool I thought that was my life – going back home, the north-west. Circumstances changed. I went to London; out to Spain. Every time I made plans, everything changed. Twenty-three years later, I sit here thinking I might be out of work tomorrow.

'I try hard, but I'm also fortunate.'

CHAPTER FOUR

Cult Zeros

MACKEM, David Hodgson

DAVID HODGSON ADMITS THAT ANY IMPRESSION HE MADE DURING his two years at Anfield has probably been forgotten by the supporters who watched him play.

'They never really sang my name while I was there,' he says, with a heavy blow of the cheeks that suggests he wishes it had been different. 'I craved acceptance, but it never really happened for me. I won the treble at Liverpool, but people that know me still ask what contribution I made. My answer is always the same: "I helped build team spirit."'

It is for this kind of reason that Hodgson was popular inside the dressing-room. Like Michael Robinson, who arrived a year after him, on the pitch he struggled with the responsibility of being back-up to Ian Rush and Kenny Dalglish. Off it, though – and unlike Robinson – Hodgson fitted right in.

During other interviews in the making of this book, different players said that Hodgson was a well-appreciated member of the Liverpool squad. He was still invited on the club's end-of-season trip to Marbella in successive summers after leaving for Sunderland in 1984.

His humour was well received. Before Liverpool played Roma in the European Cup final in the same year, Hodgson soothed tension inside the tunnel as the players waited to enter the Olympic Stadium.

'I was substitute, of course, and I could see how much everyone was really pumped up,' he recalls. 'So I broke into song. It was the Chris Rea number, "I Don't Know What It Is But I Love It". I was in charge of the music box and had been listening to it that day.

'All the Roma boys were there: Falcão, Conti, Cerezo, looking all serious. So I led: "I don't know what it is but I love it . . ."

'Craig Johnston followed with the next line and then all of the Liverpool joined in.

'It was spontaneous. The Roma boys seemed unnerved by it. We could hear the fans outside whistling – Rome was an intimidating place to be that night. But that was us. We were telling them: "We're not scared and we really don't give a shit where we are or what you can throw at us, because we're going to win this game."'

Hodgson, who is now in his early 50s, speaks with a well-defined north-east accent similar to Bob Paisley's. Gone is the moustache sported by him and so many other Liverpool players from the '80s. He is smartly dressed (pinstripe shirt, jeans and loafers), courteous and polite, taking you into his confidence by using your name repeatedly and leaning forward intently to listen to any response as if he were an old friend. But you also know that he is tougher than that.

He is persuasive – a charmer – traits that have developed in the years after retirement: first as a manager with Darlington, then as a football agent and now as a senior scout with a funding group that signs players primarily from the South American market before selling them on at a profit.

Based in the countryside near Barnard Castle, Hodgson picks

me up right on time outside Darlington train station on an early May afternoon in his Mercedes C class. In the next three months driving will be replaced by flying as he travels to Mexico – 'I'll miss the wife's birthday' – Colombia and Uruguay on separate trips across the Atlantic.

He enjoys the work. He has chosen it. He decided to depart the agency business after a saga involving one of his clients, Dan Gosling, who left Everton in 2010 for Newcastle, much to the chagrin of the controlling powers at Goodison Park. He is candid on the issue as he drives to a wine bar in Darlington's town centre.

'Dan's move to Newcastle portrayed me in a bad light,' he says, steering his car with one hand on the wheel and the other hanging out of the window. 'Because of that, I made the decision to walk away. Although I still represent Dan, I had to get away from the day-to-day garbage of the agency world. It's gutter-level work, it really is. The vast majority of people who move in those circles belong at that level. Being an agent is no longer an image that I want to be associated with.'

It is quickly established that Hodgson isn't afraid to abandon something if it compromises his principles. He has straightforward morals, which he reveals are the result of learning from the mistakes of a rebellious childhood.

'I grew up on the wrong side of the street,' he continues, as we sit down to lunch 20 minutes later. 'I had a good family – my dad ran a social club in Gateshead and we lived in a bungalow – but it wasn't the greatest area.

'The rules of our household were simple: as long as I was home at 11 at night before my father closed the door, I was OK. But it meant that I was never at home. I missed school regularly. One year my report showed that from something like 190 academic days, I was absent for 100. My behaviour was unquestionably bad. Until the moment Middlesbrough signed me as a teenager, I brushed with the law on many, many occasions.'

Hodgson did 'all of the stupid things'.

'I shot people five or six times with air rifles from two metres away; I pinched cars; I even stabbed my sister once when a prank went wrong. I was an idiot.'

Hodgson found succour playing football for the Redheugh Boys, a club based close to the southern banks of the River Tyne. Soon, he was asked to go on trial to Ipswich Town, who offered him a two-year apprenticeship.

'They wanted me to go to school in Suffolk, but I was unhappy about it. They put me up in a hotel, but because I didn't want to go, I decided to blow the hotel's lighting system up by setting fire to all of the fuse boxes. It didn't go down too well at the club or at home when they were told about it. But it was my route out of there.'

While many youngsters progressed from the esteemed Wallsend Boys' Club to the north of the river and into Newcastle United, Redheugh acted as a feeder team to Middlesbrough. There was, however, only one place where Hodgson dreamed of playing.

'I supported Sunderland,' he grins. 'Some people may say it's a bit strange – a lad from Gateshead being a Mackem. But I followed my dad who was a Mackem too. Gateshead is divided like that. I remember going to the derby once at St James' Park and standing in the Gallowgate End. One of the lads from school spotted me and started giving me stick. I got kicked everywhere and I desperately tried to escape. I ended up bunking over the fence at the front and running out of the ground via the players' tunnel. It was worth it, though, just to see Colin Todd play. Toddy was my hero.'

Hodgson would stretch the boundaries to get tickets for big games at Roker Park.

'The year Sunderland won the FA Cup [1973] we played Man City in the quarter-finals. The game was a Tuesday night and you could only get the tickets on one particular morning a week before the match. So I bunked school to queue up. The school found out. They told my father and he agreed that they should confiscate my tickets. The school sports day was coming up and they said that if I ran the 100m, 200m, 400m, 800m 1500m and competed in the high-jump event, they would review my performance and, subject to how I did, they may or may not return my ticket. I won every one, apart from the 800m where I finished second. They gave me the ticket back.'

Hodgson's performances with Redheugh continued to gather interest and, despite another offer from Bolton Wanderers, he ended up at Middlesbrough.

'I was put up in digs in 'Boro and still got into mischief,' he recalls. 'One Saturday afternoon, I played for the 'Boro in a youth-team match and we lost. When we got back into the changing-room, I found out that Sunderland had won that day. I was jumping about. "Get in; get in." Before I knew it, the coach grabbed me by the ear. "You little bastard . . . don't you ever, ever, ever show any signs to Sunderland Football Club while you're a Middlesbrough player."'

There were other incidents.

'One day, me and the other apprentices trashed the house we lived in by spraying liquid gumption all over the place, causing mayhem,' he continues. 'Harold Shepherdson [Alf Ramsey's assistant during the 1966 World Cup] found out about this and called a meeting with all the players. He was holding a pair of boots in his hand and started giving a speech about the importance of discipline. He went on and on. Eventually, he turned to me and said, "Are these your boots?" Then he threw them right on my forehead. "Get out of here and don't come back."'

Wondering how to explain to his parents that he'd been banished from another club, Hodgson returned to his digs to pick up his belongings.

'Bobby Murdoch had just retired after a long career with Celtic and Middlesbrough. He was the youth-team coach and liked me. Luckily, he had heard what'd happened back at the training ground and phoned up. Although Shepherdson was above him in the food chain, he said, "Look, we've got this Youth Cup game coming up against Everton. I want you to play. Make sure it's the game of your life."'

It was an epiphany for Hodgson, and he performed well in

the match. He eventually made his full first-team debut under Jack Charlton but only started making a genuine impression under John Neal, later to be Chelsea boss.

'He [Neal] had this wonderful ability to extract something from you. He made me feel like I wanted not just to do it for him but for myself as well. I would later see at Liverpool that players like Kenny and Souey would do it for themselves because they're winners and didn't need extra motivation. Me, I was different – I was motivated by what I saw. I needed inspiration from others.'

Despite being the youngest player in the first-team squad, Hodgson felt at ease in an adult dressing-room. 'I would say that I was cocky. I knew how to look after myself, and especially at Liverpool, where the atmosphere was ferocious, my experiences early in life helped me survive.'

He also believes that the hard work he put in as an apprentice helped the senior pros accept him.

'I took my apprenticeship very seriously, and if a senior pro asked me to do something for him, I'd make sure it was done to the best of my ability. The PFA have a lot to answer for. Over the years, they have stopped youngsters doing the kind of things that used to be a rite of passage, like cleaning boots. I was the best apprentice, and I was probably the nastiest too, because I made sure that all of the other young lads did the same. It meant that when I went into the pro environment, they respected me, because as an apprentice I took care of them. People like Terry Cooper – an England international – Jim Platt [the Northern Irish goalkeeper], even Souey – I took care of them all. When I got the call to the first team, none of them thought, "Ah, he's not done this for me", so they didn't make life difficult. There needs to be a rank and file within a dressing-room. Unfortunately, the PC brigade doesn't allow that in the modern game.'

Hodgson combined well with Mark Proctor – a fellow Geordie – and Billy Ashcroft, the auburn-haired centre-forward from Garston in the southern end of Liverpool.

'Billy wasn't the most gifted player, but we complemented each other well. One season he scored 18 goals and I set up 16 of them. We went to Magaluf for a piss-up, and Billy pulled me to one side. I was still in my late teens and he was really experienced. He said, "Without you, I wouldn't have scored so many."'

Hodgson admits that he too, wasn't a natural goalscorer.

'I could make a goal where others couldn't,' he analyses. 'I had pace and could go past people for fun and deliver exactly what was required to get the goal – I was like that all the way through my career.'

The statistics prove this. He scored just 29 times in 120 games for 'Boro, but it was enough for others to see potential. First, Ipswich came calling again, with Bobby Robson offering Alan Brazil in part-exchange. Then there was Liverpool. Hodgson believes the Reds wanted him as a long-term replacement for Kenny Dalglish.

'OK, we were quite different as players. He was cleverer than me, but I was faster than him. They saw me as a creator of goals rather than a scorer. Liverpool liked to press high up the pitch – both forwards had to work hard, and I was a hard worker. I think Bob appreciated that the reason he was signing me was not for my goals. After training one day, where I'd missed a hat-full of one-on-ones, he pulled me to one side and said, "When you're in front of goal, think of it as a pass rather than a shot and believe me you will score goals for fun." I'd always rather let someone else take the responsibility of shooting than myself. I didn't have that killer instinct – the composure – that, say, Rushy had. He was a simple footballer: one touch, two touch, goal.'

Hodgson says Rush came alive on match-days.

'For the rest of the week, he was the worst trainer in the world . . .' he laughs, '. . . the worst I've witnessed in my life. His work rate in matches was phenomenal, but I think he saved his energy during the week. He once got carried off at Melwood for hypothermia because he was standing still so much – he never moved an inch.'

Hodgson recalls the day Liverpool offered £450,000 for his services.

'I was at the opening day up at 'Boro, signing autographs, when Jim Platt, who was one of the club's senior players, said, "Hodgy, you're going to Liverpool." I just laughed, then within a minute the public address system came on asking me to go to the manager's office. Everybody was there – the manager, the assistant and the secretary, who stood up and said, "We've accepted a generous offer from Liverpool for you. We need you to accept it otherwise the club could go bust."'

Hodgson wasn't desperate to leave Ayresome Park, even though Liverpool were prepared to make him the club's highest-paid player on £450 a week.

'En route to Merseyside, I stopped at Knotty Ash and sat on the bridge that runs over Queens Drive. I thought to myself, "Am I doing the right thing here?" I nearly got in the car and drove back to Teeside. I was comfortable there and didn't want for anything. I'm the type of person that if I'm happy, I don't look for something else – I've always been that way. To make the kind of decision that took me to Liverpool was quite unlike me.

'Even after I had been at the club for a few months, I had my doubts. It's only when you get there you realise the calibre of player you're playing with. Rushy had gone through the same thing as me when he first went to Liverpool from Chester. The difference between me and him, aside from the fact that I was a player that already had 100 league games under my belt when I signed, was that I tended to dwell on things. Rushy didn't. That's why he survived.'

Hodgson met up with the rest of the squad in Marbella, where they were preparing for the 1982–83 campaign with a pre-season tournament that included fixtures against Real Betis and Malaga. He was greeted by an unhappy camp. On arrival a few days earlier, Bob Paisley and his coaching staff were informed that the Reds would have to play on two consecutive evenings, rather than enjoying a day's rest in between, as agreed previously in a contract with the tournament's organisers.

'This seems to be a complete shambles and we are not having anything to do with it,' Paisley seethed, after then discovering that the number of beds at Liverpool's allocated hotel was disproportionate to the number of players in his squad. Paisley was also unhappy with the training facilities. Although his side managed to complete a comfortable 2–0 victory over Betis (with a debut strike from Hodgson and the other from Dalglish) before drawing 1–1 with Malaga (Alan Kennedy) in a match that finished at 1.15 a.m., the whole experience was labelled 'disappointing' by Peter Robinson, Liverpool's general secretary.

'We've been going abroad pre-season for 17 years and we've only had trouble twice – both times in Spain,' he said. 'Clearly we shall have to look at any future invitations very carefully before we accept them.'

'It was a daft experience,' Hodgson remembers. 'When I took a penalty in the shoot-out and missed [after the draw with Malaga], I turned around and all the lads were running towards me to jump on me and celebrate. We just wanted to go home. The place was a complete shithole.'

The tour did have its lighter moments.

'The first person to greet me at the hotel when I arrived was Phil Thompson. He took me down to the port and we hit the ale big time straight away. All the other lads were waiting for us. The next morning I had a stinking hangover. I was thinking, "Is this really Liverpool – the biggest club in Europe?" It was bizarre. Liverpool were champions and this was pre-season with the big kick-off just a few weeks away. Everyone was plastered.'

He was woken the next morning by Ronnie Moran.

'I knew about Ronnie, but I'd never met him. He said, "At last – we've got you." Liverpool must have wanted me for some time. Then off we went and trained all morning – sweating off all the alcohol we'd consumed the evening before. It was a rude awakening for me. There were no passengers in training.'

Hodgson found the play hard, drink hard attitude difficult to get used to.

'One of my biggest strengths was my fitness,' he explains. 'I was 22 when I signed for Liverpool, and even though I was a lad from the north-east that enjoyed a night out as much as the next person, I wasn't a big drinker. The reason behind that was because I felt I'd been given a second chance with football and I didn't want anything to get in the way of being successful. When I went out on the piss, I wasn't the kind of lad that was able to wake up the next morning the way I always did and train to the levels that I knew I could. I needed to be 100 per cent fit to be right on my game. Otherwise, I wasn't as effective.'

Hodgson recalls the game, mentioned in this book by Bruce Grobbelaar, when Liverpool travelled to 'Boro after clinching the title – a trip that resulted in Terry McDermott injuring himself in a pre-match drinking session. He was in the 'Boro starting XI.

'I remember receiving the ball to feet and running past Alan Hansen like he wasn't even there. I'm pretty sure he didn't know what day it was. We still couldn't win, though. Liverpool were so far ahead of everyone else, they could still get a draw when the whole team was steaming.'

Marbella was one of the few occasions when the whole of the Liverpool squad socialised together.

'Most weekends, everyone went in different directions. I lived on Wirral with Cat [Michael Robinson], Stevie Nic, Jan and latterly Bruce. There was no way I was going to live with all the fuddy-duddies in Southport.'

The biggest change he had to get used to was the intensity of the training.

'It would be easy for me to say that the training at Liverpool was shocking. But how can I say that when the club was winning the double every season? The work ethic at 'Boro was more intense in terms of fitness. After training, you would do extra training to try to get your fitness levels up. At Liverpool, you learnt quickly to love the ball, and as soon as the five-a-sides were finished, that was it – you went home and rested. Because everyone had the ability to retain the ball, we had possession in matches the same way Barcelona dominate today. That's why we scored so many goals late on – the other teams would be knackered chasing around for 90 minutes. We let the ball do the work, and eventually it would wear the opposition down.'

When the season started, Hodgson went straight into the starting XI and scored four times in his first six starts. Such success, though, brought added expectation.

'Some established players went to Liverpool and never got anywhere near the first-team squad for two years,' he says – blowing out those cheeks once again. 'After starting so well, scoring goals, people believed I would score every single week. That brought its own pressure. Maybe if I had more time to settle, feeling the Liverpool Way, I wouldn't have fallen so flat so quickly afterwards. I'll admit that I struggled to meet expectations.'

By November, the striking status quo of Rush and Dalglish had resumed, and Hodgson was restricted to the substitutes' bench or the stands.

'I got an injury and didn't expect to play for a few weeks, so a night before the derby when Liverpool beat Everton 5–0 I went out for a few drinks. It ended up being a bit of a session, because I knew that with the injury it was impossible for me to play. But I still had to report for duty the following day, and when I did, I found out I was selected on the bench. You had to have your leg in plaster to prove you had an injury at Liverpool. I was hungover and got on for the last ten minutes.'

Hodgson was getting a reputation amongst the squad as the type of lad that was up for a laugh. Away from football, he was interested in racing pigeons and dressing eccentrically.

'It meant I had a lot of stick come my way,' he laughs. 'Leather was a favourite material of mine. I had leather pants [meaning trousers], shorts, shirts, shoes. The other lads killed me for it.'

The worst for verbal executions was Alan Hansen.

'He only ever spoke when he had a chance of ripping you,' Hodgson remembers. 'I cannot believe to this day that he's become a successful TV pundit because he said so little unless you said something wrong or made a stupid comment. He'd have your life. I honestly can't remember having a long discussion with him about anything. Kenny always says that he has this amazing ability to retain information: reciting players, clubs, dates of births, nationalities. Maybe that's why he's done so well on TV.'

Dalglish was different.

'Kenny is such a humble person, if I had any problems in my life, I'd ring him first. His opinion counts. My boss at 'Boro before leaving for Liverpool was Bobby Murdoch. Bobby was Kenny's hero at Celtic, and they knew each other well. Bobby told Kenny to look after me, and although it wasn't his responsibility to look after newcomers – he wasn't captain – he still took a personal interest in the welfare of others. He sorted out everything for me: a house, a car, even football boots.'

Souness, or 'Charlie', was another friend.

'Everyone had run-ins with Graeme at some point or another – mainly because he was the most competitive player I've ever played with or against. When I was a reserve at 'Boro, we had a training session with the first team and I managed to dribble it round him. Next time I tried it, he just smacked me in the mush.

'At Middlesbrough, Charlie was the biggest fish about the place. Towards the end, it showed because the club wasn't progressing to the next level and he was. It caused some unrest, because Graeme is pretty unforgiving when he feels that standards aren't being met.

'In Graeme's final game for 'Boro at Ayresome Park, the final whistle had gone and he was walking off the pitch. Everyone was applauding him as he held the match ball. He then booted the ball 60 metres into the air and the whole place seemed to fall silent. What would he do? He caught it between his calf and his thigh and continued his walk towards the tunnel. He never played again for 'Boro. But only he could have done that.'

On the bigger stage of Anfield, Souness grew more confident.

'Arrogant. Charlie is arrogant,' Hodgson continues. 'It's just the way that he is. You can see it now the way he sits and talks to Jamie Redknapp on Sky: arrogant. But that's just him; he's Graeme Souness for Christ's sake. He's one of the greatest players of all time, and that supreme confidence made him great. I love him to bits for the way he is – you need that in a dressing-room.'

When Souness became Galatasaray manager in 1995, Hodgson was a part of the appointment process.

'I speak to him a lot still, and if there's a position going somewhere that suits him, I'm always happy to put his name forward. I am good friends with Howard Wilkinson, and, initially, Galatasaray wanted him as their manager. He phoned me and said, "It's not for me." Then he asked whether I thought Souey would take it instead. "Moving over there in a new culture with the fans being as excitable as they are, it wouldn't faze him one bit." So I phoned Graeme, told him, and that was the start of it. He loved it in Turkey. But only someone with Graeme's kind of confidence could succeed there.'

Craig Johnston was the second teammate at Anfield with 'Boro connections.

'If there's an individual in the history of the game that wanted to become a footballer more than Craig, then I'm yet to hear about him. He became a professional through sheer effort. He wasn't gifted – he had limited ability and was a fabricated player who made himself what he was. His energy and commitment were unbelievable. Even after he'd earned his big move to Liverpool, he'd be down at the training ground every single day for hours, long after the other players had gone home. Nobody tried harder.'

Hodgson had much in common with Michael Robinson – despite the striker being brought in later as direct competition for his position.

'Me and Cat were similar. We lived in the same place [on Wirral] and often travelled in together. We were both the type of strikers that needed praise; maybe massage our egos a bit.'

Robinson, indeed, was one of the brighter members of the Liverpool squad.

'Michael was Michael. You couldn't call him Mick; you couldn't call him Robbo. He was quite particular about things like that. He and Souness got along well because Souey considered himself different and was probably intrigued by Michael's aloof behaviour.'

The only person that could match him for unconventional antics was Bruce Grobbelaar, who was exactly the same in character as he was on the pitch.

'Brucey got along great with everyone – mainly because he was so daft. He had this habit of exaggerating stories to a ridiculous level . . . beyond belief, and everybody knew about it. I remember he was looking for a house and I came into the changing room having told the lads that I was going to wind him up. I said, "Brucey, there's a development I know about being built. It's right up your street." I'd completely made the thing up. The next day, I asked him about whether he'd gone to see the place. Brucey goes: "Fantastic – I loved the shower." The place didn't even exist. Bruce was different. But a complete nutter.'

Not everyone got along, though.

'Alan Kennedy was normally involved,' Hodgson says. 'And they nearly always also involved Souness. There were a few little scraps. There was only ever going to be one winner. I had run-ins with Ronnie Whelan once or twice.'

The different backgrounds of all the characters that made up each Liverpool team throughout the '80s contributed towards a unique collective identity. Hodgson believes that no player during his time at Liverpool could be labelled as 'complete'. As a group, however, Liverpool were a 'complete' team.

'Each player complemented each other,' he insists. 'That was the genius of the management and scouting system. You look at Kenny – sometimes he wouldn't touch the ball for ages and when I was on the bench you would hear fans saying he was lazy. But he was still always two steps ahead of everyone else. He would drop into the hole between midfield and attack, and create space for someone else to run into. Supporters sometimes didn't see that. Then you had Graeme – he wasn't a great runner, but he was strong. He had an arrogance about him that intimidated the opposition. Ronnie Whelan – he sometimes got stick in the stands, but I always remember Bob Paisley saying he was the best two-touch footballer he'd ever seen. OK, Ronnie wasn't anything spectacular in terms of driving through midfield and providing that killer pass, but he'd keep things ticking over. With Graeme alongside him, it worked. All of these different attributes made Liverpool a complete team.'

At the end of his first full season – a campaign where Hodgson had scored nine goals in thirty-seven games – Liverpool cantered to the title, finishing eleven points above Graham Taylor's Watford. Amongst his teammates he had settled, yet Hodgson admits that he was struggling to match the superior mental attributes of other Liverpool players.

'Some may argue I didn't have the ability, but I did, because I'd have never played for Liverpool without ability. I would have gone further, though, if I had been mentally stronger. At Liverpool – like at other clubs – they had excellent players. But there was something about Liverpool and the mentality there that set them apart. The Sounesses . . . the Dalglishes . . . the Hansens . . . little Sammy Lee: they could be nasty bastards when they had to be – in order to get that win.

'The one thing that Liverpool didn't do was praise you. I found that difficult to deal with, because I was used to being told that I was the bees' knees. I'd react well to praise and badly to criticism. Sometimes at Liverpool, it seemed like you'd only get criticism. Around ten games into my first season there, Tom Saunders came to me and said, "Listen: you're the best player of your type here – relax and enjoy yourself." That was the only bit of encouragement I ever had.

'At Middlesbrough, I'd have run through a brick wall for Bobby Murdoch and John Neal. But the relationship between manager and player wasn't there at Liverpool. Once you signed, you were left to your own devices. But can I say that was the wrong way to do things? Absolutely not – the policy brought about success. Collectively, it worked. But as an individual, it didn't get the best out of me.'

Hodgson's doubts didn't stop him enjoying himself when in the environs of the dressing-room. On the bonding trip to Israel ahead of the European Cup final at the end of the following season, he, Hansen and Dalglish played a trick on the hugely talented but gullible Steve Nicol.

'Kenny was a very sensible lad and would go to bed very early. If he was tired, he wasn't afraid of breaking away from the group and returning to his room. We arrived in Israel and for three nights on the trot, rather than stay out, he went to bed early.

'Stevie Nic didn't understand this behaviour, so he asks Hansen what's wrong. Jocky seizes on the opportunity. "The prognosis isn't good," he goes. "The doc says it could be terminal." Jocky then takes it to another level and tells Kenny about the joke. So Stevie goes into his room while Kenny clings to the bedsheets pretending to look ill.

'Stevie Nic says, "Kenny, you've done so much for me; Jocky says you're going to die." He's practically crying by now and the atmosphere inside the room is sombre. Then Kenny jumps up, puts his clothes on and walks to the dining room for his dinner. Everyone was in bulk.'

Nicol, Hodgson says, was a brilliantly unsung footballer who lived on crisps but made the game look easy.

'Nothing fazed him, you know? He didn't think about things, and that meant he could walk into a battle without any fear. Everyone loved him.'

After collecting the European Cup in Rome, Liverpool were on tour again a few months later – this time to South Africa for the Royal Swazi Sun Challenge.

'We had a laugh, but it was a long way and we didn't want to go back a year later,' Hodgson recalls. 'Everyone agreed on it – we'd rather play Tranmere than travel all the way to South Africa for a few friendly matches. We beat Spurs and were set to be presented with a trophy. The lady who organised it all was making a speech, so I filled up a bucket of ice water and poured it all over her. Unsurprisingly, we never got invited back and nobody from the club's board bollocked me – not even Peter Robinson. I did everyone a favour. It was a relief.'

Hodgson may have been quick to join in a joke, but privately the doubts about his long-term future at the club remained. His rapport with Joe Fagan, particularly, was breaking down.

'Before facing United in the Milk Cup final, we were due to play Brighton. When I got to the ground ready to fly down south, I felt dreadful. I was in agony. So I told Joe about it. "I got up this morning and I could barely walk." Although I got through the game – a game I can't remember much about – I came off the pitch and my temperature was 120 degrees. It was horrendous. But Joe thought I just wanted to miss the game – to make sure I didn't get injured for the final at Wembley. He said to me, "You're pulling one here – you just want to be fit for next weekend."'

After tests, Hodgson discovered that he'd developed quinsy (a more aggressive version of tonsillitis). It kept him out of the team for three months, and he lost three stone in body weight.

'When I fully recovered, I went to see Joe, who was manager by now. I said to him, "Listen, Joe, I think you owe me an apology."

'"Why?"

'"Because I said I was ill and you questioned my integrity."

'He didn't say sorry. I knew from that moment I was on borrowed time at Liverpool, because our relationship had soured.'

By the spring of 1984, and with Hodgson only featuring occasionally in the team, Fagan approached him with a solution.

'He pulled me aside and said that he wanted me to become a right-sided midfield player. Sammy Lee was Liverpool through and through, but Joe was looking for an alternative. Sammy's natural competition in that position was Craig Johnston, but he and Joe didn't see eye to eye either. I saw myself as a forward, so I said to him, "Nah, I don't fancy that."'

After a few months of considering what to do, Hodgson decided to continue his career at Sunderland – the club he supported as a boy.

'Everything was agreed, but before I went up to finalise the deal Joe had asked me to ring him before inking the contract.

I just thought, "Nah, I won't be doing that." So I ignored what he said. I only phoned him afterwards, at which point he told me that I'd made the biggest mistake of my life.'

Fagan added, 'I won't tell you what I was going to tell you, but all I will say is that I wish you well and that I didn't open any of the numerous transfer requests you had sent to me over the last few months.'

'It meant that, legally, I was still entitled to the money Liverpool owed me on my contract. It was a kind gesture from Joe, and I appreciated it.'

Hodgson regrets the decision to leave.

'To leave Liverpool just two years into a four-year contract – it was completely stupid. It's a huge, huge regret. Kenny said, "Don't go." But I was young, impatient and pig-headed. I won so many medals at Liverpool in a short space of time. But for me, life is about happiness. I wasn't playing enough at Liverpool, so I wasn't happy. That's why I had to walk.'

He also believes that if he had had the blessing of a stable relationship during his time at Liverpool, things might have been different. He married his wife, Debbie, at the end of his playing career.

'Bob Paisley always said to me, "Y'need to settle down, son. Get y'self a nice woman." I genuinely believe that had I met my wife then – at Liverpool – I would have had all the stability that I needed to make myself a success. Having the right woman offers a man balance.'

The move to Sunderland didn't work out.

'Len Ashurst was the manager. We did the press conference and he turns to me. "Listen, lad, you're not at Liverpool any more . . ." He was trying to dominate me. "You're going to have to change if you want to be successful here." It was bizarre. He'd just signed me and straight away was trying to undermine me.'

Hodgson later spent time playing in France, Spain and Japan. Despite not being a prolific goalscorer at any of his clubs, Hodgson is proud of his achievements.

'When I left Gateshead as a teenager, I had nothing. From there, I played and won medals with the biggest club in the world at Liverpool, lived in many different countries and learnt different languages. My Spanish, now, is particularly quite strong. I also managed a lower-league football club, won a few cups and kept the place financially sound.'

As he has already mentioned, he is less proud of his association with the agency world. Such was his disappointment with the Gosling affair, Hodgson and his family moved to Buenos Aires while he decided what to do next.

'That experience helped me to evolve into the job I'm in now. Essentially, it's a scouting role. I go to youth tournaments and it's my job to identify players and make a decision quickly. The pressure for me is to say, "Yes, this is the boy we should sign." After that, I negotiate with the player's current club and his family, then the funding group places an investment in that individual.'

Players that have come under Hodgson's radar include Bolivian midfielder Samuel Galindo, now of Arsenal, 'Everton had a look at him but dithered for too long', and Juan Manuel Iturbe, a winger regarded as Paraguay's answer to Lionel Messi.

'We signed all of the agreements and he [Iturbe] was offered to an English club. Unfortunately, he was then asked to play for Argentina [Iturbe was born in Buenos Aires to Paraguayan parents] and this complicated his contract. Originally, we paid $50,000 for his signature, but he's since moved on to Porto for around £4.2 million.'

There have been others that Hodgson has missed out on. He liked the look of Fluminense's Wellington before understanding that the player had already signed for Arsenal. Then there was Ángelo Henríquez, a then 16 year old from Universidad de Chile who had already agreed a deal with Manchester United.

'I think I'm as good as anyone out there – despite the relatively short time I've been doing this kind of thing. I had to make quick decisions in the transfer market when I was in management, and I thought I did particularly well. I signed players for nothing and made the club millions.'

Hodgson cites Jason de Vos, a Canadian defender who had been rejected by three other English clubs before signing for Darlington. 'We made £450,000 on him,' Hodgson beams. 'Others were David Preece, a goalkeeper who was sold for £100,000 to Aberdeen a year after his release from Sunderland, and Neil Heaney – another released by Manchester City before being moved on to Dundee United at a considerable profit.'

Such talk makes him realise how much he misses management.

'I think about a return most days,' he sighs. 'I have a strong moral conscience, and if somebody is wrong and I know they're wrong, I won't work for them. That's the reason why I have resigned on three previous occasions from Darlington. The only thing that is right in football is what is right for the football club itself. Egos shouldn't come into it, and unfortunately there are a lot of people involved in the game that believe they are bigger than the football club. It's remarkable how selfish people can be.'

Hodgson hints towards the present Liverpool as an example.

'It's sad that, gradually, it seems like the club's traditions are being eroded. Sacking Kenny Dalglish did not help.'

Dalglish was the first person to ring Hodgson when he first became Darlington manager in 1995.

'He just said to me, "Fantastic news. I'll just give you two pieces of advice: 1) Don't ask the players to do what you could do, because you played at a higher standard; 2) Be lucky."'

CHAPTER FIVE

Cult Zeros

ARRIVING LATE, John Wark

THE ADDICTION REMAINED. LONG, LONG AFTER PROFESSIONAL retirement and beyond his 51st birthday, John Wark was turning out for a team in the Licensed Trades Sunday League in deepest Suffolk. The Glaswegian signed for Sophtlogic FC in 2003 after being asked to do a favour by a friend.

'I was working as a personal trainer for this guy, and he had a few bob,' Wark explains from his home near the unremarkable town of Stowmarket. 'Part of the deal was that I coached him during the week and played for his business's team at the weekend. I ended up as manager and took them from the Fifth Division to the Premier Division in successive seasons.'

Liverpool's former goalscoring midfielder retired from professional football in 1996, aged 39, while still a Premier League player at Ipswich Town. But he missed the game, the joshing and the beer – ingredients that are as much as part of a dressing-room as Deep Heat.

'It's inaccurate to say I missed the beer, because really that's never been away,' he jokes – adding that soon after obliging with this 'favour', his responsibilities on a Sunday morning also involved devising appropriate warm-up routines, physio work, washing heavily soiled kits and organising social gatherings such as Christmas parties.

'We often got changed in car parks and round the back of pubs,' he continues in a remarkably gentle accent. 'If we had an easy game, I'd play as a striker and terrorise the opposition defenders. If the opponents were good, I'd sit at the back and try to blag it as a hatchet man. It was just great to be a part of a group again.'

Sunday League football had its pros and its cons.

'For every person that wanted to join us, there were quite a few that wanted to get one over on us as well. In one of my first games, I was playing up front and headed home a cross to give us the lead. This centre-back comes running in from nowhere and head-butted me. He looked at me and just said, "Oh, sorry – I was a bit late there."'

Wark disbanded the team in the summer of 2009.

'We were only getting seven or eight turning up regularly. I was spending Saturday nights calling ringers in.'

He now considers himself in semi-retirement.

'I've been missing it – I can't deny it,' he admits. 'On Sundays, I'm itching for a game. I still look for the same buzz now that I did when I started all those years ago playing parks football in Glasgow. My friends think I'm daft.'

In his heyday, Wark was one of the few players to achieve just as much if not more at another club as he did at Liverpool. With Bobby Robson's Ipswich, he won the FA Cup then the UEFA Cup three years later and twice finished runner-up in the league championship. In the first of three spells at Portman Road, he became the 1980–81 PFA Player of the Year – a campaign in which he scored 36 times.

Upon moving to Anfield for £450,000 in 1984, he immediately helped the Reds to the league title, and the following season outscored even Ian Rush with a tally of 27 goals. Many of them were a result of him arriving late onto a cross. At times, it seemed he had permanent residence on the edge of the opposition box, poised and waiting for the right opportunity to attack.

'John had great timing,' Bob Paisley observed. 'You could set your watch by him.'

Of all the tough men to play for Liverpool over the years, Wark's appearance perhaps made him seem the toughest. His hedge-thick moustache was of the butch kind – not the pencil-thin lip hair that passed Derek Mountfield off as an off-duty quantity surveyor.

'There were a lot of tough players at Liverpool,' he insists. 'When we went onto the pitch to play together, the camaraderie was such that at any given moment – if we had to – we'd die for each other. When I see some of the players now that represent the club – the ones that lack heart – it kills me. Quite a lot of them wouldn't have even got into my Sunday League team with attitudes like that.'

Wark admits that he followed a trend by growing a moustache. It meant that he was often mistaken on nights out.

'I was in a pub in Glasgow and this old-timer came up to me. He stopped and stared in my direction before poking me, "You're that fella off the TV, aren't ye?" He glared at me for ages. "You were that footballer – played for Scotland and went down south, didn't ye?" Before I could respond, he disappeared with his pint and a cigarette for a few minutes and I could see him scratching his head. About an hour later, he came back over smiling broadly, and I thought he'd figured it out. "I know you – you're Graeme Souness." He was hugging me, shaking my hand, and I didn't want to disappoint him so just went with it.'

Wark was born in Partick, Glasgow, in the summer of 1957. He spent his earliest years two streets north of the River Clyde in a four-storey tenement block that backed onto a police station.

'It was really basic,' Wark recalls. 'My mum and dad couldn't afford a cot, so I had to sleep in a drawer. Because the place only had two rooms, my parents slept on a bed settee in an area of the flat that doubled up as the kitchen. There was only one window in the place, but we had a premier view for the goings-on down at the cop shop. Quite often, you'd get all of the women from the other houses hanging out their windows trying to find out the latest husband who'd been detained on drunk and disorderly charges. Or sometimes worse.'

Life was far from easy. While his mother worked as a part-time cleaner in a hospital, his father, like many working-class men in the area, was employed by a shipbuilding firm.

'Mum was an alcoholic. She died at 57 because of it. Her disease caused a lot of heartache within the family. By the time we managed to afford a phone, we'd often receive a call. "Come and get your mum." Really, it meant, "Your mum's pissed." It clearly affected my dad, and he died earlier than he should have too because of the stress.'

Although the family eventually moved to neighbouring Scotstoun, an area that was slightly more salubrious, Wark became used to the struggles that inner-city kids face.

'We never left Scotland; the furthest I went away on holiday was Ayr and that was only for a day trip. The first time I ventured south of the border was for trials at Manchester City. I didn't even own a passport until I travelled away with Ipswich in Europe.'

The Wark family were Protestant, and that meant following Rangers. Later, during his time at Liverpool, he would share a wager with Kenny Dalglish – a Protestant-raised Celtic legend – on the outcome of the Old Firm game.

'It was made very clear to me that Rangers were the team to support in our family,' he continues. 'There was no alternative. My uncles went to every single game throughout the '60s and, more often than not, I went with them. I'd always wear the blue, red and white scarf, and for home games we'd travel across the Clyde on the Govan ferry. The queues were massive, and there must have been thousands of fans boarding the boat. It was a tight squeeze and, because I was so small, I could hardly breathe or see any light in front of me.'

Wark waited after matches to claim players' signatures on a tatty notepad.

'John Greig was the captain of the club, and I loved him,' he recalls. 'He was a leader, and I tried to play like him during my career later. I also liked Willie Johnston, a nippy winger, as well as Colin Stein, a giant centre-forward who seemed to spend most of his time trying to win the physical battle with the centre-half. Willie was later banned from the Scotland squad that went to the World Cup in 1978 after testing positive for a banned drug. He was a great player, though, and he had an edge. I liked that.'

Fortunately, Wark wasn't at the Old Firm game in 1971 when a stairway collapsed at Ibrox, killing 66 supporters and injuring hundreds of others.

'I always thought that the attendance figures given by the club were a wee bit inaccurate, because it was common for kids like me to squeeze in between the turnstile with a paying adult. When we got to the top of the terrace, the kids would get lifted over heads and down to the front where we'd watch the match. It was risky.

'My brother Alex was there when the disaster happened, and we didn't know whether he was OK because we didn't even have a phone in our house, never mind a mobile phone. We'd been up and down that stairway hundreds of times, and there was a good chance that he'd have been in that area when it fell through. The fact that he came home unhurt was purely down to luck.'

Wark says that the only regret in his career is that he didn't play for Rangers. Instead, at 15, he could have signed for Celtic after being spotted playing for Drumchapel Amateurs, the famous boys' club that also launched the careers of, amongst many others, Kenny Dalglish, Archie Gemmill, Frank McAvennie, Walter Smith and Alex Ferguson.

'I was pretty thick in school but obsessed with football,' he concedes. 'I left education with no qualifications. A lot of the teachers said it would be my failing that I didn't try harder academically, but because I was so determined to become a footballer I managed to make a career out of it. There were loads of boys where I grew up who were better footballers than me, but they didn't have the discipline that I had. My brother, Alex, was a professional with St Mirren, and he inspired me to try to go all the way with it.

'I was privileged to play for Drumchapel, because they were the premier boys' club in Glasgow. You had to be on your best behaviour to play for them. They were big on sportsmanship and not swearing as well as punctuality. The only problem with them was the fact they played in green and white hoops.'

David Moyes, the father of the current Manchester United manager, was Wark's first coach.

'Drumchapel was funded by a man called Douglas Smith. He'd become a millionaire through the shipping industry and treated the kids at the club like they were professionals. We'd go for pre-match meals at a restaurant. It made us feel like we were better than all of the other teams, and we won the league year in, year out at a canter.

'David Moyes snr was heavily involved at the club. Young David was about five or six when I was a teenager, and he'd always come to games with his dad and stand on the touchline. It's quite strange when I see him on the touchline barking orders at players these days. In my eyes, I remember him as a skinny ginger kid. But he's become a fine manager in his own right – nobody can argue with that.'

Wark trialled at Celtic for two months, often 'turning up in a blue tie', and was offered schoolboy terms, but he instead decided to try out in England before making a decision. After trialling at Man City, he signed for Ipswich after being recommended by the same scout that took George Burley to Portman Road.

'I was ordered to get on the next available train from Glasgow Central. So, with a day's notice, I left home, my family and friends. I was crying my eyes out, because I genuinely didn't know whether everything was going to work out.'

Ipswich manager Bobby Robson was waiting for him at the platform in Ipswich.

'He made me feel like I was his major signing rather than a thick schoolboy from Scotland,' Wark says. 'He was very understanding of my situation and realised that I would get homesick. The same thing had happened to him when he left the north-east to play for Fulham in the '50s as a teenager. So he let me travel back to Glasgow at regular intervals, and gradually I got used to living in Ipswich. When my own dad passed away a few years later, Bobby became my father figure. He took care of me and made sure I wanted for nothing. He offered all kinds of advice, "Save some money, son – put it in your pension." When I needed somebody throughout my whole life, he was there.'

Wark's football career, though, could have been over before it even began.

'After I'd progressed through the youth teams, as a reserve we were asked to travel with the first team to their pre-season training camp. There was a routine whereby one of the senior lads would drive us youngsters, and on one occasion I was in the car with Kevin Beattie and Dale Roberts. As we went down the coastal road, Kevin had difficulty on a bend, and his Opel car spun over. It somersaulted and landed upside down. Bobby [Robson] was in one of the cars behind us, and my first memory after the crash was of him with a worried look on his face shouting for help. He later told me that he thought we'd all died. Luckily, somehow, none of us even had a scratch. The car was written off, but it affected me and it took me another ten years before I decided to learn to drive. Instead, I was always bumming lifts.'

Having played only a few times for the reserves, Wark was surprisingly called up to the first team for an FA Cup quarter-final third replay against Leeds United in March 1975.

'Kevin Beattie had an injury, and I was way down the pecking order, but everybody else in front of me also had injuries or suspensions. I'd been playing for the youth team in a Youth Cup semi-final against Huddersfield as a midfielder two days before, so the decision by Bobby to play me as a centre-back was a bit of a risk.'

The replay was held at Leicester City's Filbert Street.

'When I arrived at the hotel, the phone rang in my room. There was a guy on the line who said he was from a newspaper and wanted to chat to me about the prospect of making my debut. Quite soon, I'd given him my whole life story, warts 'n' all. I think I even told him what I'd eaten for lunch. When I got downstairs, all the lads were laughing and it turned out that the "journalist" was really Eric Gates [the Ipswich forward].'

Ipswich won the game 3–2 and progressed to the semi-final for the first time in their history. Wark was given a hostile introduction to league football by robust opponents in Leeds, however.

'I was playing against some of my heroes – Scottish internationals like Billy Bremner, Joe Jordan and Eddie Gray – and at first I was a bit starstruck by being on the pitch. Then someone whose name I won't mention spat in my face and tried to unsettle me. It was disgusting. He realised I was a young boy and thought that he'd shit me right up. Luckily, Allan Hunter was playing centre-back alongside me and saw him do it for a second time. He ran over and threatened to break this fella's "fucking jaw". That quietened him down. It taught me a lesson, and years later when I was the experienced pro, I made sure that I protected all the young boys in my team.'

Ipswich, who appointed Robson as manager in 1969, had improved gradually to the point that, in 1980–81, they won the UEFA Cup, finished runners-up in the league and reached the semi-finals of the FA Cup – all in the same season. Wark insists that Robson should take much of the credit.

'He was an excellent coach and tactically aware, but the way he dealt with players was second to none. He was tough when he needed to be as well. There was a situation before I signed for Ipswich where two of the more experienced players in the dressing-room were causing problems. They were two of the club's best players, but Bobby didn't care. He made Mick Mills the captain, and it angered them because he was so young. Bobby came to blows with the two players, then chucked them out of the club soon after. He wouldn't get very angry too often, but when he blew his top, we knew about it.'

Aside from having the right manager, Wark says there were other reasons for Ipswich's success.

'The club had an excellent scouting policy. Most of the squad was made up of northerners and Scots, without disrespecting the local talent or southerners. London clubs like Arsenal, West Ham and Spurs would underestimate us, "Here come the Tractor Boys." But we weren't from Suffolk.'

Two of the players came from Holland, Arnold Mühren and Frans Thijssen.

'The squad was very surprised when Bobby came in and told us that he was signing Frans and Arnold, because signing players from abroad wasn't the done thing then. Ossie Ardiles and Ricky Villa had recently gone to Spurs, but they were a London club with lots of money and history. We were tiny Ipswich and had somehow managed to get hold of two Dutch players in a decade when Holland were the masters of football.

'They proved to be two fantastic signings, which Bobby bought for peanuts; two completely different players, with Thijssen being a dribbler and Mühren having a left foot like a wand. From a personal point of view, they transformed my game. Before they arrived, I was more of a defensive midfielder, but in a 4–3–3 and with Eric Gates off the main forward, the set-up allowed me to get forward. The whole team expected me to arrive late and get on the end of crosses, and soon enough I was a goalscorer. I had a desire to get in the box, and that enabled me to score regularly throughout the rest of my career.'

Ipswich came close to toppling Liverpool at the summit of the First Division two seasons on the run.

'We feared nobody – apart from Liverpool,' Wark continues. 'They were our bogey side – but they were the bogey side for most teams, weren't they? Whenever we went to Anfield, we never seriously believed that we could win – something that wasn't the case when we went to places like Old Trafford, Highbury or Villa Park. Apart from being a brilliant football team, you never got anything at Anfield – no penalties, no corners or even generous throw-ins.'

Wark argues that football has always been a squad game – only squads in the '80s weren't as big as they are now.

'We had a group of 15 players performing in 60–70 matches a season. It just wasn't enough. Liverpool had a few more players than us and were experienced in such situations. It was as simple as that, because, man for man, the difference in quality wasn't too big. Winning the UEFA Cup cannot be underestimated. The UEFA Cup had many of Europe's top teams and was a huge competition to win. But, ultimately, it was one of the reasons we didn't win the league, because we were playing three, sometimes four, games a week. By the end of the season, many of the squad were dead on their feet.'

Ipswich were ambitious, and hindsight would suggest perhaps too much so. Directors ordered the building of the new Pioneer Stand at Portman Road.

'They should have re-invested in the team instead,' Wark insists. 'The club ran out of money to build it, and soon enough players started being sold. United were rumoured to be in for me, as were Verona in Italy. Then, within six months, Bobby got the England job, so we lost our leader, inspiration and manager as well as some key players. The squad was too small already. When that happened, I said, "I'm off." I needed to get away to improve my career. It's a shame, because we weren't too far away from achieving even more than we did.'

As respite, Wark spent the summer of '81 filming *Escape to Victory* on location in Hungary with a host of other professional footballers with time on their hands.

'I didn't realise how big the film was going to be until we got out there and Bobby Moore and Pelé were waiting for us,' Wark remembers. 'They were good lads, and we'd sit in the hotel and have a good few drinks every night. Pelé was 40 at the time, and I couldn't believe the skills he had with a ball. When he scored the overhead kick that you see in the film, he did it in one shot. I was 15 years younger than him, in the prime of my career, and it would have taken hundreds of cuts for me to get it right. He did it perfectly in one go. A lot of the movie guys didn't realise the significance, but all the footballers in the film just stood there in awe. I only had two lines in the whole film and they were dubbed because they felt viewers wouldn't be able to understand my Glaswegian accent. I wouldn't have minded, but I only found out when I went to watch the premiere. Nobody noticed at first, but I was watching the film with all my teammates at Ipswich and I told them. I got a lot of stick for that. They replaced my voice with a posh Scottish accent.'

Other stars in the film included Sylvester Stallone and Michael Caine.

'Stallone had done *Rocky I* by then and was a bit big-time. He stayed in a different hotel to us because he was the film star. He didn't have a Scooby Doo about football and asked us whether he could score the winner when the POWs beat the Nazis in the final scene of the film. He didn't understand that he was the goalkeeper and that just wasn't possible. In the end, he had it written in that he saved the penalty because he was so big-time. Michael Caine was a good lad and wasn't a bad footballer. But his legs had gone and he couldn't run. Kevin Beattie was Michael Caine's legs.'

Wark remained at Portman Road for another two years as Ipswich regressed under a series of managers. Finally, in the spring of 1984, his consistent performances earned him a move to Liverpool. He signed forms at the St George's Hotel – a favourite watering hole of Liverpool's board of directors.

'All I could think about was whether I'd be good enough to get in the team. I had a lot of doubts in my mind and because United had previously registered an interest in me when they thought they were going to sell Bryan Robson to an Italian club, I asked my financial advisor to ring Martin Edwards [United's chairman] and see whether they still wanted to sign me. I was really panicking because I wasn't going to sign for a club, Liverpool or otherwise, if I wasn't getting picked. I thought I'd have a better chance at United. But in the end, Edwards said that Robson wasn't going to Italy and therefore they didn't need a replacement.'

Negotiations with Liverpool were swift.

'John Smith, Peter Robinson and Joe Fagan were waiting downstairs for me. There was no messing around. John handed me the contract and basically said, "You'll be wanting to sign this if you want to come here," before giving me a pen. It was worth £851 a week, which seems like a bizarre figure. It wasn't much more than I was on at Ipswich, but the bonuses for cup runs were a lot better. Because the transfer deadline was approaching, Liverpool knew that if I tried to barter a better fee, I might've had to stay at Portman Road. So the deal was done in less than ten minutes.'

All Wark had to do now was complete a medical. Again, it was basic.

'They took me down to Anfield and we waited in the Bootroom. This old fella comes in who looked more like a retired doctor than a practising one. He took my blood pressure, nodded, then I went to the door because I anticipated that I'd be going out on the pitch for a run. Instead, the doctor called me back, asked me to bend down and touch my toes. That was it. I was signing for Liverpool, but the whole regime looked a shade *Dad's Army*.'

Wark recalls his first training session at Melwood the following day.

'The ball came to me and I sprayed a 30-yard pass down the touchline. I was standing there admiring what a great pass it was then Ronnie Moran marched over and gave me a right bollocking. He was screaming at me, waving his hands everywhere, going, "We pass and move it nice and short here – don't ever stand there admiring what you've just fucking done." He was a very angry man. Then he gave a free-kick against me. It was a bit of a culture shock, but it was the right way to train. Ronnie was a tough guy, and he kept everyone on their toes.'

A week later, Wark made a goalscoring debut in a 2–0 win at Watford. Craig Johnston was the player dropped.

'Craig was really pissed off, because he started in the Milk Cup final win over Everton and by all accounts did very well. Then he was left out and started ignoring me as a result. For weeks, he wouldn't speak to me, and he endured a frosty relationship with Joe, so he didn't seem very happy at Liverpool. Eventually, we became quite close because our kids went to the same school and we lived in the same area.'

Wark bought a house in Sandfield Park, West Derby.

'It was burgled twice just after we moved in there,' he explains. 'My car got pinched as well after I eventually got round to passing my driving test. It was a nice place to live, but because it was closer to the city centre than say Wirral or Southport, where a lot of the other lads lived, there were times when you had to keep your wits about you. I liked that, though, because it reminded me of Glasgow – a place with an edge. Myself, Sammy [Lee], Souey, Craig Johnston and Bruce all lived within a mile of one another, so it was convenient for socialising.'

Wark was soon to experience more misfortune behind the wheel of a car.

'It was my birthday and we went straight to the Jolly Miller after training. By the time we left, it was 11 p.m. I jumped in the car and got 100 yards away from home before the police pulled me over. I was three times over the limit. I spent the night in the cells and the police said I could make one call, so I rang Kenny Dalglish to explain why I'd be late for training. He went ballistic.'

Before moving into the Liverpool suburbs, Wark lived at the St George's Hotel, along with fellow new signings Paul Walsh and Jan Mølby.

'I was married, but the wife was back sorting issues in Ipswich for quite a lot of the time in my first few months. Jan and Paul were both single lads, and living in the centre of town meant they were out pretty much every night. Some of the lads could deal with the drink and play the next day without a problem, but Jan struggled with his weight.

'But that was Jan. Despite his size, he didn't have too many problems on the pitch, and for a period of time he was the best passer of the ball in European football. Had he been a bit slimmer, who knows what else he might have achieved, because he could pass 60 yards with either foot quite comfortably.'

Mølby was just one player in the Liverpool squad up for a laugh. Wark says success on the field was founded by a well-drilled changing-room camaraderie.

'The Christmas party was always one event in the year that I looked forward to,' he explains. 'Each year, it was fancy dress, and we always tried to outstrip the previous year's antics by wearing costumes that were even more outrageous than the last. At Ipswich, all the lads did at Christmas was go for a pint in a smelly local pub. At Liverpool, though, it was the most important event in the social calendar, and a lot of time and effort went into the preparation.'

The night would usually conclude at Tommy Smith's nightclub, the thoughtfully named Smithy Manor.

'We'd usually start the evening at Sammy Lee's wine bar on Aigburth Road and gradually make our way towards town. By the time we got to Smithy's, everybody was well oiled, and part of the ritual was to make any of the new signings or apprentice boys sing an initiation song. At my first party, I did Frank Sinatra's "My Way", and Paul Walsh did a Chas & Dave number. Paul was pathetic, and everybody started throwing sausage rolls at him from the buffet. He was covered in sausage.'

Wark emphasises just how important the costumes were.

'My first effort wasn't the best, and I went in a fat clown costume. Kenny came as the Hunchback of Notre-Dame and Tommo [Phil Thompson] was Boy George. On my first year, Craig [Johnston] arrived the next morning at training in his Fred Astaire outfit – he was still pissed. Kenny felt rough as well because he wasn't the biggest of drinkers and somebody decided to drop a little mixer in his pint. We carried him to the taxi, but by the time the party came around the following year he was the manager, so nobody could touch him.'

Wark was signed by Joe Fagan – a person he likens to 'your

favourite family relative'. Despite the apparently benign persona, Fagan was not to be crossed. On one occasion, Wark, Alan Hansen and Bruce Grobbelaar got into trouble for eloping to Belfast.

'There are loads of supporters groups over in Ireland, and a few of them asked us to appear, to hand out awards.'

Crucially, each event provided a free bar.

'We left Bruce to clear the trip with Joe, and immediately he refused. Bruce didn't tell us and we went anyway. They put us up at the Europa Hotel – a place the IRA had targeted so many times, it became known as the most-bombed hotel in the world. It meant we had to have bodyguards on us at all times, even when we went for a shit. It turned out to be a really edgy weekend, because at one event all of the Protestant supporters were singing sectarian songs and at another event our driver showed us a revolver because we were at a Catholic social club. Thankfully, everything passed off without any trouble, but our main problem was getting home. The airport in Belfast was shrouded in fog, and it meant that we couldn't get to Melwood for training on the Monday morning. When Bruce called Anfield to tell Joe, he was furious and fined us a week's wages. It meant that we lost all the money we'd earned from the weekend.'

Despite other indiscretions off the field, Wark admits that those in charge at Liverpool were generally happy to look the other way if the team was playing well. Personally, Wark had good reason to be in a celebratory mood. In his first season, he was the club's leading goalscorer.

'Many of my goals came from arriving late in the box. It was my forte and quite surprising considering I probably was never the most inconspicuous person on the pitch. I had it [the ability of timing] as a teenager, I improved on it at Ipswich, and then I probably mastered it at Liverpool. The reason that happened was probably because Liverpool created so many chances. I didn't just score from crosses at Liverpool as well. When you've got Kenny, who drops deep – the calibre of player we didn't have at Ipswich – it allows you to sometimes get ahead and join the strikers. A lot of my goals were the result of Kenny's movement.'

Despite finishing runners-up to Everton in the league, the campaign finished with a European Cup final in Brussels.

'I'd played at Heysel a few times with Scotland,' he reflects. 'Even in the late '70s, it was a shithole and in desperate need of redevelopment. When it was announced that the European Cup final was being held there, I convinced myself that they were going to do some work on the ground to make it worthy of such an important game. Instead, when we arrived, it was exactly the same as it always had been. I said to one of the lads that they should have filmed *Escape to Victory* here. The stadium was so outdated, it wouldn't have looked out of place in a Second World War movie.'

Nightmarish scenes on the terraces were to follow, but on the morning of the game, however, all the talk inside the Liverpool camp was of Joe Fagan's impending retirement.

'He walked into the dressing-room and told us, "After tonight you can call me Joe." The news spread quickly. I thought it was strange that Joe would make such an important announcement before such an important game. Sometimes, it can take a player's concentration away if he knows there is going to be a change in management. Personally, it made me want to turn around what was a disappointing season domestically for the club by winning the European Cup for Joe. Others may have thought differently.'

On an unforgivingly hot day, Wark remembers driving to the game on the team bus through the centre of Brussels, where he saw Liverpool supporters in bars sharing drinks and singing songs with Juventus fans.

'It was 45 minutes before kick-off when we first heard about problems inside the ground. The dressing-room was cramped and, once again, backward in terms of facilities. There was a loud bang and all of the lads stopped talking. Within minutes, a gang of riot police came bouncing through the door. Everybody looked at each other and it was one of those moments when we all understood that something was desperately wrong.'

A UEFA bod wearing an official blazer called Phil Neal into the corridor. He reappeared 25 minutes later.

'When he came back, he told us that some fans had been killed. As the minutes passed, the number of dead began to rise. Phil told us not to play the game, and all of the lads agreed. We were still in our kit with our socks pulled up, but everybody was wandering around in shock.'

UEFA insisted that Liverpool and Juventus played the game.

'Phil still didn't want to, and most of the lads agreed, including me. I felt sick at the thought of people dying. It just didn't seem right that we should play a game of football on that backdrop. But we also realised that if the game didn't go ahead, it might encourage more violence. In the end, we figured that it was best that we went and got it over with. The game was played like it was a testimonial.'

Juventus won 1–0 after a penalty from Michel Platini on the hour mark.

'Gary Gillespie tripped up Zbigniew Boniek, and it was definitely a foul. But it definitely wasn't inside the area. Normally, we'd have complained all day to the referee, but it didn't seem right in the circumstances, so we got on with it and Platini scored. When I think about that game now, my mind is a blank and all I can think of is the 39 people that died.'

After such an effective debut season, Wark's second campaign was blighted by injury. Given that Alan Hansen once admitted 'you were persona non grata if you were injured', being on the outside wasn't a pleasant place to be.

'It was made pretty clear from an early stage that if you were injured you were blanked, because I'd seen the way the staff acted with other players when they were out,' Wark adds. 'One day, I felt a twinge on my Achilles after an obstacle course. So I told Ronnie Moran. He looked at me like I was an alien and told me to get myself off to the hospital. "Make sure you've got your kit with you, though – you'll be back to training in the afternoon." I went off to A&E in Walton, where I joined the queue with the other patients. By the time I eventually got to see a doctor, he told me that it was a good job I'd gone to see him, because the Achilles was on the verge of snapping. Had that happened, I'd have been out for six months, because in the mid '80s there was no fast-track to recovery. He put my foot in plaster, handed me some crutches, and I headed back to Melwood. When I saw Ronnie, he shrugged his shoulders and just said something like, "So you were injured after all, were you?"'

Wark did return from that injury, but a broken ankle suffered soon after ruled him out of the majority of the 1985–86 season as Liverpool completed the double.

'The treatment of players at Liverpool when it came to injuries was very basic. In fact, at times it was laughable. There was an occasion when the coaching staff were getting very frustrated with Paul Walsh because he wasn't responding to ultrasound. He was given the silent treatment and we all got the impression that the staff thought he was crocked. It was only when a maintenance guy turned up to service the equipment that it was established the machine hadn't been working for months.'

When out of the team, Wark admits that the free time allowed him to drink more and play snooker. 'I wasn't the golfing type.' He says that before he'd arrived in England as a teenager, he'd never been inside a pub, but by the mid '80s he was well grounded in the art of combining an afternoon in the boozer followed the next day by a strenuous training session at Melwood.

'The regime at Ipswich wasn't quite as tough as it was at Liverpool, but saying that Liverpool took a hard and fast attitude towards drink would be a lie too. Bobby Robson never had a problem with us having a pint – even on the night before a big game. In hotels before away games at Liverpool, each room would have a visit from Ronnie Moran and Roy Evans. "Anyone want a sleeping tablet?" they'd ask, before nosing around to check we weren't up to mischief.'

For a time, his best buddy was Bruce Grobbelaar, 'a crazy man with a deeper side'. The goalkeeper's ritual before a game would be to visit the Holiday Inn on Paradise Street for a meal of steak and chips.

'Stevie Nicol had the biggest appetite, though,' Wark insists. 'On away trips, he'd have an evening meal then return to his room and order room service. It wasn't just a snack either. He'd have a burger and chips with all the garnishing. Later on, he'd have a midnight snack of crisps, chocolate bars, fizzy drinks and Haribo sweets, which he carried in a holdall. We were never allowed to take beer into our rooms with us, so Steve often carried a couple of cans of Tennent's with him as well.'

Wark concedes that Nicol was the dressing-room buffoon.

'He did so many soft things,' he says, before clearing up a story about Nicol being abandoned near Gretna by Graeme Souness and Kenny Dalglish on a trip back to Scotland. 'Souey had asked Steve to wipe the back of the window as it was steaming up because of the snow outside. As soon as he got out, Souey drove 50 yards up the road. When Stevie caught up, Souey would drive off in the car again. This went on for half an hour or so before they got bored and allowed Stevie back into the car again.'

There were other humorous moments.

'We were inside the dressing-room and a load of brown envelopes were being handed out by the club secretary. Stevie assumed that money was being exchanged and was pissed off that he wasn't given one. So he marched over to the manager's office asking questions. Kenny then informed him that the letters were from the Inland Revenue over unpaid taxes. Stevie walked out with his tail between his legs.'

Nicol's nickname was 'Chops'.

'He couldn't say the word "chips" because of his strong Ayrshire accent,' Wark laughs. 'Unfortunately for him, he loved chips, so he was saying "chops" all of the time. We'd deliberately send him around to the chippy for lunch after training, and it took him a while to figure out why we were doing it.'

Nicol was, however, well appreciated as a player by the squad.

'He was underrated – could play anywhere and still give an eight out of ten every single game. Everybody had complete faith in him, and he had a brilliant football brain. The goalscorers tend to get the accolades, but every successful team needs a player like Stevie.'

Wark left Anfield in 1988 after playing only a handful of games in the previous two seasons. Despite being a close personal friend of Dalglish, having been an international and club teammate for the best part of a decade (Wark made his Scotland debut at Ipswich in 1979 and played 29 times for his country), the Liverpool boss wasn't in the business of dealing favours for friends.

'I could have stayed – sat out the contract for another year. But I dropped 50 per cent of my wages to play football again. I had offers from Watford and Coventry on the table, both of whom were in the old Second Division. My stock had dropped because of the injuries, so in the end I decided to go back to Ipswich – somewhere I knew well and somewhere I would enjoy the game again.'

Ipswich were not the side of the Bobby Robson era, however, and after a year at Portman Road, he moved on again to equally struggling Middlesbrough. Financial difficulties at Ayresome Park meant another return to Ipswich twelve months later, where he remained for another six years until his retirement.

'I never fancied management,' Wark says. 'I took temporary charge at Ipswich for nine games as player-manager. It really opened my eyes. As a player, you're only out for two or three hours a day. As a manager, you have to be on the go 20 hours a day, training, in the office, then out watching matches at night. I was offered jobs at Ipswich coaching, then at Cambridge, but I didn't even go to speak to them. The stress would have been too much, and I wanted to keep playing at any level for as long as I could.'

His only regret in a 20-year career is suffering the injuries that kept him out of the Liverpool team for so long.

'Before and afterwards at other clubs I was as fit as a fiddle,' he concludes.

'I was a bit unfortunate on that front.'

CHAPTER SIX

Cult Zeros

ISOLATED, Kevin Sheedy

LIKE AN INJURY-PRONE LIVERPOOL PLAYER IN THE 1980S, FINCH FARM
feels isolated. Geographically just as close to Widnes as it is to
Liverpool's city centre, the grim Fiddlers Ferry Power Station
pumps hot air from aged cooling towers into a sky that cloaks
Everton's training ground in a colourless haze.

It is easy to appreciate, however, why in 2007 Everton decided
to move here. The facilities rival that of any other Premier League
club. Even though Everton do not own the land, it offers the
opportunity to keep academy and professionals on one site and
gives the impression to any potential signings that this is a club
with ambition. The complex is modern, vast and clinical.

It could not be any more different than the old base of Bellefield,
located in West Derby less than a mile away from Melwood. Used
as the tournament camp for the Brazilian national football team
at the 1966 World Cup, it was once considered so advanced that
the Brazilian FA took photographs to inspire clubs at home. Yet

for a long time after, Bellefield – a small piece of land sandwiched in between attractively whitewashed pre-war houses – was, at best, basic, intimate and atmospheric.

It was at Bellefield that Kevin Sheedy emerged as a top-class winger. Having spent four years impressing in Liverpool's all-conquering reserve team, he was injured too many times for Bob Paisley's liking and considered too callow to replace the buccaneering Ray Kennedy on the left of Liverpool's midfield. In 1982, at the end of his contract, he signed for Everton and soon became a key component in Howard Kendall's team that challenged and, for two seasons, overtook Liverpool to become champions of England.

That Everton side was perfectly balanced, where no player other than goalkeeper Neville Southall was greater than the sum of its parts. Sheedy proved to be a performer who oozed sophistication, complementing those around him: Trevor Steven rampaged up and down the right, Peter Reid and Paul Bracewell hustled in the centre, and up front there was always someone to finish a move off.

Sheedy was particularly remembered for his set-pieces. Against Ipswich Town in 1985, he exquisitely curled one in from twenty-five yards only to be asked to retake it. Sheedy promptly pearled the second effort into the opposite corner. In a perfect storm, he was reliably calm.

On one occasion, though, he lost it. When Sheedy scored for Everton against Liverpool in April 1987, he ran towards the Kop before flicking two fingers. The Blues were edging towards the First Division title, their second in three years. It was a crucial game. The action was met with bewilderment. For someone who was renowned as being mild-mannered, the act was out of character. The media, both sets of supporters and the managers questioned his motives. At first, Sheedy pleaded that he was merely recreating a hand gesture made famous by the popular Ted Rogers in his show *3-2-1*. Years later, Sheedy admitted to the Everton fanzine *Blue Kipper* that it had simply been a release of emotion.

I decided to speak to Sheedy because Liverpool's story in the '80s is intrinsically linked to Everton's. In the interest of balance, it makes sense. Additionally, there is no other player in the history of Liverpool to have become an undisputed top-class player elsewhere having been disregarded by the club following just a handful of first-team appearances. Sheedy is unique. I am keen to know precisely why he did not convince Paisley that he was worthy of a regular place.

I meet Sheedy nearly 12 months after he was diagnosed with bowel cancer. There was a history of the disease in his family and he caught it in time, meaning that soon enough he was able to return to coaching Everton's Under-18 team, initially alongside Duncan Ferguson.

'I received all kinds of letters from the football community at a difficult period of my life,' Sheedy says, as he walks me through Finch Farm's atrium and into his office, which is adorned by pictures of Alan Ball. 'Many of them came from Liverpool supporters. They were very powerful. It makes you realise how special this community is.'

Sheedy speaks quietly and quickly. Despite living in Southport for the last 30 years, his Welsh border accent is clearly detectable. He was brought up as the second son of a publican in the village of Allensmore, just outside Hereford.

'I lived with my parents and grandmother inside a place called the Tram Inn,' he recalls. 'Fortunately, we had quite a big car park outside. I spent most of my time kicking a ball against a big wall. Being in the country, there were too many hills and no street football. I had a brother, but he wasn't too keen on joining in, so I played by myself most of the time.'

During his years at Everton, Sheedy was capable of any kind of pass. He could ping, curl, float or drill with an air of cultured elegance. From his childhood, purely by having nothing more practical to do, Sheedy's skills improved through repetition.

'I was naturally balanced, but I practised with both feet every single day until my legs were practically falling off. One of the walls had a window in it and I'd take free kicks from different angles trying to hit the target. Without me actually knowing, I was getting all the ammunition to become a professional. The basics are essential: you have to be able to pass and receive the ball properly. I used three walls to test my movement. If you can't do things like this when you're not under pressure, you're not going to be able to do it when people are closing you down.

'You see the academies and the levels of control on young footballers now, but I was self-taught. It helps having a coach or someone to guide you, but it's important that a player can make his own decisions. That's always in the back of my mind when I coach.'

Sheedy's first experience of competitive football was at a church fete. He started out as a goalkeeper.

'My dad organised a six-a-side team, and we travelled around the county. They were really intense, with some big country boys ready to knock you about. I'd rush off my line and sweep. It helped my understanding of how the game was played, as I could see everything in front of me – how a game developed, if you like.'

Having progressed to an 11-a-side team and after playing in the Forest of Dean League, an invitation for a trial at nearby Hereford United arrived through the post. Few players in the area could use their left foot like Sheedy. He stood out.

'There was a shale car park outside Edgar Street, and we'd train with the floodlights on. You'd finish every session with cuts all over your legs. Other players didn't hold back on tackles. Monday was a hard running morning whether the team had won or lost. We'd run until we were physically sick. But I was able to handle it.'

Sheedy trained at Hereford while still at school. He'd long since decided that he was not going to follow an educational path.

'John Sillett was the manager and he told me to ask my headmaster to see if I could miss lessons to train during the day. My heart and mind was set on football, so I plucked up the courage to knock on his door. We came to an agreement that I only needed to go to school in the afternoons. I know clubs have regular contact with schools now, but this was unprecedented.'

It is unimaginable in the modern era that a teenage footballer would be asked to scrub mud from the communal bathtub inside a club's dressing-room with such intensity that his hands would wither in the detergent. But as one of six apprentices, this was one of Sheedy's jobs, along with cleaning boots, kits and sweeping the stands on Mondays.

'It continued throughout the summer. As an apprentice, I became an amateur horticulturalist, learning how to weed the pitch and sow the seeds for a relay. We'd be out there come wind, rain or shine. It taught me to get the job done; no excuses.'

Sheedy made his league debut aged 16.

'I was surrounded by some great characters. Up front we had Dixie McNeil, who was a lower-league goalscoring legend. At the back, we had John Layton and Billy Tucker. Both of them were very protective of the young boys. If I ever took a buffeting from an angry right-back, they'd be right in their faces. It usually happened against Cardiff, who became a regional rival for a period. It was an opportunity for the Welsh to get one over on the English, whether that be in terms of the result or, instead, in terms of the physical battle.

'Hereford was the perfect environment for a young player entering professional football for the first time. There was a hierarchy, and that was a good thing within the framework of a squad. As a young player, it gave you something to aspire to.'

Wolverhampton Wanderers and Bristol City sent scouts to Edgar Street the season after Hereford clinched promotion from the old Third Division. On the recommendation of chief scout Geoff Twentyman, however, Liverpool were the first club to make an offer.

'I knew that Liverpool had a policy of signing players young and preparing them for first-team football by playing them in the reserves for a couple of years, but that put me off to be honest,' Sheedy insists. 'I went there not really wanting to sign, because I felt I was good enough to start every week. Bob Paisley showed us around Anfield and I got a photograph of the European Cup with my dad. But I must have been the least enthusiastic signing the club has ever made. I really didn't think it was the right move for me. I explained this to Peter Hill, the chairman of Hereford, but he said the £100,000 that Hereford had accepted was going to save the club because they faced going out of business. A gun was put to my head a little bit. I felt pressurised. I had to go with it.'

It was agreed that Sheedy would live seven streets down from the old Kemlyn Road on Elsie Road in lodgings with a Mrs Edwards. For the first six months, Alan Hansen called it home too, and afterwards Ronnie Whelan moved in.

Signing for Liverpool brought added attention. Soon, he was offered the opportunity to represent the Republic of Ireland at Under-21 level. He qualified through his father's family, and after Wales 'dithered' for too long about selecting him – even in any of their youth squads – he rang the Welsh FA to ask whether they had any intention of changing their stance. 'Yet more dithering.'

Sheedy chose Ireland, and in the decade that followed he would become a key part of Jack Charlton's side, qualifying for the World Cup in 1990. His success at international level served to support his idea that he was ready for first-team football at Liverpool.

'All the reserve boys were frustrated,' he says. 'It was a very good team performing very well in a competitive reserve league. We won the Central League four times on the trot. It was probably one of the best reserve teams there's ever been. Unfortunately, the first team were cruising. They strolled through games, seasons even, and rarely picked up injuries. There were few opportunities. It was a bottleneck. I was probably at the right place at the wrong time.'

Sheedy regrets not speaking to the management about his lack of opportunities.

'I should have been a bit more forward,' he says. 'Sometimes it helps to go knocking on your boss's door. But I was brought up with the idea that your talent and ability will always take you far. In competitive environments, though, that isn't always the case. I wasn't a confrontational type; it just wasn't in my nature. I'd gone from playing for Hereford, watching Kenny Dalglish score the winner in the European Cup final, to sitting next to him in pre-season a few months later and then going to a barbecue at his home in Birkdale. As an 18 year old who hadn't done much, it was difficult to find a space in a dressing-room that included some of the continent's best players.'

For two and a half years, Sheedy remained in Liverpool's reserves. In February 1981, he was given a first-team debut against Birmingham City.

'Football is dictated by small margins. I hit a shot early on that whistled towards the top corner right in front of the Kop. Instead, it hit the angle of the bar and the post. If that nestles, you get probably selected the following week. Instead, I ended up on the bench at Brighton.'

Inside Anfield, there were already doubts about Sheedy's fitness. During his first six months as a Liverpool player, he suffered a serious back injury.

'The people at Liverpool didn't take too kindly to any player spending time on the sidelines. They saw it as a sign of mental and physical weakness. I thought that was unfair, because sometimes players are genuinely unlucky. It probably stems from the fact that those in charge at Liverpool came from a different era – an era when people were told just to get on with things and shrug off their problems. We were athletes, though, and injuries are part and parcel of football unfortunately. When my back went, Ronnie Moran and Roy Evans tried to get it better. I don't think they had any qualifications, though. The treatment certainly didn't work for me.'

Liverpool's attitude towards injured players had been legendarily brutal. In Bill Shankly's era, a centre-forward called Jack Whitham, signed for a considerable fee from Sheffield Wednesday, spent more time on the treatment table than on the training pitch.

'Training for Jack was like jogging in between injuries,' Ian St John recalled. 'Finally, one day Shanks marched up to him and said, "You, go up to the corner [where the pigsty was] and train up there. I don't want you to contaminate the rest of the team."'

With history against him, Sheedy was in an awkward position. For a long time he felt pain in his back and struggled to find consistent form.

'The injury was absolutely genuine, but Liverpool didn't see it like that. Liverpool was such a successful club; it's difficult to argue with their methods generally. But I think my early struggles with fitness were bad for me in the long term. Immediately, there was a perception that I was a crock. And when you had that reputation at Liverpool, it was a difficult tag to shake off.'

When the possibility of a first-team outing arrived, injury struck again.

'I played for Ireland Under-21s, ironically at Anfield, and took a heavy knock to the ankle. It ruled me out for a month. Straight away, Ray [Kennedy] got injured too, and my opportunity passed by. I was playing in Ray's position for the reserves, so I was his deputy. Ronnie [Whelan] was left footed and Bob gave him the chance. He took it with both hands. It felt like everything was conspiring against me at Liverpool.'

Even by the time Sheedy made his debut, he'd informed the club of his intention to leave. On a four-year contract, exit routes were limited.

'It was the most difficult period of my career. I felt like I was banging my head against a brick wall for a long time. Mentally, it was impossible. I felt I was good enough for first-team football at a top club, but Liverpool weren't in the business of letting a player go to a place where they might end up proving the decision makers wrong. Blackpool and Derby County both made firm offers and Liverpool accepted, but I didn't want to go to either of those clubs.'

This was before players had the power to force moves away from clubs they did not want to be at. Sheedy's long-term contract meant that, unless all parties agreed, he would have to wait until it ended and then have a choice of destinations, albeit the buying club would still have to pay a fee for his services.

'It made me tougher mentally. I knew that no matter how well I did, there was a bit of an impasse between me and the club, and in the long term I would have to get away. My parents helped me through it, coming up for all reserve games both home and away. It would have been easy to let my performances drift off, but because my parents were in attendance I didn't want to let them down. Thankfully, Everton saw enough to take me on.'

Initial contact from Goodison Park arrived through a local press man.

'Football clubs were and always have been secretive. They trusted certain aides to make confidential calls for them, and when my phone rang I thought he wanted a quiet chat about my future, as it was common knowledge my time at Liverpool was coming to an end.

'Elsie Road was right next to Anfield but a stone's throw away from Goodison Park, so every midweek home game when Everton were playing, I'd walk over and sit in the top balcony of the Main Stand. I wasn't a well-known face in Liverpool, but I still wore a heavy coat with a hood to make sure nobody recognised me. I was lucky enough to watch Graeme Sharp make his debut. I could see Howard [Kendall] was building a young team centred on players like Adrian Heath and Kevin Ratcliffe. Without knowing it, I'd done my homework. I knew what I was going into. I also knew Evertonians were thinking that if I wasn't good enough for Liverpool, why would I be good enough for Everton, so I knew I had to get off to a good start and, luckily for me, I did.'

Sheedy's initial form was steady. But it took another 18 months for Everton to take off. By November 1983, inconsistent league form had seen only four wins in twelve matches. A new nadir was reached as table-topping Liverpool cruised to a 3–0 derby victory. There were rumours of Kendall being sacked. But what appeared as a moment of misery acted as a catalyst for future achievements. Although the Blues would continue to struggle until the beginning of January (a month where Kendall was rumoured to again be on the verge of dismissal), the defeat in the derby prompted Kendall to install Colin Harvey as first-team coach.

Although Harvey's appointment received recognition in the press, that story was overtaken by Everton's attempt to sign Brazilian João Batista Nunes. In an attempt to boost morale on the pitch and on the terraces, Kendall targeted the ageing striker who two years earlier had finished as the country's top scorer in domestic competitions with Flamengo. Had the deal been concluded, Nunes would have been the first Brazilian to play in England. At the last minute, though, Nunes decided to remain in South America. Instead, Kendall moved for Andy Gray. Gray would score goals in the FA Cup final at the end of that season, as well as in the Cup-Winners' Cup final a year later.

'Howard gave the younger players as much respect as the older ones. He treated us like adults,' Sheedy recalls. 'It was a good young team, but it was a good young team that wasn't getting consistent results. Howard was really clever with the press, and that bought him a bit of time when things were at rock bottom. People look at various moments, like Adrian Heath's goal at Oxford when we were 1–0 down in 1984 during the League Cup. [Everton went on to reach the League Cup final as well as the FA Cup final.] There was a theory buzzing about the place that the directors were prepared to sack Howard if we went out.'

While Harvey's influence on the training field improved Everton tactically, the belated flowering of Peter Reid in the heart of midfield was crucial to the team's development.

'We needed a few more experienced pros to help the youngsters out through the sticky patches. Andy Gray's arrival and Reidy's emergence as one of the best midfielders in the country helped a lot. When Reidy came in from Bolton, it did not look like a big signing. Peter had been through a lot of injury problems.'

A fee of £60,000 reflected that.

'We heard someone had sent Howard a letter warning him against signing him because he could not pass the ball more than 40 yards. But Howard went with his instincts.'

Sheedy believes the impact of Reid and Gray on an Everton dressing-room filled with ambitious young players was 'to turn us into men'. Gray was the type of striker that could wage a one-man war against opponents, flattening defenders like a cruel cyclone.

'There is a perception now that Gray scored a lot of goals, but if you look at his record, that wasn't the case. His influence over the team, though, was very important because his presence meant we weren't going to be bullied any more.'

With Harvey taking charge of training and Kendall observing and trusting his own judgements, the regimes at Bellefield and Melwood were very similar.

'There wasn't a lot of coaching at Liverpool. It was more a case of the management recruiting good players with the intelligence to figure it out themselves. People say, "Surely it wasn't just five-a-sides . . ." But it was.

'At Everton, there was the odd tactical drill, but generally it was uncomplicated. It was a case of getting it down, passing and moving – one and two touch. For me, it proves that if you've got good players who are bright enough, they can self-teach and take their findings into a match.'

Not much could divide the quality in the Liverpool and Everton teams. Sheedy believes, however, that Everton had an advantage in their goalkeeper. Neville Southall was probably the best in the world during the '80s. Usually with his socks down and shin-pads flapping, Big Nev was a man who bore an appearance of someone whose job it was to drain dregs at a dreary speakeasy. Instead, he had remarkable acrobatics and could deny any of the English top flight's clinical best.

'Nev was better than Bruce [Grobbelaar] by far,' Sheedy insists. 'He didn't make any daft mistakes, rushing off his line or coming for crosses when he should have stayed on his line. Bruce was helped by the fact that the Liverpool defenders always knew that he was coming, meaning they could get back on the line and prevent the ball from going in when he didn't meet a cross. To a certain extent, they knew what they were going to get.'

Despite Southall's greater reliability, like Grobbelaar he was different to the outfield players, marked out by the fact that he did not drink. I remember a story told to me by ex-Everton midfielder John Ebbrell. Whenever Everton travelled to away games, Southall would collect Ebbrell from his home on Wirral en route to the team's rendezvous point. The reason was simple. Ebbrell would like to unwind on the way home with a few beers, and, as Southall wasn't a drinker, he became the regular designated driver.

'He used to come and park his Volvo estate on my front lawn,' Ebbrell explained. 'I used to live in a cul-de-sac and I'd be sitting in my living room watching TV, waiting for him. Suddenly I'd hear the screech of this car speeding around the roads nearby, then this filthy Volvo would come in and pile through my driveway. Nev would be sitting there in front of the window having mowed down the flower bed, looking like Mad Max.'

Sheedy continues: 'Bruce was an eccentric while Nev was plain crazy. He was the '80s version of Peter Schmeichel. It was his dedication that set him apart. He hated conceding goals. If anyone scored a hat-trick against him in training, he'd be chasing them around Bellefield for a week. With respect to the other goalkeepers at the club, you knew that if you had a shot, you didn't necessarily need to put it right in the corner to beat them. That wasn't the case with Nev. A shot had to be perfect. That also improved the precision of the strikers.

'The best goalkeepers always make the goal look smaller. The failing of some goalkeepers means that draws can sometimes turn into defeats and victories can turn into draws. The opposite was the case with Nev. They used to say at Liverpool that Ray Clemence won the team a minimum of twelve points a season in an era when there was only two points for a win. I'm not sure whether Bruce could claim that.'

Everton's social scene was founded on mass gatherings around a table at one of any number of Chinese restaurants in Liverpool's city centre. Kendall's policy was to make sure the players met when results were lean.

'It meant that, one way or another, any issues would get ironed out quickly,' Sheedy remembers. 'We had a stringent disciplinary system at Everton, where players would get fined for the slightest indiscretion. It was a great idea for team spirit, because it meant that people would try to be on their best behaviour, but at the same time if anyone went out of line the group would benefit by coming together for a night.'

Compared to Liverpool's fourteen major honours in the '80s (excluding Charity Shields), Everton won two league titles, one FA Cup and a Cup-Winners' Cup. Their threat to Liverpool's domination was genuine. But after the Heysel disaster, Everton – like all English clubs – were prevented from competing in Europe. As reigning First Division champions, the restriction was particularly damaging to Kendall's team, who believed they had a chance of winning a first European Cup.

'All the momentum was with us,' says Sheedy, who eventually left Everton in 1992 for Kevin Keegan's Newcastle before a spell at Blackpool. 'English clubs had dominated the European Cup for nearly a decade, so we thought it was going to be our time. After Heysel, there was a lot of disappointment that we didn't get a chance to prove it. But we were not alone. Liverpool were in the same boat. So, who knows, if things were different, Liverpool could be sitting here now with seven or eight European Cups. I have a lot of sympathy for their players, too.'

CHAPTER SEVEN

Cult Zeros

SKIPPY, Craig Johnston

'I WAS CRAP, MATE,' SAYS CRAIG JOHNSTON IN A BEGUILING MANNER, while he redresses his thinning top curls into a ponytail. 'I had a dream to become the best player in the world, but I failed miserably. In fact, by playing for Liverpool, I was the worst player in the best team in the world . . . you really have no idea how crap I was.'

The genial Australian, known as Skippy to Liverpool supporters, could be readying himself for a beach party at Surfers Paradise rather than an afternoon slurping Earl Grey inside his partner's penthouse apartment in Knightsbridge, central London. He is bereft of footwear when I meet him, wearing a checked shirt with sleeves rolled up and a pair of ripped jeans. 'I go for the Status Quo rather than the Brian May look these days,' he jokes. Of all the characters interviewed for this book, the former winger would be the most unassuming and engaging in equal measure.

Johnston, who won five league titles, an FA Cup and one

European Cup at Anfield between 1981 and 1988, had to prove a lot of people wrong before making it on Merseyside. At Middlesbrough, during his first trial match in England, he was labelled by Jack Charlton as 'the worst player I've ever seen', before being told that it would be in his best interests to 'fuck off back to Australia'.

It toughened him up, and those words have been buzzing in his ears ever since – as a constant motivation to improve. Past his 50th birthday, Johnston has maximised his talents both during his football career and afterwards. Since retiring at the age of 27 to care for his sick sister, he has invented a football boot, created software for hotel businesses to monitor minibar thefts, made up a revolutionary system for coaching children, developed computer models for analysing football statistics and, most recently, established himself as an award-winning photographic artist. At one point, he was also bankrupt and made homeless.

Johnston's memories from matches, moments and medals over his playing career have faded – something he admits. It probably has something to do with the fact that he's done so much since deciding to quit the game. Unlike many other ex-pros, he has a lifetime of alternative achievements to reflect on.

'One day, I'll have to research and try to remember exact games and goals,' he says. 'Instead, I am more analytical of people and attitudes. I wasn't an intelligent footballer. I was called an idiot on a lot of occasions because my understanding of the game wasn't as good as other players'. Away from the pitch, I was and still am streetwise, and I reckon I've got a better grasp of the way the world works. That has been my saviour, because football doesn't prepare you for what happens after you quit.'

Johnston spent the first four years of his life in an apartment block in the Berea district of Johannesburg.

'My parents were Australian and met on a boat. They were travelling independently around the world. Dad was going to Scotland to try to be a footballer, and Mum was going to London to be a teacher. After a year or so, Dad was frustrated with

Aberdeen reserves, so he travelled south to catch up with my mum. Before long, she gave birth to a daughter.

'They lived near Craven Cottage, so my Dad went to watch Fulham a lot. His heroes were Johnny Haynes and Jimmy Greaves. He tells a lovely story about going to the ground before they moved to South Africa when Mum was pregnant with me. There was nobody there; it was during the week. He rubbed her belly and said, "One day my boy will come back here and play soccer." Years later we drew Fulham in the League Cup and Kenny [Dalglish] got injured. I wore the famous number 7 and we won 1–0. Dad's prediction was right.'

After his parents decided to return to Australia when Johnston was six, the family settled in Boolaroo on the outskirts of Newcastle, a coalmining and steel town about 100 miles north of Sydney.

'It was very working class,' he says. 'The miners from the collieries in the north of England had come over to work. They named places after towns back home – there was Morpeth, Gateshead, Wallsend – all towns being built on the east coast of Australia.'

The coalminers brought football with them.

'Sydney and Brisbane are rugby league towns. Everywhere also had cricket, rugby union and Aussie Rules. But soccer was a big, big thing in Newcastle where I lived. It was soccer, soccer and soccer. That's the main reason I became a player.'

Johnston later starred at cricket for New South Wales state at junior level as a medium-paced bowler. But he was obsessed with 'soccer'.

'I grew up with my dad telling me stories about his early 20s when he tried to make it as a pro. I made it my mission to retrace his footsteps but this time to make it as a professional – even if it was just for one game. The team of the day that we saw on Australian TV was Leeds United: Billy Bremner, Johnny Giles and Sniffer Clarke. I liked them because they were tough men.'

Johnston watched football a lot following an enforced break from school.

'I got involved in a bad fight one day,' he recalls. 'I really got beaten up by this English kid. I developed a disease, osteomyelitis, which is a form of polio. It rots the bone. In the '60s, it was incurable. I spent six months in hospital and at one stage doctors said that the only option was to cut my leg off. My mum signed the form giving the order to amputate. Luckily, there was a doctor visiting Australia from abroad who managed to save it. While I was recuperating, all I did was watch English football.'

At 15, he saw a touring team from Middlesbrough beat his local side, Newcastle. Afterwards, he wrote to 'Boro boss Jack Charlton asking for a trial. He also penned letters to Dave Sexton at Chelsea and Tommy Docherty at Manchester United.

'Middlesbrough were the only ones to respond,' he remembers. 'But they told me I had to pay for my own flights and boarding. It meant some big sacrifices for the family. We had horses and they used to shit a lot and people needed it for their gardens. So I collected horse manure for money. My family eventually had to sell the house and move into a smaller property out of town to fund the plane tickets. They understood that I'd struggled with the osteomyelitis and understood what it was like to have your dreams taken away like it did with Dad. So they supported me all the way through.'

One condition of the trip was that he left Australia having achieved straight A grades in his final exams, so it was lucky that Johnston was academic.

'I was really good in school and at first I wanted to be an architect because I've always liked building things. Then, once, I went on a soccer trip to Sydney and I got violently sick. I must have had a dodgy meat pie. I thought I was going to die. Then a doctor came in and gave me a drug to knock me out. When I woke up, I felt better immediately. From then on, I wanted to be one of those people who could take the pain away. I thought about medicine. Very easily, I could have been successful in either of those professions. In the end, I studied, studied and studied like no kid had ever studied in science, maths and English and aced them all. So I was off.'

Middlesbrough was very different to Newcastle, Australia. Although similarly dominated by the heavy industries of mining, railways, iron, steel, shipbuilding and the docks (later petro-chemicals), by the late '70s it afforded few prospects of employment. Middlesbrough was depression-stricken, a land of everlasting fog. This was the town of J.B. Priestley's *English Journey,* 'whose chief passions . . . were for beer and football'. It was, Priestley wrote, 'a dismal town, even with beer and football'.

'To go from the hot, steamy beaches of New South Wales to the cold, cobbled, misty streets of north-east England on a wet, gloomy winter's evening was a shock, even though it was fascinating to me,' Johnston says. 'That was when I started taking photographs. I'd walk around the town and try to capture the little quirks of life in the north of England.'

Jack Charlton attended his first trial match.

'It was at a place called Hutton Road,' he continues, grimacing. 'We were 3–0 down at half-time. For whatever reason, the manager of the first team turned up – something that never happens. He went around the dressing-room bollocking everyone. "You – where are you from?" he asked me.

'I'm from Australia, mate.'

'"I'm not your mate and well . . . you . . . kangaroo are the worst fucking footballer I have seen in my whole fucking life. Now fuck off."

'I burst into tears and couldn't play the second half. I got my bag and found my way to the digs. I had to tell my mum. This was 1975, so phoning Australia meant a lot of hassle with reverse charges. It took me an hour to get through. "How was your big trial? We're so proud of you!" she said. "Have you met Jack Charlton?"

'I told her that Charlton thought I was one of the finest footballers he'd seen in his life and that he wanted me to stay. Then I put the phone down as quickly as I could. They'd sold the house for me, so I couldn't tell them I was fucking crap like he'd told me, could I? They had taken so many risks just to see me happy.'

However ruthless he may have been, Johnston insists that Charlton was right about his ability.

'He wasn't wrong; I was that bad,' he smiles. 'There were all these cultured, elegant European footballers to pick from, and I had bleached blond, almost Rastafarian hair because I was a beach kid. He really wasn't wrong. I met Charlton years later at a function on the Gold Coast [in Australia] where his son was then living. I told my story and he told his side of it. "You needed a kick up the bum." Charlton got the most out of people, not that he intended to get the most out of me. But I suppose had he not been so harsh I wouldn't have bounced back with so much desire to prove the bastard wrong.

'Since then, I have met him five or six times and I have found him to be a funny, clever guy, and people don't give him enough credit for what he achieved – especially at Ireland. He got results. He was no-nonsense and straight-talking. I've always admired Charlton. Otherwise, I wouldn't have taken any notice of him.'

For the next six months, however, Johnston hid from Charlton's wrath and trained alone in the club's car park.

'Some of the professionals like Graeme Souness and Terry Cooper [ex Leeds] had heard what he said to me and felt it was a bit harsh. They said that if I cleaned their cars, they'd give me enough money to stay at the digs. So whenever Charlton came into work, they'd give me a shout and I'd crouch behind the vehicles to keep out of his way.

'After the Charlton episode, I thought to myself, "How do I become a footballer?" They dribbled, they passed and they headed the ball. But I couldn't do any of those things particularly well. So I started watching Souness and [David] Mills in training, then I'd return to the car park and try my best to develop my skills and techniques by using garbage cans to dribble in and out of at full speed if I could. If I hit one of them, it didn't count, so I had to do it again: ten left foot, ten right foot. Every time I hit the can, I had to start again. There was a mortuary next door, so you never wanted to hit the ball over the wall because it was a nightmare getting it back. I'd do this all day until seven or eight o'clock at night – whenever I'd fulfilled my quota of skills. It was the only thing that kept me sane and focused. I had to be a better player at night than I was when I woke up in the morning.'

It was a lonely existence.

'It's a bit of a hard-luck story here, but I couldn't share it with anybody else. I knew the other apprentices that had been taken on were back at their digs eating their Spam and watching *Coronation Street*. When you're in a football club, your self-worth and value as a human being is only marked as a footballer. All of the great, naturally gifted footballers are like mini gods. All of the clodhoppers like me are worthless. Nobody says it, but that's the way I interpreted it. People thought I was a joke – bloody hilarious – running around on my own. I was resented from the start because I was crap, they resented me also because I tried to get better, and they resented me because I was a proud Australian and was a lot brighter than many of them. I wasn't a dope, so if shit came my way, I wouldn't just stand there and take it. I used to get in all sorts of arguments and fights. But the car park was my penance for being a useless footballer.'

Eventually, Jack Charlton moved on to Sheffield Wednesday and was replaced by John Neal.

'On his first day, he saw me training in the car park and asked, "Who's that scruffy guy?"

'The older lads just said, "Ah, that's Kangaroo – he always practises in the car park – he's crap."

'John then invited me over and said I could train with the youth team. From then on, I think I became a concern to all the players that doubted me because my style was harem-scarem. I was keener than them. I had no natural ability, but I had an engine and a huge heart. Because I practised hard, I showed all of them up for effort and attitude. Gradually, I got better. Soon, I'd have one touch rather than three. I also bought a cinema projector and watched a lot of old shows about Pelé and the greats. I tried to learn from their attitudes off the pitch. Eventually, the other apprentices came to my room to watch the movies. Then they'd start playing one on one in the car park because they liked the games that I invented.'

A flu epidemic at Ayresome Park gave Johnston his chance in the first team. Just two years after being brutally discounted by Jack Charlton, he was lining up in the FA Cup against Everton.

'Six of the squad were wiped out,' he says. 'There wasn't a big squad at Middlesbrough, and because I'd played well in the reserves, John Neal put some faith in me. It was on television and I played really well. I'd spent my whole life watching English football on TV and now I was a part of it. It was like when you're young and a fair comes to town and you watch it roll down the road. All the people are on floats. All of a sudden, I was on the field and I was on one of the floats. I wasn't waving at the floats. The people were waving at me. It was a strange feeling, given what I'd been through in a short period. At 17 I became the youngest player at the time to play for Middlesbrough. I'd set out what I aimed to do when I left Australia.'

Better was to follow. Following 64 games and 16 league goals on Teeside, Liverpool made an offer for him. But there were other proposals to consider.

'The first call came from Brian Clough at Nottingham Forest,' Johnston recalls. 'The fella on the end of the line said, "Hello, young man, it's Brian Clough here," in that unmistakable accent.

'I was like, yeah, right. "No, it really is Brian Clough here and I'm in Benidorm . . . and I'd like to sign you."

'I thought it was somebody taking the piss.

'"No, no . . . I'm very serious. This is an expensive call . . . I'll be back next week, we'll see you at our place and we'll sign up the details."

'He put the phone down and I said to myself, "Wow – that really was Brian Clough."'

Twenty minutes later, the phone rang again.

'"Erp . . . erp, it's Bob Paisley 'ere like y'naw," this bloke says.

'"Aw, piss off," I responded.

'"No, it's Bob Paisley . . . I've heard all aboot ye from the lads, Graeme Souness in particular. We'd like to sign ye, like."

'I knew it was him because the accent was too perfect. He told me that we needed to do the deal quickly because he understood that Clough was interested and because Liverpool were on the verge of selling someone in my position [Jimmy Case was the player set to leave, although the transfer to Brighton didn't happen for another four months].

'When Bob put the phone down, I immediately rang around to get hold of a solicitor, because I didn't have an agent. Eventually, I spoke to my dad. He went straight to the point. "Brian Clough is a man. But Liverpool is an institution." Forest were winning European Cups and all the buzz was about Clough. He'd played for Middlesbrough after growing up there, and people like the old groundsmen who knew him said we had similar personalities. Like me, he was the only other footballer they knew that would spend hours on the training ground after a session had finished to practise technique. Despite this, I realised that I had to go to the institution.'

There were other interested parties.

'Bill Shankly recommended me several times to Everton,' he insists. 'I had word that because the Liverpool board had peed him off by distancing themselves, he agreed to some scouting work with Everton on the quiet. They were looking to move for me but because Middlesbrough said no initially, they signed Gary Megson instead. I could have been an Evertonian.'

Liverpool agreed a deal worth up to £650,000 with Middlesbrough.

'It was the first time I really felt wanted. To go from the situation with Jack Charlton to being signed by Liverpool in no more than four to five years was quite spectacular. In one of the national newspapers, the headline ran "Craig Johnston: Take your pick". It had a picture of me with a list of over a dozen clubs underneath that were trying to buy me. It was solely down to the four or five hours I'd spent in the car park every day.'

Like many new signings, Johnston was accommodated in the Holiday Inn on Paradise Street after agreeing a contract with chairman John Smith. He soon moved to Sandfield Park in West Derby.

'Kenny Dalglish wasn't the captain, but he was a leader in the dressing-room,' Johnston insists. 'Within the first 24 hours of me being there, he took me around Southport to look for property and went out of his way to make me feel at home and comfortable.'

The next day, Souness warned Johnston against living in Southport.

'He told me that it was where the posh guys live. "Come and see where us working-class blokes live." So he took me for a pint in the Jolly Miller then around West Derby. Davey Fairclough and Sammy Lee also lived there, along with Chris Lawler. Melwood was just around the corner, so to me it was perfect.'

Later on, when Johnston was out of the Liverpool team, his home on Sandfield Park would provide a convenient location for sneaking back into the training ground for some extra sessions.

'I was so embarrassed that I didn't meet the required standards for a Liverpool player that I had my own key cut for Melwood. Nobody knew about it. I did everything I could to become better. One time we were training and Ronnie Moran stopped us. "What the fuck is this?" There was a set of cones in the figure of eight. He thought that kids must have broken into Melwood and had a kickabout. "Bloody kids." After training, I admitted to Ronnie that I'd been there the night before practising by doing some shuttles with the ball. "What for?" I explained that I needed to work on my left foot.'

Johnston arrived at Liverpool in April 1981 but didn't play for the first team until the following season. By then, the Reds were struggling in the league. On Boxing Day, they had lost five and drawn six of the seventeen games, occupying a place in mid-table. Sceptics argued that Liverpool's dominance of the English game was on the verge of a collapse.

'I was completely naive to the situation because I was used to rocky times at Middlesbrough,' Johnston says. 'I was slightly disappointed that I wasn't called on a lot more, because I felt I'd earned the right to play by training hard [Johnston only appeared in 18 league games that season]. In the second part of the year, we managed to turn things around and eventually pipped Ipswich to the title. I was pleased we did it, but I'm an Aussie and I'm competitive. I wanted to play an important role in a successful team.'

In the summer of 1982, Johnston was late turning up for pre-season training after his then wife, Jane, gave birth to their firstborn in Australia. Already, he was beginning to feel unsettled at Liverpool. Bob Paisley wasn't quite the genial person he appeared to be.

'I provided enthusiasm and effort for the team. I tried to spark and provoke other players to do the same. But I wasn't sure that was appreciated. Bob kept his distance from me and all the players – as did Joe Fagan and later Kenny. It was the accepted Liverpool style of management. I didn't feel like I could go to Bob, and Joe especially, with the concerns that I had. It's a macho responsibility to sort yourself out mentally and physically, so I never, ever went into the manager's office. I wanted to prove myself at Liverpool, but I wasn't given a fair chance until Kenny took charge.'

Johnston fell out with Fagan upon his appointment as manager in 1983.

'I thought Joe was being unfair to me. Here I am 25 years later and I still feel the same way about what happened. I was dropped from the team for not playing well, which was fine. But then I worked hard in training and played really well in the reserves, so I thought that I deserved a recall. He said, "I can't change a winning team – I can't put you in." Then somebody got injured and I went in and we won the next three or four back to back. But he dropped me again. So I went into his office and said, "I thought you said you can't change a winning team?" Joe replied, "That was then and this is now."'

With that, a bristling Johnston became even more frustrated at Anfield.

'Maybe there are players that can pick up their wages and sit on the bench, but I wasn't one of them. I'd fought too hard as a youngster in the hospital and dreamed too hard to not contribute. It ate me away. I couldn't train all week, knowing that I wasn't going to be in the team. Every time the team was read out on a Friday or Saturday, I'd sit there with my palms sweating nervously. Rushy used to laugh at that, but it used to hurt me so much. A couple of times, I shouted out, "You've gotta be fucking kidding here." Nobody ever spoke out of turn to the manager. It probably didn't help my chances.'

Johnston considered leaving Liverpool, with both Chelsea and Ron Atkinson's Manchester United making offers.

'There were times when I'd go out drinking with players in a similar position to me – players dumped from the first team and into the reserves. We'd bitch about the manager and we'd do it for two or three weeks. But then I thought that wasn't my style. I had to extract my aggression out on something else. It was my own fault – I wasn't good enough to be in that particular team. So I trained harder. Under Joe, I played eleven games in the 1984–85 season. But when Kenny took over, he knew I was doing extra training and rewarded me for it. To have the balls to come back was something I was very proud of.'

Given the difficulties during his first three seasons at Liverpool, it is easy to forget that he was a major part of the squad that won the club's fourth European Cup in Rome. Johnston believes a major reason behind Liverpool's success was a well-oiled team spirit.

'I never drank at all at Middlesbrough,' he says. 'I didn't particularly like the taste of beer. I made up for it when I got to Liverpool, let me tell you. I began to enjoy it. It was a very sociable dressing-room. The guys appreciated each other's company. There was a genuine cultural connection. You were either English, Scottish, Irish or Welsh. There were those that weren't – the Australian, the Zimbabwean [Grobbelaar], the Dane [Mølby]. We all understood the Liverpool culture, spoke English and loved a beer.

'The reason why we won everything hands down was because of team spirit. It was remarkable. If you look at people like Dalglish, Souness, Lawrenson and Hansen, they've all gone on to do extremely well in life because they were all gentlemen. They understood what professionalism means, what delivery means and most of all what being a man fucking means. They really did. There was no hiding place in that dressing-room. Nobody got away with one shirked tackle, because we understood what it means to play for Liverpool.'

The spirit at Anfield was founded on verbal wit rather than practical jokes.

'There were no examples of a poo being left in somebody's lunch box to my knowledge. But each person was funny and had a sense of humour. Me and Bruce would be the butt of everyone else's displeasure and piss-taking at times. But that was part of a great team spirit – somebody always has to be the fall guy. There were others as well – for their lack of intelligence, naiveness or because they told porky pies, exaggerating things. The dynamics of the dressing-room was fascinating to me.'

The atmosphere at Everton was similar.

'We were very alike. For Rushy, there was Kevin Ratcliffe. For Souness, there was Peter Reid. Culturally, they were very similar people and performers. Howard Kendall understood the importance of team spirit and instilling a drinking culture that would inspire success.'

Manchester United were full of drinkers as well.

'United had better players or individuals than us,' Johnston maintains. 'It would be a wrongful statement to say we were individually superior. But we had the better team spirit, which was founded in the pubs and bars of Liverpool as well as the training ground. What set us apart from United and the rest was the running off the ball. Football is all about movement. In the game today, there is more focus on the player in possession, but they miss the players that make the space. Kenny was and still is regarded as one of the greatest players of all time – rightly so. But at any one time he had three players running off him, making the defenders move into places where they didn't want to be. We were ahead of our time. The dummies and the dopes were as important as the artists. We had a better balance of people and players in the squad, and that's why we won a lot more than them.'

Ian Rush initially struggled to become a part of this 'spirit', but after two seasons at the club he became one of the dressing-room leaders along with Souness, Hansen and Dalglish.

'At first, Rushy was dressed like Tom Jones, and some of the boys used to call him "ET" because he was phoning home all the time and he looked like he was from Mars. But he got into the swing of it pretty quickly and became one of the major piss-takers. In Liverpool, if you can score goals like him you can walk on water. People would laugh with him even if he wasn't funny.'

Johnston's room-mate was Grobbelaar.

'We were seen as two exotics. They used to say we were stupid, thick and crazy – especially Ronnie Moran, who seemed to have a fear of anything different. Anybody who came from Australia or Zimbabwe must be a fruitcake, so Ronnie thought that anything me or Bruce said made little if any sense at all. At one away game, somebody brought a game of Trivial Pursuit. For once, because it wasn't cards or piss-take jokes and rather something about general knowledge and how the world works, we managed to win it hands down.'

Michael Robinson was also different.

'He was not your typical footballer at all. He was on another planet – like me and Bruce. It was considered that anything he might have to say that embraced a cultural subject was fluffy, fairy and for poofters only, so to speak.'

A player wasn't encouraged to break from the often-burdensome results-orientated climate that emanated from the Bootroom.

'Tom Saunders was the only person who saw the world like me. Being an ex-headmaster, he'd already worked with kids from all kinds of different backgrounds. Bob and Ronnie were more basic but equally effective in their methods. Ronnie particularly set the tone for everything that went on in training. He would call Dalglish and Souness "Effing bigheads". He was the sergeant-major type who'd say, "You think you're clever; I'll show you who's clever." When we won the league, his attitude was, "I'll show you clever – put your kit on and let's train for two hours and see who drops first." Ronnie and the management just wanted to win, and win with style, class and charisma – it was so comprehensive that it was beyond reproach.

'This attitude originally came from Shankly and was carried through time by the people he brought to the club to pass on that message. They all had football intelligence beyond the years of any other management team in Europe. They were all canny and streetwise in the bucketload. Shankly understood that a successful team must have Jocks, because they too were canny. Bob Paisley was clever enough to carry that on with Hansen, Souness, Kenny and Nicol. They were all professionals who were prepared to go all the way to win. In life generally, the guy in a fight who is prepared to die is the one that wins, and our team was full of those guys.'

Johnston insists that he shared those qualities, but because he thought deeply about other issues in life away from football he was sometimes viewed as 'a bit soft'.

'Maybe I came across as someone who wasn't as committed. There were a lot of other things that entered my head after a game, which made me stand out as a bit fluffy or woolly. On the field, you couldn't find a more committed player, and I think that's why the supporters took to me. It was like winding up a toy and letting me run around for 90 minutes. Bruce and Hansen have both said since that I was the fittest player in British football. I was like that during matches, but once it was over and we'd won, I was interested in the arts and interested in photography. I think that came across badly. If I had my time again, maybe I'd keep it to myself, because to the old guard, maybe they thought I was a bit of a flake and that caused friction. Really, though, I was more committed than them because I did it when it mattered.'

Unlike the more instinctive players, Johnston also suffered from nerves.

'We played Everton once in the derby and I was really shitting myself. When you play for Liverpool, it's the best club in the world to be at when everything is going well and you are performing. But you get nervous because if you make a mistake or, like me, you're not this wonderful footballer that other people are – if you're this guy that comes from northern New South Wales that misses an open goal – your confidence can go. That's why you become so scared – because you fear letting yourself down, your teammates down, the fans down and the manager down, especially in the derby. So I started to look around at my teammates and I began to think, "Really – how bad can it be?" I had Souness standing next to me. I had Dalglish and Rush in front of me. All I had to do was half pass a ball and they'd get there. Then I looked at Lawrenson and Hansen. I realised that if I was nervous, how much must they be shitting themselves next door? I started laughing and all of a sudden I relaxed and started to believe in myself.'

By 1986, Johnston was playing some of his best football. With Dalglish now in charge, he was a regular on the right-hand side of Liverpool's midfield, making sixty-one appearances in total that season, scoring ten times. A week after securing the title against Chelsea, the Reds travelled to London again for the FA Cup final against Everton at Wembley.

'Everton were a brilliant football outfit – they were tough and they were hard. Anything we could do, they could do too. Neville Southall was unbelievable. He could save everything. I was fast, but Pat Van Den Hauwe was just as quick. I was thinking about how to get out of his way for 90 minutes, because he'd justifiably earned the nickname "Psycho". It all meant I was very, very nervous. It affected my performance, and both teams didn't play as well as they probably should because it was so intense.'

Johnston recalls his goal with a grin.

'Everywhere I went, Van Den Hauwe was with me. Box to box. Then one time, I remember going back to our box and he followed me. I saw a space down the wing and I started to sprint into it. The ball was on our left wing, but Van Den Hauwe followed me all the way for 70 or so yards. By then, Jan Mølby had the ball. I knew he'd try to find Kenny first, but something prompted me to make that last ten-yard dash. Instinctively I went, and it was only because I had a bigger heart that I connected with the cross. Psycho Pat didn't have any legs left in him, and it was the easiest goal I've ever scored.'

Ian Rush and Ronnie Whelan still make fun of Johnston for what he did next.

'I shouted, "I did it . . . I did it." Ronnie and Rushy were the first over and whenever they see me now they scream like girls, "I did it . . . I did it." I didn't mean that I'd just scored. I was actually talking about the journey to get there: the polio, the television, the Jack Charlton stuff, the car park every day and the tough times at Liverpool. It sounds corny, but it was my dream to play in an FA Cup final and to score a decisive goal was unbelievable. If somebody would have shot me then, I'd have died a happy man.'

Another goal from Rush secured a 3–1 victory.

'I scored the most important one in the match, but the turning point was the skirmish between Bruce and Jim Beglin after a misunderstanding at the back. Everybody reacted to it. The celebrations afterwards were special. We all jumped in the bath inside the changing-room at Wembley with the cup. The baths were huge, and you could fit a whole squad in there. Suddenly, these two Liverpool supporters burst through the door and jumped in with us. Somehow, they'd passed through security with their bobble hats and scarves on. The beer flowed.'

Two years later, Liverpool were in the cup final again with Wimbledon the opposition. Johnston decided to contribute something even more special than the promise of a goal ahead of the match. This time, he created a song. Twelve months earlier, before the League Cup final defeat to Arsenal, Johnston had written, produced and released 'The Pride of Merseyside', a tune that reached 41 in the charts. The 'Anfield Rap' was different.

'I liked "Pride of Merseyside" more than the "Anfield Rap",' he says, like a musician who resents his most famous work. 'But the "Rap" was an achievement because people remember it today. It was my idea, I paid for it, I wrote it, and I did the video. But I did need a bit of professional help and I got it from Derek Bee, who was Britain's first rapper. I had the idea for the rap, but I needed a musical hook with something to do with The Beatles and "You'll Never Walk Alone". So he came up with using "Twist and Shout". The whole concept of the song was to reflect accents. There were only two Scousers in the team – Aldo and Steve McMahon – so they opened it.'

Johnston breaks into the song. Then he pauses. 'Every time I hear it, I cringe. I even exaggerated my Australian accent for effect, and it sounded crap. I think when I initially said it in recording, everybody laughed. I regret it now.'

What people didn't know at the time was that while Liverpool were doing so well on the pitch and Johnston was producing music off it, he was also going through a personal trauma. His younger sister, Faye, had an accident earlier that year while on holiday in Morocco, leaving her in a coma. Johnston was at the annual Christmas party with his Liverpool teammates when he was told of the news.

'I was dressed as Dame Edna Everage and a call came through. I realised that I had to drop everything and hired a private plane – something that wasn't easy to do. I flew to Morocco straight away and had to get her out the same night. The place she was being kept in was such a hellhole. It was like the *Midnight Express* if you dreamed about a hospital or a prison. It was horrible. She was all blue and I didn't recognise her. When we arrived in London, I had to get my parents across from Australia. Because I was in the team at Liverpool, I was up and down the motorway every other day. Only Kenny knew about it, but maybe he didn't understand how dire her situation was. Faye's husband had just died in mysterious circumstances in Afghanistan and they'd just had a daughter. It was a terrible situation.'

Johnston, believing his sister would emerge from the coma,

placed all of his energies into her recovery. At the same time, he played 20 times in Liverpool's first team as the club eased towards the 1987–88 title, playing some of the most exhilarating football ever witnessed at Anfield. The pressure took its toll.

'I was a substitute against Southampton with a couple of games to go, and for the first time my mind wasn't on the game [it finished 1–1]. I was thinking about my sister and a million miles away from football. Kenny brought me on and I should have scored in front of the Kop. I should have used my right foot and I used my left foot instead. But I didn't care about it and it felt strange. Afterwards, I didn't go into the players' lounge and headed straight home. I was living on Wirral by then and we were driving through the Birkenhead Tunnel. I just said to the wife, "Do you want to go home?"

'"We are going home – I'm driving . . ."

'"No, home – Australia. It's time. I need to look after Faye."' [Faye had subsequently been moved back to Australia.]

Johnston decided to retire from football, informing Dalglish the week before the cup final against Wimbledon.

'Kenny wasn't happy with the timing,' Johnston recalls. 'I felt I'd achieved everything and more of what I'd set out to do. When your sister is there sitting in a coma, it makes you look differently at life. For so many years, I lived my life around a football result at a weekend, but now something else had taken the focus away from that. Liverpool thought that because I hadn't been in the team as much as I would have liked, I was trying to engineer a move away. To Kenny, everything happened quite suddenly, so I can understand why maybe he felt that way.'

Liverpool placed a freeze on Johnston's wages.

'They seized my assets and took control of my bank accounts. They'd [previously] bought Ray Houghton in my position, but I was prepared to fight him for a place in the team before this all happened. It was quite a sad way to end everything.'

When Johnston did not return for pre-season training, Liverpool finally realised that he had gone for good.

'I was unlike other footballers because I loved pre-season. It was my time of year when I could achieve more than others. I was the benchmark that every other player went by, because nobody could touch me in terms of fitness. When I didn't show up, maybe then the penny dropped with Liverpool.'

Twelve months after retiring, news made its way to Australia of a stadium football disaster involving Liverpool supporters in Sheffield.

'I was surfing on a Malibu board decorated in Liverpool's colours when someone called me back to shore and told me something awful had gone on at Hillsborough. I was working for Channel 9 and I dropped everything to get the first flight back to the UK. I was there for about three weeks, doing what I could by talking to people. I could relate to the families because most of the injuries were suffocation and therefore brain damage – exactly what had happened to my sister.'

Before he returned to Australia, Johnston was asked to visit Dalglish's office at Anfield.

'He told me that they really appreciated me coming back. He said that I'd had my tragedy – admitting that they couldn't quite understand it at the time. Maybe I wasn't as forthcoming with information as I should have been. "We've had our tragedy now." Kenny added that if I ever wanted to come back, there was a contract waiting for me on the table. "Thanks, boss." As I was walking out, he added that there was one other thing. "You forgot this when you left." Out of the drawer he pulled out a league championship winners' medal from the season before. "Have that – you deserve it."'

The meeting with Dalglish settled Johnston's differences. But even after a contract offer to return to Anfield from Graeme Souness in 1991 after he took over from Dalglish, Johnston remained in Australia. His sister, Faye, remains there, still in a vegetative state.

By the early '90s, and without the kind of money a footballer would retire on today, Johnston was pioneering a television show in Australia called *The Main Event*. 'When I walked away from Liverpool, I had to use my mind to earn a living.' Soon, he would make more money from clever inventions. The one most people haven't heard of is The Butler. 'Moving around so much, I've spent a lot of time in hotels. Minibars are one of the biggest drains on hotel revenue. So I surrounded each item in the bar with sensors so that if you took a bottle of beer out it sent a signal to the room's telephone and it would appear on your bill. Simple really.'

His most successful invention has been the Predator boot. He may have designed it with a children's market in mind, but as soon as it was licensed by adidas it became the must-have footwear of choice for football's nobility – David Beckham, Zinedine Zidane and, latterly, Steven Gerrard.

'I went to Reebok and Nike, but they weren't bothered about it. Then I went to adidas in Munich. Beforehand, I spoke to players that adidas would respect – Beckenbauer, Rummenigge, Breitner – and videoed them trying out my prototypes. They said a whole load of stuff in German I couldn't understand. When I showed adidas the film, they went, "Oh my gosh, don't leave the room."'

Johnston sold his idea to adidas, not fully appreciating the boot's potential.

'I took the money. Since then, they've sold millions of boots, at over a hundred quid a pair. And I was on 2 per cent of the action, so you can do the mathematics. It left me much shorter than I should have been.'

A person of energy and creativity, Johnston continued to dream big. He used his adidas pay-off to develop other inventions, including a football-coaching system for children called SoccerSkills. Despite gaining official FIFA approval, the English Football Association was uninterested by the idea and the system failed to take off. He found himself penniless and, eventually, divorced.

He told *FourFourTwo* magazine: 'Because of the FA's delaying tactics, incompetence and gamesmanship, I went bankrupt. It cost me £1.5 million and my marriage. At one stage, after countless pointless meetings with them, I lost it. I nearly punched one of them out. Instead, I ran around the car park with a pair of women's knickers on my head shouting, "You're a bunch of twats!"'

'SoccerSkills is so far ahead of its time in certain ways, the governing bodies will eventually take it up,' he tells me. 'I also think that the Predator hasn't reached its potential as product yet. One day, I'll go back to that and do a much better version.'

Johnston became depressed. Then he pursued photography. In an interview with the *Daily Telegraph* in 2010, he described what happened next: 'I broke up with my wife, the kids had gone back to Australia; I had no house, no car, nothing. It would have been easy to hit the bottle. But I had my old camera. I went for a walk, it was pouring with rain, and for me photography is like meditation. I suddenly saw this mannequin, beautifully dressed in beautiful light in a window. Just then this nasty tramp was coming along the road, swearing at me. And I saw him in the window, and I thought how interesting – the haves and have-nots in the same picture. I got his reflection in the window, with this lovely model; it was a great moment. It really lifted my spirits. It took me to a different place.'

Later, Johnston shows me a selection of personal photos from his iPad – many black and white – taken during his decade in English football. He bought his first camera with an £8-a-week pay packet from Middlesbrough. Many of the pictures are from nights out with the Liverpool team: Rush slumped in a chair; Souness caked in mud during an end-of-season trip to Israel; Beardsley dressed as a sheikh; Barnes infamously in Ku Klux Klan apparel at a Christmas party.

There are others pictures not related to football that are equally atmospheric, many of which have featured in successful London gallery exhibitions. Ahead of this interview, Johnston had been to Las Vegas to take snaps at the wedding of Australian midfielder Tim Cahill.

His rebirth as a photographer has coincided with a new relationship. Together with partner Viv, he now lives in Orlando, Florida, but travels to London and Australia throughout the course of the year. Despite resuming a nomadic lifestyle he is so used to, he still has regrets as he returns to a mood of self-reproach.

'I never fulfilled my potential as a footballer because the older I was getting, the more I understood it. I was finding that the simple things in football are the most important. It's a real shame and it still frustrates me.' He also wishes he'd represented his country at international level. 'Bob and subsequent managers said that if I went and played for Australia, I wouldn't be in the first team when I came back.'

He'd still like to try football management.

'I've got some very strong ideas about it. I think a lot of it is about getting the most out of a person. Up to a point it's a bit of a con game, because you've got to get people thinking that they're better than they really are. If I do it one day, I'll do it in my own style.'

Johnston says his life has been littered by lapses in judgement. 'Buying a Porsche when I first went to Liverpool was a biggy,' he laughs. 'The boss thought I was really flash. But when you're on your deathbed, I'd imagine that you look back and think about what you've achieved. Not everybody can live through truly great football moments – moments when you stand there and say, "Oh my god – how did they do that?"

'When I'm at death's door, I'm sure I'll be thinking about my family, but I'll also be thinking about a crisp, sunny morning at Melwood with a slight bit of dew on the field. Ronnie Moran will be in an aggressive mood screaming, "One touch, you big-headed bastards" – ensuring that everyone would be thinking about the next pass before the ball had even come to you. Dalglish, Souness will be dominating the play. And every now and again, I'll be a part of the move.'

CHAPTER EIGHT

Cult Zeros

SOUTHERNER, Nigel Spackman

WHEN NIGEL SPACKMAN TOLD A NATIONAL NEWSPAPER THAT HE would always support Liverpool, a group of Chelsea supporters lobbied for the removal of the 'Spackman Hospitality Entrance' that leads inside Stamford Bridge's West Stand. 'It should be replaced with a title more historically fitting and appropriate,' read the petition.

'It's unfortunate they feel that way,' Spackman says, eyes radiating hurt. 'But Liverpool have always been my club. I get stick all the time at the Bridge for pledging my allegiance. Even though I was at Chelsea for longer than I was at Liverpool, I can't help but feel the way I do.'

Spackman, who played 63 times for the Reds between 1987 and 1989 without scoring a goal, appreciates that he also divides opinion at Anfield. Some Liverpudlians feel that he should have defended Liverpool as a club in the time after Roman Abramovich's arrival in English football and the bickering that followed between José Mourinho and Rafa Benítez, igniting ire between both sets of supporters. Seemingly, he can say nothing right.

'I have huge respect for Chelsea, although they are a completely different club to the one that I played for,' he concludes diplomatically on the issue. 'But when it comes head to head, Liverpool are my team – not Chelsea. It wasn't until I went to Liverpool that I really started to learn how the game should be played.'

I meet Spackman inside a pub in Bloomsbury, an area of London where both Charles Dickens and Karl Marx once lived and drank. Spackman orders a pint of ale at the bar, which could pass for a pirate's galleon. There are wooden panels everywhere and I'm just waiting for Oliver Reed to walk in when the barmaid offers the words 'Allo, squire,' that chirpy welcome familiar to many London boozers. The exterior of the pub, consumed in ivy, has a placard covering its otherwise tastefully coloured stained-glass window: 'Watch the England 'ere.' Amidst this most London of settings, it is easy to forget that Spackman was born and raised outside of the capital.

'My mum gave birth to me in Romsey hospital, but my dad was a policeman and his work took us to Andover, so I spent my childhood there,' Spackman explains. 'Dad was an old-style policeman – a clip around the ear and be done with you. Police jobs did not earn a lot of money, and I think he relied on earning a decent pension. We lived in a police house, and it had a toilet in the back yard where there was a small area for growing vegetables. Andover was probably more middle class, but my family only had a modest income.'

Andover in Hampshire was a market overspill town originally built to deal with the increasing population of London.

'It grew in the '60s and '70s when the Twinings tea group built a factory. Nothing really happened there. The best thing about Andover was the road out of it.'

Spackman – the youngest of four siblings – grew up playing football with his older brother.

'We spent a lot of time up the rec,' he says, like one of the cast from *Grange Hill*. 'My brother was five years older than me and I played with his mates. It toughened me up quickly, because they were all a lot more physical. It also improved my dribbling because, although I was smaller, I was also a lot quicker with the ball at my feet, so I had to play to my strengths. We played on the streets until midnight – sometimes with a tennis ball. One time, I bust my toe on the kerb and because I only had plimsolls on the blood changed the colour of the shoe. Until the older ones started discovering booze and birds, it was an education for me.

'It's a shame that kids don't really do that now. The landscape of youth culture has changed. Kids stay indoors and spend hours on the PlayStation rather than getting outside and having a knockabout. The roads are too busy with cars, and neighbours complain when a ball goes in their garden because it happens to land in a bed of chrysanthemums. Attitudes like that are stunting the sporting development of our children, and it's no real surprise that fewer and fewer kids are playing football – learning in their own natural way.'

Academically, Spackman got by – without impressing.

'Every year, my report read: "Nigel does enough." At one parents' night, the teacher told my mother that if I put as much effort into my school work as I did football, then I'd achieve a lot more. "Unfortunately, your son is never going to make a living out of football," she added. I got six O levels and went on to do a diploma in business studies, but I was no Einstein.

'There has never been any incentive in this country to encourage kids to embark on a sports career. In Spain or America, they have scholarships, but here – if you don't know the capital of Lithuania or the square root of 342, you're left to one side to struggle. It shouldn't be that way, but it never seems to change.'

Spackman started supporting Liverpool before he entered his teens.

'There was a girl in my class who I quite fancied,' he smiles. 'She was an Arsenal fan and they were due to play Liverpool in the 1971 FA Cup final. Until then, although I played football, I didn't really have a team. Because I wanted to attract her attention, I made everyone know that I was supporting Liverpool. Southampton were my nearest professional team and had some fantastic players – Mick Channon, Terry Paine and Ron Davies – but I never really felt the same link with the club. Liverpool lost to Arsenal in that final, but I sympathised with them and from then on they were my team. I also liked Alun Evans because I had a similar haircut.'

Spackman competed in athletics and cross-country for Hampshire and played basketball, appearing in an England Schools Under-14s final.

'I chose football, though,' he recalls. 'Andover wasn't a hotbed of football, and it was difficult for me because Hampshire is a bit of a no-man's-land if you try to come up with a shortlist of famous footballers from the area. Scouts from the London clubs never really came that far down to look for players because there were no academies or the network of scouts that there are today. I was meant to go for a trial at Southampton in '76, but I broke my collarbone and missed out. It meant that I started out with the junior teams at Andover who were in the old version of the Conference.'

Spackman was spotted by Bournemouth at 18 playing as a centre-forward for a college team. After signing a contract with Alec Stock (famously with QPR), he made his debut under Dave Webb, a manager who brought his own ideas to the club.

'He got rid of a lot of old pros and played me 48 times in my first season. We lost 4–0 away at York on my debut. Because I was so young, after the match Dave sent me into the bath while he tore a strip off the rest of the older players. He wanted to protect the young boys.'

Webb, who had played most of his career in the First Division, managed to attract a clutch of experienced players to Bournemouth. Charlie George, Don Givens and Steve Kember all arrived at Dean Court, helping the club out of the old Fourth Division. After Webb was later sacked, Don Megson signed George Best, then 36.

'There was a rumour that George was going to sign for us,

but nothing happened. One day he was coming, the next day he wasn't. Finally, we arrived at training and he was there, kicking the ball against a wall. He was much smaller than I thought he was going to be. We were doing this session, then all of a sudden a woman appeared on the side of the pitch in a velour tracksuit. My chin was on the floor and my tongue was hanging out. I've never seen a lady with no make-up look so beautiful. It was Mary Stavin – Miss World [Stavin, Swedish by birth, was a Bond girl in the film *Octopussy*]. I couldn't believe that she'd be there at Bournemouth, watching the training. I was 18 or 19 from a country town looking at Miss World and playing with George Best. It doesn't get much better than that, does it?'

Although Best only stayed on the south coast for five games, he did enough to pass on invaluable experience to younger players like Spackman.

'I spoke to him one day in the dressing-room, and because he was just one of the lads and very approachable I asked him essentially where it all went wrong for him. He told me that when he moved from a small town in Northern Ireland to a place like Manchester, he didn't get enough support from the club or the team. He was just 18, then all of a sudden he was besieged by stardom. Having had no experience of drink, he was thrust into an alien culture. At first he said no, but eventually it became easier to say yes rather than explain why he couldn't. Neither he nor Manchester United could quite appreciate what was happening. He said that he went from being the best footballer in the world to being the best drinker in the world. I think he felt a bit of resentment towards United for not helping him more.'

Spackman respects Best for playing as long as he could – even though many observers say he should have been at the top for a lot longer.

'By the beginning of the '80s, top professional footballers were finished at 30. Many of them – like George – had taken too many cortisones and their bodies wouldn't let them play in the First Division any more. Because they'd earned a decent wage in their career without it being enough to retire on, it meant they had to carry on playing until their late 30s – often in the lower leagues or non-league football. It was healthy, because younger players like me got to play against people like Chopper Harris and Stan Bowles. They had to earn a living, whereas that's not the case any more when players can retire after a month's wages. These guys in the '80s were pushing their bodies as far as they could just to survive. They'd open a shop or run a pub as well to keep their income ticking along. For me, that was a vital experience. I got to play with and against senior pros who were tough and knew their way around the field. It sped up my maturity as a player and meant a lot of other players at the same age as me became better as well. That's one of the reasons why there were lots of players progressing from the lower leagues to the top back then, and it explains why there are so few now. You're never going to get Alan Shearer playing for Gateshead or a player going from Gateshead to Newcastle, are you?'

Soon, Harry Redknapp arrived at Bournemouth as first-team coach. Spackman did not foresee his future career as a manager.

'Because Harry was a winger in his career, all the coaching he seemed to do was based on attacking. You could tell he enjoyed coaching the attacking players with crossing and finishing sessions but was fairly limited with his defensive work, and I know it sometimes frustrated our lads at the back. I never for a minute thought he'd go on to achieve what he has. He seemed happy as a coach in the lower leagues. The two big moments for him were beating Man United in the FA Cup after taking over as manager at Bournemouth then going back to West Ham as Billy Bonds' assistant. West Ham was his club and the fans revered him, so there was always a chance he would get a chance at management there. Things just fell into place for him.'

Redknapp was just as flash then as he is now.

'We never had a permanent training base at Bournemouth, so a lot of the time we had to go to some park covered in dog shit. One of the places was in the New Forest in Barton-on-Sea, but the pitch was terrible and I turned my ankle over. Harry had a BMW and said that I could go and wait there while we finished the training session, because there were no changing facilities. I sat in the car and his sons were in there, Jamie and Mark. Jamie must have only been 12 or 13. Because I'd been running my balls off and it was freezing outside, the windows began to steam up. To get some air in, I asked Jamie how to wind the windows down. Harry's Beemer was fancy and had electric windows. But when I pushed the button to pull them down, the window fell out and it smashed on the floor. Harry wasn't happy about it. I just said, "It was your cheap old banger, mate."'

After an enquiry from Everton, Spackman signed for Chelsea in 1983.

'Ken Bates had taken over the club after ending his association with Wigan Athletic. Because Wigan still owed him money, Ken took John Neal [the Chelsea manager] to a match against Bournemouth and hoped to cherry-pick one or two of their better players on the cheap. On a wet, cold Tuesday night at Springfield Park, they were sitting it out in the stands while we slogged it on the pitch. The story goes that Ken kept on nudging John every ten minutes saying, "Have you seen anyone yet?" In a typical Middlesbrough accent, John kept responding, "No", before probably lighting up another fag. This routine was repeated until halfway through the second half when John leant over and said, "I like the look of the number 4."

'Ken said, "The Wigan number 4 is 30 years of age – we're not having him." John then pointed out that he liked the look of the number 4 for Bournemouth. Luckily, it was me and unfortunately for Ken Bates he had to pay out. I signed on the same day as Pat Nevin.'

Ken Bates was brash in the extreme.

'He was big-time, but I was young and eager to please, so I just went along with whatever he said. He wasn't around the club as much as you'd imagine and spent a lot of time on his yacht somewhere down in Monaco, but I know he probably irritated a lot of the lads because we were just footballers but he was full of his own self-importance. Then again, I supposed he was entitled to be because he rescued the club from financial ruin.'

On one occasion, Bates's ego got the better of him. In the tunnel at Stamford Bridge ahead of a match and with a loose ball at his feet, he asked former Liverpool left-back Joey Jones to tackle him. So Jones did, leaving Bates in a heap.

'Joey was a tough lad,' Spackman says. 'He and Mickey Thomas were nutters. They drove down to London every other day for training from their home in North Wales. Every Monday morning, John Neal would come into the dressing-room and say, "Sorry, lads, training's been put back an hour – Mickey and Joey are stuck on the motorway."

'Because Ken Bates wouldn't pay for them to stay in a hotel, they'd sleep in the referee's room at Stamford Bridge on a Friday night before a game. It was a big room with a TV and a sofa, but not the ideal place to sleep if you're a footballer preparing for kick-off. They'd walk up the King's Road on a Saturday morning for a fry-up then go back to the ground and wait for everybody else to arrive. It was a ridiculous arrangement.'

Stamford Bridge was hardly a place you'd wish to watch a game of football, never mind spend the night.

'It was big but a bit of a dump,' Spackman continues. 'There was one huge stand, but the rest of the ground seemed so far away from the pitch because of the greyhound track. You needed 25,000 in there to create any sort of atmosphere. The pitch was terrible, too. I was used to a nice bowling-green surface at Bournemouth, but at Chelsea – a club then in the Second Division – the pitch was a dustbowl. It made it difficult to play pretty football. Over the years, that's probably why Liverpool found it difficult going there.'

Stamford Bridge was an awkward place to play for other reasons as well. In the '80s, a violent nihilism coexisted there with an extreme right-wing philosophy.

'I'd never really experienced racism in football before I signed for Chelsea. Bournemouth was a small place and we had a few black players in the team. I'm certain they were always welcomed by the home supporters. Traditionally, Chelsea were a club well supported with a tight core of fans getting behind the team. But in the '80s, the club became synonymous with racism and hooliganism – for good reason. Paul Canoville [the black winger] was a Chelsea boy through and through, but the abuse he took from supporters was ridiculous. There was a time when his form was really, really good – scoring some great goals – but whenever he touched the ball, they'd boo him. It has to be said that in my opinion it was a small group doing it, but they had the loudest voices. Were they football supporters or were they just thugs attaching themselves to a football club so they could mask who they really were?'

Despite problems on the terraces, Spackman became a part of an evolving Chelsea side that won promotion from the Second Division in 1984.

'We had a strong team spirit and that was founded on the social scene. A lot of the boys lived in Camberley [Surrey], so we saw a lot of each other. After a match, we'd start in the Stamford Bridge Arms, just over the road from the ground, and mix with the supporters. Gradually, we'd work our way further into the West End. Colin Pates and John Bumstead were the ringleaders at Chelsea because they were the local boys and knew their way around London. If they said, everybody else followed. I wasn't streetwise enough to guide people on a night out. I was still wearing Marks and Spencer's underpants and listening to Bruce Springsteen albums or U2. I was more of a rocker than a romantic – like Pat [Nevin], who loved Frankie Goes to Hollywood.'

Chelsea played a role in Liverpool's '86 title story. After losing at Anfield to Everton in February, the Reds were eight points behind Howard Kendall's side. Ahead of travelling to Stamford Bridge on the final day, Liverpool needed another three points to secure the championship, having won ten of the previous eleven games, inspired by the return to the pitch of player-manager Kenny Dalglish.

'I knew Peter Reid quite well and he was speaking to me

before the match. He was a boyhood Liverpudlian but obviously wanted Everton to win the title. He was saying, "Liverpool always struggle at your place – make sure you win this one." But one moment of brilliance from Kenny changed everything. He was 36 or 37 at the time, but he was the difference on the day because Liverpool were nervous and it was a rocky pitch.'

The 1–0 victory clinched the title by two points from Everton. West Ham, who were also impressive that season, finished third, only four points behind. Spackman, a prominent influence in Chelsea's midfield, helped the west Londoners to sixth place.

'It was a good season for us, and we thought we could maybe push into the top four ahead of Man United because they were in turmoil, with Ron Atkinson on the verge of the sack [he was replaced by Alex Ferguson]. But my relationship with John Hollins [who'd replaced John Neal as manager] was deteriorating. He appointed a fella called Ernie Walley as coach, who tried to change too many things. In my opinion, Ernie was the wrong person for the job and wholesale changes weren't the answer. I was one of the stronger, more vocal people in the dressing-room by then, so our personalities clashed. The manager left me out of the team, and the situation was difficult. Eventually, he brought Micky Hazard in from Spurs to replace me and although Micky did well, the team didn't. So he had to put me back in and, as a partnership, Micky and I helped turn things around. The damage had been done, though, so there was no chance of me staying when Liverpool made an offer.'

He drove to Merseyside after Chelsea accepted a £400,000 bid lodged by Liverpool secretary Peter Robinson in February 1987.

'Peter was the first person that welcomed me to Anfield,' Spackman says. 'He effectively ran the club and dealt with player contracts. He took a lot of the pressure off Kenny and allowed him to work independently with the players. They seemed to have similar ideas about football, so it was the perfect partnership. As a player-manager, you need somebody you can rely on and, in Peter, Kenny had that.'

John Smith was Liverpool's chairman – someone who preferred to operate away from the limelight.

'He lived around the corner from me and sometimes I'd see him in the pub. But he was very shy, would introduce himself, then leave me be. Every now and again, he would go in the changing-rooms before a match and wish the players well. Then he'd leave. He was a lovely fella and the kind of person you'd want at the top of a football club, hiding away from the glory. He did that because, fundamentally, he was a football supporter.'

In Spackman's first season at Anfield, he played 14 times as the Reds finished second in the league to champions Everton.

'It was hard to take. The season before, Liverpool won the double. But the year I joined, we won nothing and lost to Arsenal in the League Cup final. When Rushy had opened the scoring, everybody thought we were going to win, because when Rushy scored we usually did. I felt we'd done enough to win the game, but I guess it just wasn't our season. I was very disappointed, but you could tell looking around the dressing-room that it was even harder to take for the established boys who'd been there and won things before.'

Liverpool needed some major signings. They had always reinforced while on top, but now they were behind to their city rivals the need for change on the playing staff was critical. In the summer of 1987, Dalglish signed John Barnes, Peter Beardsley and Ray Houghton. Shortly before, he'd also brought in John Aldridge – intended as a replacement for Ian Rush, who was moving to Juventus.

'I know all of the senior players were concerned about the redevelopment of the side. There was a lot of pressure on Kenny to get it right in the transfer market. He definitely did. Each signing brought different qualities to the team. Barnesy had a bit more pace; Peter was very similar to Kenny in that he'd drop off from the main centre-forward; while Ray gave the midfield legs and intelligence. We were already very strong in midfield with Craig [Johnston], Steve McMahon, John Wark and Jan

Mølby all competing for places. Then there was Ronnie [Whelan] and myself.'

With the loss of Rush, Liverpool had to alter their tactical approach on the pitch.

'Ian's departure was a huge blow. The team had to change, because Rushy was pace whereas Aldridge was better at holding the ball up. Peter Beardsley didn't have much pace either. Maybe we became less direct and put more crosses in the box from wide areas. Everybody knew Aldo's goalscoring pedigree. If you put it inside the box, he would score. Whereas Rushy ran onto balls a bit more, Aldo was a penalty-box man. With Barnsey on the wing, we knew that he'd get enough service.'

Spackman has his own explanation for why Rush struggled in Italy.

'He was really unlucky. People forget that Michel Platini had just retired. Had he been playing, I'm sure Rushy would have scored more over there. It is true that he found the culture difficult to adjust to, but usually that doesn't become an issue if you hit the ground running on the pitch. Had Rushy enjoyed the kind of service he'd had at Liverpool with a playmaker in behind him, I'm certain it would have turned out different for him.'

While Rush failed to find consistent goalscoring form in Serie A, Barnes and Beardsley made their debuts in a 2–1 opening-day victory over Arsenal at Highbury. Safety restrictions at Anfield meant the Reds had to play their first three league fixtures away from home. After Liverpool thrashed Coventry City 4–1 in the second game, John Sillett, who'd months before steered the Sky Blues to FA Cup final victory over Spurs, commented, 'For me, that is the best football England has seen. It was lovely to watch – why don't they go somewhere else and do it instead of here at Highfield Road?'

The victories kept coming, and Liverpool went 29 games unbeaten, with a reverse at Goodison Park in March their first loss of the season. By May, Liverpool had scored four or more goals in each of eleven league games, eighty-seven in total. Barnes registered 17 of them, while Aldridge was prolific with 29.

It wasn't just the statistics that made 1987–88 arguably Liverpool's greatest league campaign. It was a season of unrivalled excellence. The quadruple coup of Barnes, Beardsley, Aldridge and Houghton signified Liverpool's most astute summer of transfer activity in the club's history. They may have arrived for a combined fee of £4.3 million, but the football they helped provide made the sum seem irrelevant. The four gelled effortlessly with the core of the side – Hansen, Nicol, McMahon and Whelan – resulting in some of the most fluid football ever witnessed by Liverpool supporters. It was close to the total perfection of the Real Madrid side in the late '50s or even at Barcelona under Pep Guardiola.

This Liverpool side was different to those before it. Shankly and Paisley's teams and the success that followed were borne out of collectivisation rather than individuality. Liverpool were efficient and ruthless. Yet they were not expressionists. Manchester United had those teams and players who were adored as darlings of the press, despite achieving comparatively little in terms of trophies.

There were times when Shankly and Paisley broke from the routine – the 1974 FA Cup final and a 7–0 dismantling of Spurs four years later – but throughout both of their reigns, the football was unfussy: no messing in defence, pass-and-move, defend from the front and generally keep it simple. The football was mechanical and unrelenting.

In 1987, Dalglish liberated the players. Barnes slotted in as a classic winger – running, dribbling, crossing; and in Beardsley and Aldridge the attacking portfolio was enhanced to compensate for the loss of Dalglish himself as well as Rush. Beardsley, despite his natural posture of a postman with a heavy sack on his shoulders, reliably managed to find pockets of space and exploit it, creating possibilities that were unselfish and devastating. Aldridge, meanwhile, was an artisan rather than an artist and squeezed the maximum out of relatively limited ability. He did, however, possess an intimate understanding of the penalty area and its complexities. He had scored goals in every team, and this trend continued in a Liverpool shirt. The fundamentals remained the same, but the additions of Barnes and Beardsley enabled ingenuity and spark. Liverpool broke from tradition. Barnes, particularly, was on a different level.

The antidote to all of the attacking creativity was Spackman. His role in the team was withdrawn and understated, although his contribution was quickly recognised by supporters, who made a song for him. Nigel Spackman became Liverpool's Batman.

'I first heard it at Dundee in a testimonial. I was buzzing. It was a proud moment because they'd made the effort to come up with something about me. I was walking off the pitch, laughing my head off because the whole of the stand were singing it . . . "DNaNaNaNaNaNaNaNa . . . Spackman!" We got back to the hotel, having a drink with some of the supporters, and they started singing it as well. Fucking brilliant.

'I became a different player at Liverpool. At Chelsea, I was an attacking midfielder. At Liverpool, Kenny wanted me to hold and allow the other three midfielders to attack – not that he told me to do anything specific; he just knew that the midfield would evolve naturally so we'd understand our own responsibilities. The only thing he did instruct me to do was take the ball off the defenders, because he knew I was good with the ball at my back to goal. I suppose I allowed the more technical players to express themselves. Over the last decade, most people have labelled it the "Makélélé role", but I was playing in that position 25 years ago. Liverpool tactically were well ahead of everybody else like that, but people didn't realise it at the time. We played one–two-touch football, just like Barcelona do today and get all the credit for it. If any of us got into trouble, we'd give Barnesy the ball and he'd do something with it. He was our Messi.'

Spackman's partner in the centre of midfield was Steve McMahon – a player whose tackles were so Machiavellian that often only the deceased knew he'd been done.

'Macca was a bit of a hothead, and even teammates had to learn how to handle him. However, I think his bark was worse than his bite. I can remember times in games when Steve's tried to do someone but ended up getting injured himself. In training especially, he was very competitive and he wouldn't be scared to go in really hard. But he was a quality player and scored some sensational goals. I was just glad I was on his team. If you were on the other side, you knew that Steve was going to be aggressive and try to upset you. When he was pumped up, he was quite frightening.'

One league performance to this day shines out above any other from that season. Liverpool achieved footballing perfection against Brian Clough's talented Nottingham Forest side – a 5–0 win that Spackman has vivid recollections of.

'Prior to the game, Aldo was desperate to score because he was on for the Golden Boot. I roomed with Aldo, and he was Liverpool through and through. I always remember one pre-season after a really, really tough session, me and John went back to our room and I collapsed on the bed like the great big fat southerner I was. John was doing hundreds of sit-ups and press-ups, and I was telling him to relax but he wouldn't. He'd always do extra work to keep on top of his game. That's why he went all the way from non-league to Liverpool – because he wasn't afraid of working.

'In the first five minutes against Forest we were a bit sloppy, and Bruce made a good save from Nigel Clough. But after that we just annihilated them. It could have been more than five. It was the most enjoyable game I've ever played in. The passing and movement was at its very best, and everything everyone tried came off.'

At the final whistle, Sir Tom Finney, in attendance at Anfield, described the display by Liverpool as the best he'd ever witnessed. Within weeks, a VHS of the match was released by the BBC. Liverpool were well on the way to the championship.

'We'd won the league by Christmas, and deep down all the players knew that,' Spackman insists. 'Barnesy particularly had raised the bar for everybody. The link-up between him and Stevie [Nicol] at left-back was unbelievable. We were organised, everybody knew their job within the team, but we were also told to go out and enjoy it. The team spirit was great at Liverpool. That's the main reason why we won things. Even now if I haven't seen one of the boys for five years, it's the same. We carry on as if it was yesterday.'

The vibrant social aspect of the dressing-room was instilled from the very top of the club.

'It was accepted by everybody that Kenny was the gaffer who played occasionally. He'd been so instrumental in helping secure the double the season before I arrived that people expected him to play. But you could tell he had confidence in his squad. The biggest thing about Liverpool was being able to cut it at training. Kenny still could.

'He was also very shrewd in dealing with team-building exercises. He'd come to social events like any player but wouldn't stay the whole night. Sometimes he'd have a Cinzano and lemonade then get off. "Enjoy yourself to the hilt, but don't let it affect the training or the matches," was his maxim.'

By the mid to late '80s, the Liverpool players were spending a lot of time socialising on Wirral.

'A lot of us lived over the water. Usually, we'd go wherever John Wark sent us. It was three o'clock closing, so Warky would arrange pool competitions where there would be some prize money at stake. Any social event, there would always be a competition with pride and money at stake – it was designed to make you want to win. There was always a champion.'

Bruce Grobbelaar enjoyed the drinking games.

'Bruce would insist on putting a depth charger in every drink, a mixer. Stevie, Bruce, myself and Craig Johnston would drink in the local pub where I lived in Parkgate [a prosperous part of Wirral]. Walshy would be in there as well. John Barnes and David Burrows lived in Neston. We'd be on the first round – I'd be on lager or bitter or sometimes a mild – then Bruce would come over with a tray of shorts: brandy, sherry or often in his case a Sambuca, because he was mad. Bruce was also a fan of the "yard of ale challenge". That was a regular on a Sunday if we had the day off. We'd do it for charity and bet each other who could drink the most. But like I said, none of that affected us professionally. If somebody was doing it too much, you'd see it in training, and if you weren't playing well in training, you wouldn't get selected on a Saturday.'

The most regular game was Fizz Buzz.

'When you've had a few to drink, you've got to be really sharp with this one. The leader of the game chose multiples of twos and fives, the cycle would go around the group. If you said buzz in the wrong place, there was a forfeit, usually involving the downing of some kind of shit mix. Some of the boys weren't as sharp as others.'

After playing Fizz Buzz, Mike Hooper, the back-up goalkeeper, was nearly barred from a plane journey.

'We played Chelsea last game of the season and drew 3–3 before going to Israel for a friendly match. So we started playing the game in the players' lounge afterwards. Then it continued in the hotel when we were meant to be sleeping, and then in the airport bar. We had to carry Mike onto the plane. When we got to Tel Aviv, we got straight back on it again. [Liverpool, unsurprisingly, lost the friendly 3–0.] It was funny on Mike because he was usually so serious. He was a passionate ornithologist and used to disappear to Devon for his bird-watching holidays.'

Steve Nicol was another 'brilliant lad'.

'Whenever we travelled to away games, he'd strip off on the bus and sit there eating crisps and fizzy drinks in his boxer shorts. He didn't like the sensation of a tracksuit on his body.

'Me and Bruce were watching an England–Scotland game in the pub one day and Steve was playing. He'd told us to wait there for him for a few hours and he'd meet up with us for a pint. The game was at Wembley or Hampden Park, but he had a good driver. He turned up at the pub with his full Scotland tracksuit on and we offered him our commiserations because the Jocks had lost. Steve loved nothing better than a game of pool, a lager top and a packet of crisps. When I left him later, he was on his sixth or seventh packet and sixth or seventh pint. The next day, I went back to the pub and it turned out that the taxi had refused to take him home at the end of the night because he'd drunk too much. Apparently, Steve started playing people at pool in exchange for a pint and a packet of crisps. In return, he gave them a part of his tracksuit. At first it was just his trackie top, but by the end of the night he was left with just his money in one hand and his keys in another. The doorman knew Steve and he knew all the punters, so he offered to pay the taxi driver personally, saying that if he didn't take Steve home, he'd never get any trade off the pub again. By the time the taxi had arrived at Steve's house, two mile down the road, with the fare already paid by the doorman, Steve insisted on paying him again. It turned out that Steve had slumped out of the car after offering the driver 20p. "Get y'zellf sumit nice." That's Steve – a typical Scot.'

Later, when Spackman was managing Sheffield United and Nicol was a player with Sheffield Wednesday, the pair met up for a pint.

'I went home at about midnight and I left Steve in the pub. The next morning I got a call off his missus. "Where's Steven?" She later found him in the utility room with one leg hanging outside the dog flap. His key was in his pocket, but for some reason Steve had climbed through the dog flap and fallen asleep.'

Nicol's antics away from the pitch never affected his performances on it.

'Steve has to be one of the most underrated players in Liverpool's history. If the manager asked him to play anywhere, he'd do it well. He was a drinker, and all the lads took the piss out of him because he could be daft, but you only have to look at his success as a coach in America to understand that he wasn't as silly as some people may have thought.'

When out in the city centre, the Liverpool squad would bump into players from Everton.

'Howard Kendall used to take his players for a Chinese at the Yuet Ben [on Upper Duke Street in Liverpool's city centre] whenever the team had a bad result. It was intended to boost spirits. We went for a Chinese regularly, too. When I first signed for Liverpool, I was invited by all the squad to go for a meal with their wives. I was alone because I'd just driven up from London. I remember the restaurant had a table that twizzled around. One of the lads did it and all the food fell on Ronnie Whelan's wife, Elaine. There was a fridge there and Rushy was in charge of replenishments, so he made sure everybody had a drink. I was thinking, "Is this Liverpool Football Club – is this *really* what they do?"'

Inside a fiercely competitive dressing-room, Spackman says that he fitted in well – despite being one of only two southern-born players in the squad. Since Bill Shankly became manager in 1959, the club had targeted players with a northern background – initially an idea to help new signings settle quickly. 'We concentrated on Lancashire and other players nearby, and we picked up Alec Lindsay and Steve Heighway. Bill wanted locally based lads, and even fellas like Clemence and Keegan weren't too far away. We didn't bring them from hundreds of miles away and that helped them settle,' chief scout Geoff Twentyman once said. Few southerners played for Liverpool with any distinction throughout Shankly's reign and then after him until Paul Walsh signed for the club in 1984, unless you include Phil Neal, who was born in Irchester and sometimes talks with a pseudo-Cockney accent. Considering Neil Ruddock (born in Wandsworth), Phil Babb (Lambeth) and David James (Watford) were all signed in the '90s with no success as well as not really feeling like Liverpool players, it's understandable why Shankly and Twentyman preferred to shop in the north. Yet Spackman was different.

'I loved the fact that I was an "outsider" inside the best team in the country,' Spackman says. 'Living in London is quite tough, and you have to be streetwise. So I was quite prepared for Liverpool. If you couldn't handle it, it would have been easy to go under. It had a positive effect on team performances as well, because if you came through it, it made you supremely confident on the pitch. You began to feel that the banter at Liverpool was supreme to everywhere else and that if an opposing player tried to take the piss during a game, you'd be prepared with something to throw back at him because you were a Liverpool player and Liverpool players were quick in the mind. It almost made you feel like all the other players in the other teams across the league were stupid.'

In 1987–88, Liverpool made a lot of teams look stupid, swaggering to the title with games to spare. It could have been a double had they beaten Wimbledon in the FA Cup final.

'Wimbledon were a side who weren't afraid to talk on the pitch,' Spackman says. 'We knew that from the occasions when we'd beaten them in the league. Always talking, trying to wind you up and put you off your game – it was the Wimbledon way. But they didn't bully us. That was all hype from the media. There were stories about them psyching us out in the tunnel, but it was a load of rubbish. I remember there was a story in one of the papers with Vinny Jones saying he was going to bite Kenny's ear off and spit it on the floor. It was total bravado. Vinny was all about reputation, but all of the Liverpool lads could see through him because he was so obvious.

'We lost because they got in front and they defended really well afterwards. We didn't defend the set play well enough. Had we scored first, we'd have probably won the game. Tactically, they put Dennis Wise out on the right to stop Barnesy, and it worked for them. It just wasn't to be. The signs were there when me and Gary Gillespie collided the week before the match and had to play with bandages around our heads. But we should have been good enough to beat them.'

When Spackman went away on holiday that summer, he hoped to return to Melwood as a regular fixture in Liverpool's midfield. Instead, Ronnie Whelan took his place, and by February 1989 Spackman was gone.

'I felt like I was doing enough to be in the team. I was training well. But me and Rushy [who'd returned from Juventus] were usually the subs, and it was getting to me. I desperately wanted to play. I was hot-headed and asked Kenny for a transfer.'

He regrets the decision.

'It was my choice to leave and I went back to London with QPR. Within weeks, I was thinking, "What have I done?" My ego probably got in the way of making the right decision. I should have stayed.'

Spackman soon moved to Glasgow Rangers after falling out with boss Trevor Francis.

'Trevor came in as player-manager and I was asked a question by a TV presenter about whether he was as good as Kenny Dalglish. I said that you couldn't compare Trevor to Kenny, because Trevor was just a novice trying to find his feet, while Kenny had a lot more experience. Kenny had won a lot more than Trevor. He didn't like it, so he sold me. I wanted to move anyway, and in the end Trevor got the sack and I went to Glasgow. So I can't grumble.'

As the '80s became the '90s, Rangers were a club on the up.

'When Graeme Souness became Rangers manager, he turned them into Liverpool by playing the Liverpool way and training the Liverpool way. He really did turn the club around, and for a period they were probably the biggest club in Britain in terms of stadium, support, success and finance. He knew exactly what he wanted and signed a lot of players, including me.

'Graeme spoke to me about Liverpool all the time, and when the job actually came up [after Dalglish resigned in 1991], I think he was frightened that John Toshack was going to get it. He was really keen on returning to the club because, even though he was happy at Rangers, he was having a lot of problems with the SFA and getting fined all the time. He was a major success as a player, and he really thought that he could do the same as a manager. Graeme tried to sign me back for Liverpool at the same time he signed Mark Walters, but David Murray, the Rangers chairman, wouldn't let me go. I would have loved to have gone back with Graeme. With hindsight, maybe he will admit that he tried to change things too quickly by throwing the baby out with the bathwater by getting rid of people that could have helped him.'

After another spell at Stamford Bridge with Chelsea, Spackman tried management with Sheffield United and Barnsley.

'At Sheffield, I took over from Howard Kendall, who had built a very good team. I added to the squad of players and we were doing very well. On the week I eventually resigned, we were fourth from top in the Championship, with a great chance of going up given the run-in we had. We were also in the quarter-final of the FA Cup as well. [They eventually lost to Newcastle, managed by Kenny Dalglish.] Unfortunately, the chairman and chief executive started selling players without my permission. I was arriving at training on a Thursday, two days before a match, to be told that Brian Deane was going to Benfica and Jan Fjørtoft was going to Barnsley. Ten days later, Don Hutchinson was sold to Everton. So I resigned out of principle. I was young to it at the time and maybe I acted too hastily, but I thought we had a good chance of success and it was being undermined. I soon got a call from Roy Evans asking me to come to Liverpool as a first-team coach, but Gérard Houllier was appointed as joint-manager instead.'

As my time with Spackman comes towards an end, he talks about his current 'project' at the Glenn Hoddle Academy in Spain. 'It's a place where young footballers that have been released by clubs get a second chance. And it means I get to spend four months of the year in the sun.'

He finishes by explaining that a major regret from his time at Liverpool was not scoring a single goal.

'I hit a post once against Manchester United. But the only time I scored at Anfield was for Chelsea in front of the Kop end. It was a penalty against Bruce. And he did the wobbly legs.'

CHAPTER NINE

Cult Zeros

GENIUS, John Barnes

JOHN BARNES SEEMS RESTLESS.

It appears that he doesn't want to be here, waiting for yet
another television appearance. He'd probably rather be on a
touchline, pointing players in the right direction; he'd rather be
in a dugout, slumped with exasperation when his instructions
have been misunderstood; he'd rather be in the office, planning
training routines that may or may not help his side to three
points.

Brief spells in charge of Celtic and Tranmere Rovers did not
work out, although an intervening 12 months with the Jamaican
national team was more successful. 'People forget about that,'
he says regretfully.

Barnes's attire may indicate that he is relaxed. But there is an
impression that he is not. He sports a silver-coloured silk shirt,
buttoned three-quarters of the way to the top, revealing a few
strands of chest fuzz. He also wears blue jeans that have certainly

been ironed. There are also those brown sandals with his toes poking out the end. These days he is a little more round than the brilliant athlete who became Footballer of the Year in 1988.

He sits opposite me on a leather couch at the studios of Liverpool Football Club's official television channel, located in the centre of the city. He twitches and re-adjusts his posture constantly. One minute his arm is draped across the suite. Then he jolts forward and suddenly his legs are crossed like the fleshy tangled roots of an oak tree. He can't get comfortable.

'I have media contracts with companies in South Africa, Dubai and Malaysia,' he says. 'But I want to manage or get a steady job at home, be closer to my family. At this stage of my life, I still think it's what I do best.' Barnes still lives on Wirral, and has seven children, three from his second marriage.

He pauses, then adds, 'Quite quickly, people forget about you. It's difficult to get back in.'

Barnes naturally talks at the kind of pace at which he used to dribble a ball. His passion for the game has not diminished, despite disappointments in management and the lack of opportunities to prove himself again. He admits that Celtic, particularly, was toxic for his reputation. At Parkhead, his voice carried limited authority, the fans wanted Kenny Dalglish, and 'the goldfish bowl' of Glasgow magnified his mistakes, such as when he referred to opponents in a press conference as 'Dundee', when really they were Dundee United. It prompted headlines across national newspapers like 'Barnes does not know who Celtic are facing'. A significant lesson, however, was learnt.

'It taught me a lot but one thing above all,' he says, leaning forward again. 'My thinking towards football used to revolve around concerning myself with what happens on the pitch: with the players, the matches. But now you have to know more about the people you are working for. That's the owners and directors. What goes on off the field really impacts on what goes on on it, when really all you want to do is get on with your job.' José Mourinho and Rafael Benítez would concur. In every managerial position they have held over the last decade, there has been a fight for a controlling influence, albeit sometimes out of choice. 'Without being the main man, you can do nothing,' Barnes insists.

For a decade after Celtic, Barnes applied for a host of jobs and in many cases was denied even an interview. At Tranmere, he was given a chance but was sacked after less than four months in charge.

'I just wasn't given enough time,' he says bluntly, without explaining the problems that went on in the boardroom at Prenton Park. Jason McAteer, his assistant, once told me in an interview that Barnes's playing budget was halved within a month of arriving at the club. 'What chance did we have?' McAteer wondered.

Barnes says now that, despite his appetite for returning to management, he would only take a job if the circumstances were right. 'I'm happy to manage at any level. I'd rather be a number one with a Conference than be a number two in the Premier League. But I'd need to be able to trust the people I work with. Without trust amongst the people that really matter at a football club, you're always going to struggle.'

Barnes has a balanced perspective on life. He says his values stem from a childhood amongst army brigadiers and generals in a prosperous barrack suburb of Kingston, Jamaica. His father, a colonel in Jamaica's Defence Force, and his mother, a senior academic lecturer on science of the mind, raised their children with a mixture of discipline and positive thinking.

Barnes was brought up with a sense of self-assurance. He understood that racism was institutionalised in the UK but viewed it as a belief of the uneducated. It didn't affect him like it might others. In his eyes, he was always better than that. Just as Howard Gayle was a creation of his upbringing, so was Barnes. Gayle was used to confronting racism for as long as he can remember; Barnes did not have to.

Barnes's personality meant that he was the kind of person that everybody could get on with. His ability helped, too. When Everton supporters hurled bananas at him at Goodison Park during an FA Cup tie in 1988, he responded by delicately flicking them with his heel back towards the touchline. His reaction on the pitch epitomised the player. Moments later he would glide down the wing and arch a cross for Ray Houghton to score at the Park End.

'I grew up in a middle-class family and I had no self-esteem issues at all. For someone to call me a black this or that doesn't make any sense to me. I consider people who use those words as ignorant. Why should I let it affect me when it doesn't? That's why I can't give advice about what to do in that situation, because you have to be true to your own beliefs. If you have to kick some guy in the chest, like Eric Cantona did [when being abused], that's what you have to do. You can't be judge and jury, because everyone is different.'

Barnes displays an impressive meld of intelligence and *understanding* (a word he uses regularly) that makes him try to look at the opposite point of view to appreciate a subject matter better.

'Racist comments remain inside football stadiums today, but the chanting, at least in this country, has gone,' he says. 'But that doesn't mean the problem has disappeared. Does that mean that racism doesn't exist? Or does it just mean that a person says nothing for 90 minutes, but for the rest of the week thinks and says otherwise? Football can try to take a lead, but people need to be educated properly to get rid of racism in society. It is not – and never has been – *just* football's problem.'

Barnes arrived in England during the early winter months of 1976. It was a time of social chaos and political shifts. A Labour government grappled with power only to let it slip during a period of sharp economic decline. The National Front, a political party that advocated the expulsion of Britain's non-white residents, claimed limited but significant success during elections. When Margaret Thatcher came to power in 1979, many NF supporters absconded to her new Conservatism. The majority of these defectors were from the white working class – a demographic that also dominated the English football scene.

In front of the terraces, black players were being introduced on the pitch. At Nottingham Forest, Viv Anderson was marauding up the wing from a full-back position and was soon to become the first black player to represent England; while at West Bromwich Albion and Watford, Cyrille Regis, Laurie Cunningham and Luther Blissett were becoming key protagonists in emerging teams.

The profile of black footballers was on the rise. But so was the terrace opposition to them. In 1978, the National Front launched recruitment and propaganda campaigns outside many London clubs, most prominently at Chelsea and Millwall.

Yet Barnes, aged 12, was shielded. In London, his family first lived in the Selfridge Hotel near Oxford Street before moving into the affluent area of Hampstead. Barnes was enrolled into one of the more reputable inner-city state schools, Marylebone Grammar.

Barnes liked football, but it was not an obsession. Before entering a career in the military, his father, Kenneth, had played as an amateur, managed and become president of the Jamaican national team and the FA. Although the West Indies is more famous for its cricket, and Jamaica, indeed, has provided both batting guile and bowling force, with Michael Holding and Courtney Walsh hailing from the island, football is unchallenged as the sport of the people.

'Cricket is for Barbados and Antigua,' Barnes insists. 'My footballing heroes were all West German. I fell in love with the team of 1974. I could not take my eyes off Franz Beckenbauer and Wolfgang Overath. I'd choose them over Pelé any day of the week. My first pair of boots were also made by adidas.'

Aged 16, Barnes joined Sudbury Court in the Middlesex Premier Division. Scouts soon became interested in the teenager with muscular thighs and ballet feet. Representatives from Ipswich Town, Watford and Queens Park Rangers all paid visits. Barnes, however, had no ambition of becoming a footballer, insisting he wanted to complete his education by taking up a degree in the United States. Undeterred, Watford finally persuaded him to sign a short-term contract at Vicarage Road.

'Watford were just very relaxed and hospitable,' Barnes recalls. 'I trained with QPR as well, but they were very pushy. QPR didn't realise I was training with Watford at the same time, and one week when I turned up to play for Watford against QPR, they weren't very happy. So I never went back.'

Watford were a club on the rise: the traditional English football team for whom a midfield was merely something to be bypassed. For their defenders, it was a case of see ball, thump ball: the quicker the route to goal, the better. Tactically, Graham Taylor, their manager, favoured the chaos theory. It was extraordinary that a player of Barnes's elegance managed to flourish in such a barbaric system.

'Watford looked after me. I was living in England on my own by then, but Graham [Taylor] taught me so many lessons. He told me to believe in myself when times were bad but also to realise that when the times were good, I should not get ahead of myself just because people were saying nice things about me. Watford was a great club for that. I saw people go to Arsenal and Spurs who were talented but went off the rails because of too much praise or too much criticism. Watford helped me to handle the pressure, as they did with all the young players: Kenny Jackett, Steve Terry and Nigel Callaghan. As players, we were taught to be well dressed, well mannered and not to drink. From an educational and discipline point of view, it was the best place for me to go as a teenager.

'We had this tag [of being a long-ball team], but if you watched us every week you'd realise that there were players like myself and Nigel – wingers that wanted to play, get the ball down and take people on. Later, Wimbledon took that tag off us. I remember on one cold Tuesday night Dave Bassett bringing his team to watch us play so they could learn the style he wanted to execute.'

In 1984, Watford reached the FA Cup final but lost to Everton. 'It was a fairy tale for us – the journey we had been on from the Fourth Division to the First. We expected to win; we'd previously finished above Everton in the league. Yet the build-up for us was like our big day out. It was a novelty, because it hadn't been done at Watford before. At Liverpool, there was more of a focus – you had to win. The week isn't important; the story doesn't matter, it's only about winning. With Watford, it was almost as if we enjoyed the week so much that we forgot to turn up on the day, because we played well below the standards that had got us there in the first place.'

Already an international, having elected to represent England, that summer he was called up for a tour to South America and his most famous moment followed. During a game against Brazil in Rio de Janeiro's Maracana Stadium, Barnes scored a fine individual goal. After initially receiving possession near the halfway line on the 44th minute, he ran diagonally past seven Brazilian players, rounded the goalkeeper and tapped it into an empty net. England won 2–0. Some Brazilian newspapers labelled it the greatest goal the Maracana had ever seen.

Barnes's act of genius was expected to launch him as a new level of player – one on whom England could rely to produce brilliance against the most potent opposition. Instead, it only offered a glimpse into what might have been. The exhilarating form he later produced for Liverpool was never matched internationally. Bobby Robson, the England manager, described Barnes as the 'greatest enigma' he'd encountered in 30 years of coaching. The player offers his own explanation for his contrasting fortunes.

'When I played for Liverpool, I would receive the ball 20 or 30 times a game. That was enough to maybe score a goal or provide an assist from a cross or a pass. For England, I would receive possession maybe five or ten times a match. This was mainly because Liverpool dominated possession whereas England did not. There was a lot of long ball. During all my time in international football, I can't remember a run of games where we passed a team off the park from start to finish like we did at Liverpool. You don't have to be a genius to figure out that, mathematically, I had less of an opportunity to impress. OK, I did all right at Watford – a team that played with a similar style to England – but the focus wasn't on Watford like it was with

England. Some games at Watford would go by without me touching the ball, but nothing would get said in the papers afterwards. Possession football suited my game, and that's why I excelled with Liverpool.'

Barnes clicked at Anfield instantly. Yet the process of his transfer to the club did not help his relationship with supporters. Barnes was supposedly keen on a move abroad and his agent, Athole Still, compiled a video showcasing his talents and distributed it to a number of Italian and French clubs. Fiorentina, Napoli, Roma, Verona and Marseille all deployed scouts to Vicarage Road, but none of his performances were strong enough to merit a recommendation. He was also misquoted in an interview reproduced in the *Liverpool Echo*, allegedly saying that the only other clubs he wanted to join were Tottenham Hotspur and Arsenal 'because he wanted to stay in London'.

'I just didn't say that,' Barnes insists. 'Think about it: I was a Jamaican living in London. London wasn't a natural habitat for me anyway. It wasn't like London was my original home.'

Archives at the *Echo* and its morning paper the *Daily Post* reveal that before Barnes joined Liverpool, racist slogans were daubed on the walls behind the Kop. The local press found out about it, but officials persuaded editors not to print the story until after Barnes was signed. Eventually, the *Post* ran an article credited to an anonymous reporter announcing that the club was determined to clean up racism. It showed a photograph of an exit from the Kop where clearly sprayed read those grotesque initials, 'NF'.

On Barnes's arrival, Dalglish spoke of the importance of Liverpool recruiting their first genuine wide player since Steve Heighway. Yet Barnes was also the first black footballer to be signed from another team by either Liverpool or Everton. While black players had become familiar and often key performers at nearly every other major club in the country, the squads of the Merseyside institutions had remained white, aside from a few appearances by local black pretenders who – as examined with Howard Gayle – failed to flourish for reasons that are similar.

'I would never judge anyone on their colour, creed or religion. All that concerns me is their ability,' Dalglish – who grew up as a supporter of Glasgow Rangers before making his name at Celtic – would later say. Unfortunately, colour did matter to some. In *Fever Pitch*, Nick Hornby claims that before his debut against Arsenal, Barnes had bananas thrown at him from the away supporters' enclosure as Liverpool warmed up at Highbury. Barnes insists that he has no recollection of that happening, preferring to focus on the football and his understanding with Peter Beardsley and John Aldridge, where the latter's ruthlessness in front of goal dovetailed with the patience and incisiveness of the former.

'People saw it click on the first day of the season, but I saw it on the first day of pre-season training. It felt like we had been together forever. As soon as we got the ball out and started passing, it felt natural. That was the genius of Liverpool: recognising how a group of players that hadn't been in the same side could come together and gel instantly. We weren't coached into being good.

'Aldo wasn't a natural footballer, but he was a natural finisher. Think about it: he wasn't tall, but he scored lots of headed goals. He wasn't really that quick, but he got on the end of crosses and through balls because of his determination and intelligence. John's timing was phenomenal. He was usually picked last in the five-a-sides, but everyone knew he was the club's premier finisher, and without him the team wouldn't have been anywhere near as effective.

'Peter's game was dropping off and picking up possession. There was a time when the crowd didn't really appreciate his work. There was an impression that he should be getting on the shoulder of the last man and reaching John's flick-ons. People quickly started comparing Peter to Kenny, but they were very different in my eyes. Peter was a lot more mobile but not as good with his back to goal. Personally, Peter was crucial to my success because we clicked straight away. Whenever he got the ball, he would look for me first and allow me to sprint off. Of everyone I played with, I would have to say that Peter was the one I enjoyed playing with most.'

Some inside the Liverpool dressing-room, however, were suspicious of Beardsley's motives.

'He was different from everyone else in that he didn't drink. He'd collect the bibs, cones and balls after training had finished. Initially, there might have been a feeling that Peter was sucking up to the manager, being a bit of a creep, and there were a few snide remarks. But, gradually, people realised that was just his manner. He was a worker and unselfish – just as he was on the pitch.'

Barnes believes the key to Liverpool's success was humanitarian. Management would target players with the correct type of character.

'Although the majority enjoyed a drink, there was not really any wild, temperamental types. Bruce [Grobbelaar] was a one-off, but he could get away with it because he was a goalkeeper. If Bruce had turned up at Melwood in a fighter jet, no one would have thought it unusual.'

Grobbelaar's eccentric behaviour was not different to other players in his position. But it was probably magnified because of his upbringing in Rhodesia.

'He would tell us stories about fighting crocodiles as a kid and getting drunk with Clint Eastwood. He was a crazy man. But we loved him for it. I'm convinced that goalkeepers are a bit odd because it can be a lonely job. They have to find ways to amuse themselves. Bruce is unfortunate that he doesn't play now because he was very comfortable in possession of the ball. With the back-pass rule now in place, he would have relished helping the team build from the back. He rarely did any specialised goalkeeping practice. It was just a case every now and then of someone suggesting we give him some shooting practice. In the five-a-sides, Bruce, instead, played outfield, and he was never the last one chosen, because he could play.'

The dressing-room equilibrium at Liverpool remained the same throughout the '80s.

'There was a status quo – a line-up. If you were Ian Rush, nobody ever gave you stick. He was one of the top players, and at Christmas we'd have a vote on the top three of everything. One of them would be the daftest lads in the squad. Even though Rushy was clearly one of those, he never got voted. Steve Nicol was always there, no matter what. Even though there were essentially no stars at Liverpool, there was still a rank and file. In sporting terms, that's important, because it meant that youngsters and newcomers would have to earn their stripes.'

Barnes preferred to socialise amongst his own group of friends.

'Although success in football can be based on camaraderie and an understanding between players based on experiences together, fundamentally it isn't too different to the average office job in the sense that you might go for a drink with co-workers after a day's work, and then if you get on really well perhaps meet up at weekends. I was always very wary of mixing at the kind of venues that footballers go to. I didn't get the celebrity thing. You look at Paul Gascoigne and Chris Evans. I suppose they were best friends once upon a time and now they probably don't see each other. You wonder how strong the friendship is. Sometimes it is out of convenience. It's OK while you're there, because you have a common interest, but when you move on, the friendship is over. I find my best friends are the ones I've always known: the ones that knew me before being a footballer.

'When I moved to the Wirral, I would see Ian Rush, Jan Mølby, Stevie Nicol and Bruce. It was only on the pre-season tours and foreign trips where the whole squad would be out together. It was a typical case of boys together, playing pool and getting drunk. There were many cases with jealous, half-cut punters and a fracas ensuing. If the media had been as intense back then, Liverpool players would have been on the front pages every single week, even though I can't remember anyone getting hospitalised. We were no different to any other group of young men having a drink to unwind. Graham Taylor [at Watford] would never have tolerated the consistent binges enjoyed by all the Liverpool players, no way.'

Barnes drank spirits rather than beer. 'I don't get why in the modern era it is such an issue if a player goes out and has a drink. Players get condemned by society because of the money that footballers earn. In my eyes, though, if a player makes £1,000 or £100,000 a week, he still has a duty to perform. If they deliver on the pitch and make people happy, what's the problem? The majority of successful English clubs that dominated Europe in the '70s and early '80s all had a drinking culture even though they didn't in Italy, Spain and maybe Germany, remember.'

Heavy drinkers they may have been, but Liverpool's players reliably delivered on the pitch. Liverpool were forced to play the first three games of the 1987–88 season away from Anfield after a sewer collapse beneath the Kop. Parts of the stand were rendered unsafe. While the club was investing almost £4 million on new players, the ground was falling apart. After two wins and a draw, by the time the new-look Liverpool finally played at Anfield in mid-September, intrigue had peaked – especially in relation to Barnes.

The winger's performances in the 1987–88 season were so good that the £900,000 Liverpool spent to bring him from Watford looked like a knock-down price. Barnes believes it was the balanced environment of Melwood that helped him settle.

'At Watford, Graham [Taylor] was completely entrenched in all aspects of the football club: from the pitch to the stands to the coaching to the administration. He did everything. At Watford, we trained 100 per cent all of the time. But at Liverpool, they were "Hey – take it easy, slow down!"

'Kenny just played five-a-side with us and didn't do much else, especially coaching. Players were left to develop alone – a natural evolution. Nobody really analysed tactics from a method point of view. The first team to come along and do it was George Graham with Arsenal. And they won the league. He was a pioneer in this country in many ways.

'The biggest lesson I learnt is to always focus on the next challenge and not get too excited or disappointed. When I won my first title, there was nothing from the management. Ronnie [Moran] came into the dressing-room and told us the first date of pre-season training then walked out. When we lost the title to Arsenal, he did the same, and the following year we won the league again. When Blackburn won the Premier League, they had the biggest party ever and were cock-a-hoop for months. A few years later they went down. To maintain success you need to be consistent on the pitch and consistent off it, especially with your emotions.'

Despite his influence often proving crucial, Barnes did not enjoy derby matches against Everton. It was not, however, a result of any taunting from the terraces.

'It was mainly because they weren't good games and, instead, full of bravado,' he explains. 'I understood why they meant so much to the fans; the sense of anticipation was intense. But I prefer games where the winners prevail because of football. A lot of players on both sides would play derby games with their hearts rather than their heads, and that's a dangerous thing. It was a mistake we kept making – why should we change our approach just because it was Everton? We were Liverpool and we were the better team.'

On the pitch, there were two significant disappointments in Barnes's first three seasons as a Liverpool player. The first came in the FA Cup final of 1988 against Wimbledon. Barnes maintains that several myths are attached to the fixture.

'It is regarded as one of the biggest upsets in history,' he says. 'Yet Wimbledon finished seventh that season and subsequently regularly concluded a campaign in the top ten for another decade. OK, some of the skill levels may have not been so high, but they were a very good, effective side who knew each other's function and contribution as well as any other team in the country.'

Then there was the issue of Wimbledon's supposed intimidating tactics.

'That didn't happen,' he insists. 'Liverpool were the top team in the country because we had one or two nasty players in the team that could mix it if necessary. On that particular day, however, we didn't play particularly well as a team and they took their chance.'

The second disappointment arrived a year later when Liverpool surrendered the league title to Arsenal in the final game of the season. 'After Hillsborough, though – to me – [losing to Arsenal] became irrelevant. It was a frustration, but I don't look back upon it holding a sense of regret.'

At his best – and that seemed to be a regular occurrence in his early years at Anfield – Barnes was untouchable. He was Liverpool's number 10, but a number 10 with a difference. Despite his starting position being on the left wing, Dalglish offered Barnes freedom to operate where he liked. He did not seem to move as fast as other wingers in the league, but he reliably found a way to influence the game. His bulk and rapid feet marked him out as a centre-forward, and when he found space in that area of the field, he was lethal. In his first four years at the club, he averaged more than 19 goals a season.

In 1991, however, Barnes ruptured his Achilles tendon.

'I couldn't sprint any more. So overnight, I couldn't do what I did well. People remember me for dribbling and taking the full-back on, but that was over. I had to change the way I played. I decided to let Steve McManaman do my role and try to play like Ronnie Whelan: not have too many touches on the ball and release it quickly. My passing and awareness had to improve, and I think they did. Maybe I wasn't as effective as I was before, but I still contributed positively to the structure of the team.'

By then, Liverpool were also in decline. He has his own explanation for the club's regression.

'The culture of Liverpool was guided by football and nothing else,' he says. 'The commercial dominance enjoyed by United in the '90s could have been Liverpool instead. Liverpool won trophy after trophy in the '70s and '80s, but Bill Shankly would never have believed in exploiting the club's commercial potential and nor would Bob Paisley or Joe Fagan. They were only interested in what happened on the training ground and what happened when Liverpool took to the field. You only have to look at

Anfield to realise that. Other stadiums in London or Manchester are grand. Yet Anfield is still very basic and spartanly decorated. The same applies to the training ground. It is true that Liverpool only existed to win trophies.

'But the club was a victim of a changing football culture and before they realised it, it was too late.'

CHAPTER TEN

Cult Zeros

IRISH UPSTART, Steve Staunton

ON A BAD MORNING LIKE THIS, THE ASPHALT CLOUD IS BARELY separated from the nightmare of lumpen grey concrete that is the Northern Echo Arena. Today, the skies are squally above the outskirts of Darlington when Steve Staunton pokes his head around the door of a spartanly decorated pressroom to check if anybody wants to speak to him. There are three: two regional media and me.

At the time (2010), Staunton, Steve Nicol and Gary Ablett, a trio of full-backs that represented Liverpool the 1980s and into the '90s, were the only players still in the game as managers, all of them in lower-league football: Nicol in the United States with New England Revolution; Ablett in administration at Stockport County; and Staunton here at the bottom of the old Division Four with Darlington. Sadly, Ablett passed away before this book was published. Nicol, meanwhile, has since resigned from his position.

On this particular Thursday afternoon, Staunton, who scored seven times during one hundred and forty-eight appearances across two separate spells at Liverpool, wears a permanent frown, which probably comes with the job. He'd arrived at Darlington the previous October and failed to prevent the club's plummet towards relegation and the Conference, despite improved results since a period when more than 20 playing staff were made redundant shortly before the arrival of former boss Colin Todd.

When the local pressmen probe, he does not dodge any awkward questions, explaining considerately why he'd decided to release captain and longest-serving player Steve Foster the week before. Staunton has a surly reputation, and I am informed that he is not the kind of person to charm the paint off a dressing-room wall. Yet here he seems to have developed a mutual respect with the writers who are sporting considerably smarter clothes than me after half-jokingly being told to scrub up by Staunton in his first week in charge if they wished to further enjoy his company.

Now, they share a gallows humour. 'We should be OK at Bradford on Saturday,' Staunton says, blowing his reddish cheeks and adjusting the thinning strawberry blond verging on ginger hair that rests across the top of his head. 'Providing the chairman's got enough money to pay the bus driver.'

One of the journalists told me later that Staunton's presence had really given the club a lift. Hearts and minds may have been secured in the media, but it can't disguise Darlington's predicament. With 17 league games to go, they are 13 points off safety; this at a time when the club have been losing a reported £60,000 a week following a decline in attendances in their under-used stadium.

Of all the people interviewed for this book, Staunton was always going to be the most difficult to arrange. As a manager, time is limited with him and there was no expectation of getting the two to three hours spent with other players. While managing Liverpool, Rafa Benítez once had a list of more than 55 journalists hoping to sit down with him at Melwood. This may be

Darlington, but it was a welcome surprise when a 45-minute interview slot was arranged with the club's press office. Staunton is not Jamie Carragher when it comes to entertaining copy, but as one of only three former players from the '80s still in management, I am keen to find out why he thinks so many former Reds have elected to go for the pundit's chair rather than the dugout.

'The one thing Liverpool instilled in me was to make time for others,' he says before leaving more than 90 generously offered minutes later. 'Liverpool was a family club, everybody stuck together and that's why we achieved so much success. It's also probably why they aren't winning much now.'

Born in Drogheda, Staunton grew up a few miles away in Dundalk's tough western outskirts on the Ard Easmuinn council estate.

'My dad was a Garda Síochána,' he says, in the thickest of Louth accents. 'Being a border town, it wasn't always easy for him – especially in the '70s when there was a lot going on politically. Dundalk was a place of two extremes: boom or bust. There have always been a lot of breweries in the town. Because it's the first place that people see when they come from the north, the first thing they always say is, "Bloody hell – the number of pubs." It's like Liverpool used to be on the Dock Road where there was a boozer on every street corner. When times are good, the docks have meant a lot of people have made good money, especially with industry and commerce from Blackthorn Shoes who have a big factory there. At the moment, it's not great with the euro and the pound. There was nothing fancy about my upbringing but nothing too bad either. Everyone looked out for each other.'

Like many Irish teenagers, Staunton supported Celtic from afar and admired full-back Danny McGrain.

'I always wanted to play in an FA Cup final. That was what I dreamed of. Most kids did. I wasn't different to anyone else. It's all I wanted to do. I was good in school, although my mother kept telling me I was lazy. I didn't have to work very hard to get good results. I could play football all day long and forget about revising but still pass exams. I was lucky like that. She always went mad, saying if I put my mind to it, I could really achieve something in life. I'd rather play rugby, Gaelic football or go running than go to school. If there was a sporting event and it got me out of classes, I'd go for it.'

Staunton later thought about joining the army and considered enrolling on a sports scholarship in America. But a career in football was what he desired most.

'I was six when I played my first game at Under-10s,' he continues. 'The leagues in Dundalk didn't go down too low, so I ended up playing in a higher age group with my brother and the bigger boys. We played football every single day on a green in the middle of Ard Easmuinn. Most of the time, there was 20, 30 or 40 lads playing in a big game. I was always the youngest and the smallest. It taught me to be streetwise, because if you wanted to have a kick of the ball, you had to do things properly and not be afraid to throw your head in.'

Gaelic football toughened him up as well.

'I loved the Gaelic, and I believe it helped me a lot when I signed for Liverpool. You learnt to keep on the move all the time and create space for yourself – like the Liverpool way. Otherwise you were going to get a wallop. When I signed for Dundalk in the youth team, they tried to stop me playing, but I carried on. We got to the last 16 of the FAI Youth Cup, and there was a final with my Gaelic team on the same day. They both said I couldn't play the other. So I turned up at the soccer, because that was earlier on in the day. We were 5– or 6–1 up. So I asked the manager to take me off. There was 15–20 minutes to go, but he told me I was staying on. In the end, I walked off and my dad took me to the final of the Gaelic. They were losing. I came on at half-time and we ended up winning.'

Despite walking out on Dundalk, Staunton's reputation as a hard-running left-winger was spreading quickly, and at 15 he was offered a trial by Manchester City.

'The youth system at City was a lot better than at Liverpool,' he insists. 'It was more organised. They had a well-run academy, and in the late '90s it produced some fantastic players. David White, Andy Hinchcliffe and the Brightwell brothers [Ian and David] were all there. They were a bit unlucky in their careers, because City later struggled off the field with finances. They were the right players at the wrong club. Unfortunately for me, City felt I wasn't good enough and sent me home. They also felt I was a year too old for them. I was devastated and went back in tears. My dad told me that it didn't matter because I was going to finish my education first. He wasn't keen on me leaving school early. He told me to be patient and see what happened when I finished my exams. That put me in my place.'

An appearance at the FAI Youth Cup final with Dundalk a year later was followed by an approach by Liverpool. This was the summer of 1986.

'I'd played in the Milk Cup before, and all the scouts were there. I know now having been in the game for so long that if a young lad has something about him, it spreads like wildfire. Liverpool came in and there were five or six other clubs ringing my house as well. My idea was to have a go at all the other teams and get fit to the highest standard possible before having a go at Liverpool. I wanted to be bang at it. They were my team in England. In the end, I was convinced to go straight to Liverpool and trust my ability to do well.

'I was at Melwood every day and training with the reserve team. Tom Saunders was overseeing everything and had picked me up from the airport. I was there for eight days, and we'd played a couple of games where I'd done OK. I knew I was due to go home and before the final trial match, which was a pre-season friendly at Stafford Rangers, Tom came up to me and said, "We all like the look of you. But I'll see how you do tonight then make up my mind up after the game." My face dropped and my shoulders seized up. Jesus, talk about a life-changing moment and all my dreams to be decided in one match. But that was the psychology of Liverpool. They wanted to see whether I would bottle it. After the game, Tom came up and said, "Well done, son."'

Staunton was offered a modest contract.

'But it seemed generous to me. I'd done odd jobs here and there back home, but I'd never really earned a wage. I didn't give a shit what money Liverpool were offering me because I'd have paid them to play. Going to Liverpool was solely about football. But the money was more than I'd ever imagined.'

His two-year deal with Liverpool coincided with the return of Phil Thompson as reserve-team manager.

'We had a few names for Tommo, because he wasn't universally loved by everyone. He got a lot of stick for the size of his nose – but that was only behind his back. Nobody would dare say anything to his face. He was a tough man and it was a tough school. Ronnie Moran was probably the toughest, though. One day, he gave me a lift home because I didn't drive and he opened up a bit. To me, he always seemed like a man of limited emotion. But this time, he said, "The minute I stop having a go at you is the day you're finished." It made me think and, with time, I understood where he was coming from. You're not going to waste your time and energy on somebody who has given up the ghost, are you?'

Despite still being a teenager in a new city, a new country and with no friends, Staunton was given limited help by the club as he tried to settle in.

'I was lucky that I had an aunt who lived in Aigburth, so I stayed with her for a while. Otherwise, I'd have had to find somewhere by myself. It was the first test by the club – to see whether you had the mental capability to sort things out yourself, because it was always going to be the same on the pitch. It was different at other clubs, where they'd put you in digs straight away and mollycoddle you like they do these days. It doesn't help in the long term, because there are footballers in the modern game who finish then don't know how to brew a cup of tea, they've had so much help. If you were very lucky, you'd be given the number of Mrs Prince, a woman who had some flats in Utting Avenue, then it would be up to you to sort out living arrangements. Ronnie Whelan and Alan Hansen had lived with her in the late '70s. I wasn't that fortunate.'

Staunton befriended two other Irish lads at Melwood, Ken DeMange and Brian Mooney.

'Like Ronnie [Whelan], they'd both signed from Home Farm in Dublin. We'd play a lot of snooker together in the pubs around Anfield after training. But it wasn't like they were the only people I spent time with. It is true when people say that everybody was treated the same at Liverpool. It didn't matter whether you cost a bag of pork scratchings or millions of pounds, everybody was equal. If your feet ever came off the ground, you were brought back down straight away.'

The transition to full-time training was difficult.

'It was a massive change – the intensity and pace we used to play at every day was frightening. I reckon we worked harder than any other team on the training ground. After four or five months, my body was close to packing in. Physically, I wasn't able to cope. I'd never done weights in my life or run for so long, so everything took its toll.

'Before, I'd been a left-sided midfielder or central midfielder, but now I was playing left-back for the reserves in a really good team. The Pontins League was very strong, and we used to win it every season. If Liverpool were playing away on a Saturday afternoon, the reserves would play the same opposition at home. There were only 13 players in a match-day squad, and Kenny would often take an extra man, just in case of injury or illness. Everybody else would play in the reserves. It meant everybody was playing regular football all the time and us young lads in the reserves were learning off the senior pros. We were playing with first-class players against first-class opposition. That experience was invaluable, and I can't understand why they don't do it that way now. The standard of the reserve league now is shite.

'The reserves and the first team played exactly the same. We trained the same way too, and that made matches seem easy. Because we'd worked our socks off, we were so fit – a lot fitter than other teams. The intensity of training was higher than in matches. So the games seemed easy.'

Staunton soon earned a nickname at Melwood – a tag that has stuck with him ever since.

'John Bennison had been at Liverpool with Shankly and was well respected. He was in the same mould as Ronnie Moran – very tough, especially on the young lads he wanted to test mentally. I could hear somebody shouting the name "Stan" during games, and I didn't have a clue who was being shouted at. One day, Beno came up to me and said, "Laddie, why do you keep ignoring me?" I was like, "What?"

'"Your name's Stan, isn't it?"

'"I'm Steve . . . Stephen in fact."' Nobody bloody even called me Steve at the time. Beno was looking at me confused. Then he told me that he'd played at Chester City in the '40s or '50s with a bloke called Stan Staunton. After that conversation, he started calling me Steve, but the rest of the lads stuck with Stan. There was a lot of bullshit about the nickname Stan coming from *Laurel and Hardy*, because people perceived me as a figure of fun. But it wasn't. It came from Beno.'

At the end of the 1986–87 season, Staunton was sent on loan to Bradford City, a club still recovering from the Valley Parade Stadium fire.

'It gave me the experience of realising that lower down the leagues you're playing for people's livelihoods. Jobs were at stake. Since, I've seen people go mad in dressing-rooms, but at least you can walk away always knowing there's a next week to put things right. At that level, a run of defeats can mean loss in match-day revenue and eventually can mean redundancies. That was the grim reality.

'Terry Dolan was the manager at Bradford, and he was experienced. But he was good with youngsters as well. I was there for two months and came up against some good players. Paul Birch, god rest his soul, with Aston Villa was one of my toughest opponents. He was small and tricky, and with me being 6 ft and slow to turn, I struggled against him. He'd never fucking stand still – a little jack-in-the-box. I always found it difficult against the little ones. Even until this day, having played in two

World Cups, I will always say that the little ones gave me more problems than the more technical ones. Later, I remember playing against Russell Beardsmore [a winger with Manchester United who later moved to Bournemouth]. That fella gave me more problems than Roberto fucking Baggio. Gary Crosby at Forest was another one at the back end of the '80s, as was Gazza. Gazza was a year older than me when I was at Bradford, but he was small and podgy. What a player he was. He was playing central midfield but got about the pitch and was a problem for every defender that day. He'd try everything to put you off your game – tickling, pinching, groping, and that when he was barely 20 years old.'

Staunton returned to Melwood over-confident and believing he was ready for first-team action.

'Within two or three days of being back, I couldn't pass a ball five yards. The staff battered me because I'd gotten too cocky. I thought I was ready to play first-team football and I was dead wrong. After a week of harsh words, they started building my confidence up again. I learnt a very big lesson – a great lesson – at such a young age. Never get ahead of yourself.'

Twelve months later, Staunton travelled with the first team for the first time for a 0–0 draw against Norwich City at Carrow Road. The following summer, he was part of the squad that went to Norway for a pre-season tour.

'We drunk an awful fucking lot,' he says, grinning for the first time. 'It was a big learning curve for me, because I'd barely touched a drop since moving to Liverpool. I was that desperate to prove myself. Then I got to the first team and all they did was drink. It was an eye opener for me. We'd travel, train, play, drink, travel, train, play then drink again. It was constant. People say that the United boys were big drinkers in the '80s, but we drank just as much. The difference was that we had better players who could deal with it, and we achieved much more success so nobody cared about it. It's only when you stop winning that it becomes an issue. If supporters saw us out on the piss, they'd come over and congratulate us for doing so well. But if the

United boys were spotted, they'd get criticised for not focusing when the team wasn't doing so well. Most Tuesdays after training we'd be out, and sometimes we'd bump into the United boys. We got praised; the United lads got bollocked. It was like that in the '90s as well. United had just as many players that were out on the town as Liverpool – all young lads. But the United lads had some more experienced pros in the dressing-room who could advise the younger boys when to stop.'

Back to the tour. There were funny moments.

'We were in a fast-food joint somewhere in Oslo and some people spotted us standing there ordering our food. Aldo was getting more attention than everyone else and we couldn't figure out why. Then one guy went running out the door shouting, "Look, I've got Ian Rush's autograph."'

As the youngest player in the squad, Staunton came in for some stick.

'I had to stand up for myself,' he grimaces. 'I quickly learnt that I couldn't hover in the background and hide. It's like that in any working environment. If you let people get the better of you, you're done for. For a time, I was the butt of all the jokes, being a young Irish lad with a strong accent. It changed for me when I was away on international duty with Ireland in Dublin and I fronted up to Liam Brady. He was one of my heroes. Liam was sitting there playing cards with Aldo, Cas [Tony Cascarino] and a few of the other boys. It was late at night and they were all having a laugh and a joke. It was the day before a game and I was doing what I was told by going to bed and getting the rest. They woke me up, so I went to see what was going on. I walked into the room and Liam tries to belittle me, "Stan, make us all a cup of tea . . . and bring those biscuits over while you're there."

'"Fuck off, you cunt," I told him.

'The boys sat there speechless and all started laughing. I was 18 and Liam was one of the best players Ireland had ever produced. He'd played in Italy with Juventus. But I didn't give a shit – not that I meant it in a nasty way. I just wanted them all to know that I'd stand my ground. From then on, I had the balls to stand up to everyone. But it didn't stop Aldo trying it on.'

In August '88, Staunton was on the bench when Liverpool beat Wimbledon in the Charity Shield alongside fellow reserve-team player Charlie Boyd (Alex Watson, brother of Dave, started the match). By the middle of September, he'd made his first-team debut.

'We were playing Spurs at Anfield and Jan Mølby had a problem and was signalling to come off. I was on the bench with John Durnin, and Kenny sent me out down the line for a quick warm-up. When I got back to the dugout, he goes to me, "Now, Stan, where do you fancy playing?" Kenny knew I could play left side of centre-back, left-back or left-midfield. I couldn't believe what he was asking me, but I had a think about it and thought, "Left side of centre-back – I'd be up against Paul Walsh", and he was on fire. I didn't fancy that for my debut. So I ended up chickening out and playing left-hand side of midfield. I put my first three crosses in the Kop. It wasn't the best of debuts.'

With Barry Venison, Jim Beglin and Gary Ablett in front him, Staunton believed his path towards a regular position in the first team would be at left-back.

'David Burrows also came in around the October time, but I could see it was an area of the team Kenny wasn't settled on. Barry and Jim were good pros but players I felt I could put under pressure. Compared to other parts of the park, the competition at left-back wasn't quite as strong.'

Dalglish, though, had other ideas.

'Kenny thought I could play centre-forward. God knows why. On the pre-season tour of Norway, I'd come off the bench a few times and in one of them I came on for Rushy and scored a hat-trick. That backed up Kenny's argument, but after a few years I think he realised that I was better at running onto things than with my back to goal. Everybody knew that my position was left-back, but I ended up playing in nearly every position for Liverpool. I played everywhere down the left, everywhere down the middle, even right-back for five minutes when a player was receiving treatment. Then, when I later came back from the club from Villa, I played in goal against Everton in the derby after Sander Westerveld got sent off. I must have gone through every single shirt number.

'It was important for my development, and I think that's why I played for so long [Staunton finished his career at centre-back]. There is a tendency now for players to get stuck with a position from an early age. They get in the comfort zone. That wasn't allowed to happen at Liverpool.'

Wearing the number 10 shirt, Staunton scored on his full debut against Arsenal in the Centenary Shield (a competition devised to compensate top English clubs for lost revenue following Heysel and the European ban that followed). After starting in a surprising one-goal defeat at home to Newcastle, who were eventually relegated, Staunton didn't appear again for a month in the league. Then, returning for a 1–1 draw at Anfield against Wimbledon, he was virtually ever-present as Liverpool gave themselves a chance of a league and cup double. If Staunton, who finished the campaign having played 29 games, believed that April and May would mark a glorious culmination to a debut season, he was wrong. Hillsborough happened.

'I was naive to the whole situation. Because I was so young, I couldn't really take in what was going on, particularly on the day. I couldn't quite comprehend what I was seeing. Because I was left-back, I was in the corner of the pitch where the worst crush happened. I could see everything . . . hear everything.

'When Peter Beardsley had the shot that hit the bar after a few minutes, there was a big surge in the crowd and seconds later I could hear screams. You don't expect such a thing to happen at a football match, so I was trying to focus on what was going on on the pitch. I went to take a throw-in and people started climbing over the fence. I could see in their faces that something bad – something out of their control – had happened.

'In the weeks and months after, I was ringing home all the

time, I had a breakdown, and my mother was a big help. Without her, God knows what I'd have done. It was probably after the season had finished when I went through the worst of it. Physically and mentally, I was a wreck for a few days. I was crying all the time, like shell shock. It hit me like a steam train. The memories are still with me. They are vivid. I think about it most days.'

Staunton was not selected for the Hillsborough memorial match at Parkhead against Celtic.

'Kenny pinned the team on the board and I wasn't in it. He knew I was a young boy and that's probably why he played the older ones. It wasn't easy for anyone at that time, but it was just his way of protecting me – like he did for everyone.'

Liverpool returned to competitive first-team action three weeks after the disaster, against Everton in a league match at Goodison Park.

'The families got us back playing,' he maintains. 'I think a lot of the boys wanted to finish the season there and then. There were some discussions and a lot of the lads thought it wasn't right that we continue. We were going for a league and cup double, something few teams had achieved. But the morale was so low; nobody cared. The FA Cup became more important than the league, because we wanted to win it for the fans after what had happened in the semi-final. We weren't really focusing on the league but somehow managed to claw it back after being a dozen or so points behind. Arsenal were going for the title and on a really bad run, so they went away on holiday to Ibiza and only started winning when they came back. After Hillsborough, we had a load of games in hand again and it was a bit too much for us. Everybody knows that the season went until the final minute. I think our legs and minds had gone by then.'

Defeat to Michael Thomas and Arsenal came after a 3–2 victory over Everton in the FA Cup final.

Still in his teens, Staunton believes he was blessed to have two Liverpool legends close to him in positions on the pitch.

'For three years, John Barnes was unbelievable. I knew from

day one he was one of the best players in the world. Liverpool liked to play the ball on the ground and pass it with pace, and before my debut I was told this again in the dressing-room. The ball came to me a couple of minutes in, and I was down the Kop end just at the edge of the box. I've gone to hit this nice side-foot down the line, and the ball hit a bobble. I could see it going into the Main Stand, but Barnesy came from nowhere, rose and took it on his chest. Not only did he control it, but with his next touch he beat the onrushing defender. I thought, "Oh, yes – I can't lose here." Another thing we were taught at Liverpool was that you needed to turn a bad pass into a good 'un. I was lucky in that respect because I had Barnesy in front of me. It meant I could get forward all the time because the oppo only cared about stopping John Barnes.'

If Staunton was fortunate to have Barnes as an option down the line, he was blessed to have Alan Hansen inside.

'That was another blow,' he jokes. 'Again, how could I lose? If the ball to Barnesy wasn't on, I had Jocky inside, who was one of the best ball-playing defenders of the previous decade. Then there was Ronnie Whelan on the inside, who in my opinion is one of Liverpool's all-time most underrated players as well. As a one-touch player in that period, I can't think of anyone better. Razor [Ray Houghton] was a great player too. He'd make unselfish runs across the pitch just to take one touch and set it up for you. I can't think of a player who'd do that today – make a 60-yard run just to receive a pass and lay it off first time. All I needed to do was as I was told.'

Another undervalued performer was John Aldridge.

'Aldo wasn't as pleasing on the eye as other strikers because of his style, compared to Rush or Kenny, but Aldo was the best finisher I've seen. He was better than Rushy. Inside the box, he was phenomenal. I remember once in a game smashing the ball across on the half volley and it was rising all the time. It was head height, but he put it in the net with his right foot. Aldo then comes rushing to me in celebration shouting, "You nearly took my fucking groin off there." I told the soft bastard it was meant to be for his big fat head! That was him – he had a predatory instinct of where and when to go, and his goalscoring record speaks for itself. It's better than any other I've known.'

One player that struggled at Liverpool was Swedish defender Glenn Hysén.

'He was clearly more used to playing in a sweeper system – something he'd done at Fiorentina. There's a big difference between playing in a three or a four. Some of the best defenders who have played in a four all their lives can't get used to playing in a three and vice-versa. Personally, I can't understand it, because it's only a mental blockage. It's 10 v 10 outfield, but Glenn couldn't seem to get his head around the way we played. So he found it really hard.'

Liverpool finished the '80s with a title – Staunton's first – but he says the FA Cup semi-final defeat to Crystal Palace had long-term implications for the team.

'It may have been a watershed moment. We were so comfortable against them and 1–0 up at half-time. Then they roared back into the game and we didn't seem to cope. It was an ageing squad, and I was the youngest player in the team. I remember some of the lads telling me that I would have other cup semi-finals to put right what had gone wrong that day at Villa Park. I got the impression that they were saying it because they knew they didn't.'

Liverpool comfortably secured their 18th league title in May 1990 after beating QPR. Yet there was no feeling around the club that more than 20 years later they'd be waiting for their 19th.

'I don't remember any special celebrations. It was typical Liverpool. Ronnie Moran came in with a box of medals and said, "If you've played more than 12 games, take a medal. Make sure you're ready for next season because it's going to be a lot fucking harder."'

It was. Arsenal cantered to the title with Liverpool finishing second. After a 4–4 FA Cup draw at Goodison Park against Everton, Dalglish resigned as manager, and a month later Graeme Souness was appointed his successor.

'People ask me all the time about the day Kenny resigned, but it was just an average day at training. We were all tired after the Everton match and were preparing to go out when Ronnie [Moran] came in and said Kenny had had enough. We were all shocked, because he didn't show any signs he was unhappy beforehand. My personal feeling is that he needed a break from football after what had happened at Hillsborough. He took everybody's problems on his shoulders and didn't ask for any help himself – at least he didn't appear to. After the Ibrox disaster, Heysel and Hillsborough, Kenny must have felt the strain. It could have easily broken lesser people.

'When Graeme [Souness] initially came in as Kenny's replacement, he had some fantastic ideas. Training was a bit different. I was flying the following pre-season, playing in all the games. I'd never felt fitter.'

Ahead of a flight to Germany for a friendly against Bayer Leverkusen, Staunton was called into Souness's office.

'Graeme told me to go and speak to Ron Atkinson [Aston Villa's manager]. I was devastated. It had never entered my head that Graeme was thinking about letting me go. He said that Ron had made an offer of £1.1 million and he felt that because I was going to be classed as a foreigner under new laws (at a time when no team was allowed to field more than four) and because he already had three English left-backs, it represented a good deal for Liverpool.

'So I went down to Birmingham and initially told Ron, "No." Villa were offering me a big contract and long-term security, but it didn't bother me – I didn't want to leave Liverpool. Big Ron told me afterwards that he'd initially enquired about David Burrows but Graeme said, no, he could have me instead. In Ron's mind, I was twice the player of Buggsy, so he couldn't believe his luck.

'The whole experience of being let go by Liverpool toughened me up even more. From then on, I always thought about myself first rather than the club, because I realised that any club could dispense with a player at any given moment. Liverpool hurt me, if I'm totally honest, and for a long time I didn't even bother looking out for their results.'

Atkinson – originally from Old Swan – had managed Manchester United in the '80s. He coaxed the best out of Staunton.

'I was 22 when I signed for Villa, and I was only going to improve. Villa probably saw my best years, and now I have just as much affection for them as I do for Liverpool. When Graeme had left and Roy Evans took charge, he tried to sign me every summer and it was always in the papers. It peeved a lot of Villa fans off.

'We played some great football under Ron, and we probably should have won the Premier League. [In 1992–93 Villa finished second behind Man United.] I knew a few of the boys there already and there were some great times.'

With Paul McGrath in the squad, the craic at Villa was good. When Staunton signed for the club, all the talk inside the dressing-room was of McGrath's antics on a pre-season training camp in Hamburg a few weeks earlier.

'Everyone knows Paul had drink problems, and it caused difficulties for him in his life. But there were some funnier moments. Around the time I was signing, Ron was travelling to and from Hamburg to be with the team and sign players back in Birmingham. Andy Gray was the assistant manager and in charge of the squad while Ron was away. Andy was a bit of a lad in his playing days but naive to the coaching and discipline side of things.

'One day, Paul went out on a binge, because the tour was basically a big piss-up, and he didn't turn up for training. Later that night, he turned up at the team hotel and went straight to his room. Andy was trying to bang the door down to see where he'd been, but in the meantime Paul climbed out of the window, down a drainpipe for five or six floors and out to freedom – or at least the next bar. Hamburg has a great nightlife.'

Ray Houghton, a former Liverpool teammate, soon joined Staunton at Villa Park.

'Ray would moan all day. He had little man's disease. At Villa, the lads couldn't understand how we put up with each other. We lived in the same village and drove to training and back every morning. I think the lads saw us as a bit of an odd couple because we'd be arguing all the time. They'd say, "What happens after training, when you've had a barney and one of you has to drive the other one home?" I'd tell them that we wouldn't speak to each other in the car, then eventually one of us would pick up the phone and say, "Fancy a quick pint?"'

Staunton won the League Cup twice during his time in the Midlands.

'In '94, we beat United 3–1 and I was marking Andrei Kanchelskis. He was a real flyer and up for player of the season that year. United were battering everybody, and we weren't expected to win the final. Dalian Atkinson gave us the lead early on, but I was really struggling with fitness after being rushed back for the final after injury. By the end of the first half, Kanchelskis could have walked around me – I was struggling that much. So I told Ron that I had to come off. Coxy [Neil Cox] came on, and Kanchelskis was giving him the runaround. I was sitting on the bench, and Ron turns to me and goes, "If we lose this fucking game – it's on your head." I didn't know whether to laugh or cry, because when Ron lost his temper, you didn't want to be in the same room as him. Luckily, Deano [Dean Saunders] scored two late on, and Kanchelskis ended up getting sent off.'

A second League Cup medal followed in 1996 with a 3–0 victory over Leeds United, although Staunton was an unused substitute. By 1998, he was ready to move on, and he returned to Liverpool.

'You always think that you should never go back, but I did. It proved to be the wrong decision,' he says. Within months, Gérard Houllier was appointed joint-manager with Roy Evans. 'That was possibly the most annoying part of it all, because I didn't sign for Gérard; I signed for Roy. I thought the writing was on the wall straight away, and I wasn't wrong. Me and

Gérard didn't see eye to eye, and he wanted his own men in.'

Staunton signed for Villa again before moving on to Walsall, where he was on a short-term contract before making his first steps into management with Ireland.

'I didn't apply for it – the IFA sought me out,' he insists. 'I received a phone call and the person on the other end of the line said, "Stephen, would you like to manage your country?" I'd played 102 times for Ireland – more than any other player in history – but it was a huge surprise and a big honour. If I'm honest, I wasn't all that taken with the idea because I thought it might have come too soon. Then I questioned whether I'd ever be offered the opportunity again, so I had to take it.'

Life back home wasn't easy. Only three matches into the job, Staunton was confronted by a man with a plastic imitation Uzi sub-machine gun in Portmarnock, north of Dublin, while the team prepared for a friendly against Holland. Then, he was lampooned by the Irish public for an embarrassing 5–2 away defeat by Cyprus. Ireland failed to qualify for Euro 2008 and at the end of the campaign Staunton was sacked.

'I appointed Bobby Robson as an advisor, and he helped me through a lot of difficult times. What didn't he teach me? The big thing is not to get carried away when you do well and not beat yourself up when doing badly. Simple as that. And then there was his relentless enthusiasm. You only have to meet him to know that. If you show enthusiasm, it improves your players.

'It was disappointing how it all ended [with Ireland]. My record stands up for itself. The most pleasing part was the number of young players that came through under me – players that have since done well under Trapattoni. I can feel very proud of what I've done with my country.'

Staunton refuses to label his time in international management as a failure, adding that it only made him more eager to succeed in club management in order prove the detractors wrong. Unlike a lot of his former teammates, he never considered media work and soon returned to football as Gary McAllister's assistant at Leeds.

'A lot of the lads that were at Liverpool – they're all pundits, aren't they? Is it because they want an easier life? All of the lads know Kenny and saw what management did to him, so maybe they don't fancy it. They're all bright lads – footballing brains – and people who think about the game in depth. But management isn't as easy as you think. It's not like being a footballer, where you come in, have your dinner, do a bit in the afternoon and go home. You have to worry about your job 24/7, because the sack is only a couple of results away. Maybe they could see how it changed Kenny – they were all coming towards the end of their careers at that time – and maybe they thought, "Nah, that ain't for me." It probably put them off, whereas I was only young and had my whole career ahead of me.'

Staunton became Darlington boss after several failed applications with other clubs in League Two, one of them being Port Vale. He soon made Kevin Richardson his deputy. Richardson, or 'Ricco', was a former teammate of Staunton's at Villa and ironically a midfielder that lined up against Liverpool in the 1989 title decider at Anfield.

'Mick [McCarthy] had Ricco as reserve-team manager at Sunderland. He's from the area and knows the league, so I gave him a call. He's a bit of the old school. He can be calling them all sorts but still have them eating out of his left hand. I'm a bit too black and white for all that. That's why he's a good coach and why I'm the manager. I had interviews at a few different clubs, but they weren't taken on the idea of someone managing at the bottom having played their whole career at the top.'

Aside from Richardson, Staunton employs a skeleton staff with a physio, a kitman and two youth-team coaches as well as one scout. Money is tight at Darlington. Problems stretch back a decade. In 1999, George Reynolds became chairman, proclaiming, 'One day we will be in the Premiership with millions in the bank and others will be wondering how we've done it.' Orphaned at eight, Reynolds had previously competed in bare-knuckle fights in his native Sunderland and in the '50s and '60s had dabbled in crime – namely safe breaking and drug smuggling – for which he served a six-month prison sentence. He completed another two stretches before learning to read in jail. Subsequently, he went straight and earned a £300 million fortune from a business making kitchen worktops in Shildon, County Durham. When he took over Darlington, he immediately paid off the club's £5 million debt.

After vainly promising to sign Paul Gascoigne, he built the 27,500-seater 'Reynolds Arena' at a cost of more than £25 million. Soon known locally as 'George's White Elephant', fans pined for Feethams, their rustic if rather more atmospheric former home in the centre of town. It was 'built more on personal vanity than business sense', according to the club's supporters' trust.

With administration beckoning, Reynolds departed and was soon arrested for tax evasion when £500,000 was found in the boot of his car. In 2005, he was sentenced to three years in prison but released twelve months later with an electronic tag, which remained in place until April 2007. Maybe the flamboyant Colombian striker Faustino Asprilla, who fled the UK on the day he was due to sign for Reynolds' Darlington, had the right idea after all.

Today, Staunton's struggling team play at a latter-day footballing folly in front of crowds that have dipped just above the 1,000 mark. Upon my arrival, I noticed the gold taps, the escalators, the marble flooring encrusted with club badge as well as the opulence of the boardroom. That's why the money ran out. Over the last two seasons, the club's budget has been slashed by £2 million. The escalators have long been turned off to save cash, while the lift intercom has had the 'Going down' voice removed so as not to tempt fate. Inside, I walked free as if in an empty mansion and onto the pitch before an aged groundsman that looked as if he should be growing spuds on an allotment asked me what I was doing. This is life at the bottom of the bottom division.

'It is quite a responsibility to be fighting for an old club's existence with players' livelihoods in your hands,' Staunton says.

'But that's football. That goes from the top right down to the very bottom. There isn't a problem motivating the players, because if they are fighting for their lives that is the best way of motivating them – dangling the carrot. They do not earn as much as those in the Premier League, but they have got a wonderful opportunity, a wonderful stage to progress their career. So if they are doing really well here, I hope my phone is ringing all the time because clubs are wanting to buy them.

'You know, we are not daft. We are coming in with our eyes wide open. We know it is a tough job, and we have ideas to get the best out of what we have got in the squad at the moment. There are a lot of tough jobs out there in football at the moment. If you ask anyone, they are all tough. Not one manager will say it is easy.'

New Darlington chairman Raj Singh, a care-home entrepreneur, insists the club is on a firmer financial footing than during the extravagant Reynolds era, and says 80 per cent of clubs in the lower divisions are fighting for survival.

Staunton is settled here, living near Yarm – a well-to-do area where the glitterati of Middlesbrough reside. 'I like it in the north-east,' he reflects. 'But sometimes there aren't enough hours in the day to do everything. I can see now why everybody at Liverpool said you needed a good staff – people you can trust. Without that, you're fucked.'

***Three weeks after this interview, I was watching *Sky Sports News* when a story broke about Staunton being sacked. Three years on, he has not returned to football management. Darlington, meanwhile, were relegated to the Conference National before dissolving in 2012. A reformed club known as Darlington 1883 finished the 2012–13 season as Northern League champions, while sharing a ground with Bishop Auckland, once a great name of amateur football.

CHAPTER ELEVEN

Cult Zeros

DISCIPLINARIAN, Ronnie Moran

IN THIS BOOK, RONNIE MORAN HAS SEPARATELY BEEN TERMED A 'barking dog', a 'Rottweiler' and a 'very angry man'.

I find none of those descriptions absolutely accurate when I meet the oldest living member of the famed Bootroom a few days ahead of his 79th birthday in the Liverpool suburb of Crosby.

Using a walking stick to manoeuvre his hulking body through the front door of a bungalow where he lives in a luxury retirement complex, it is imaginable that, in his prime, Moran was not a man to be crossed. In his playing days, indeed, he was a fiercely competitive left-back and in an alternative life would surely have had the physique and tactical sporting mind to compete as an amateur boxer.

Placing his paisley-patterned flat cap and heavy winter coat onto a wooden stand, he invites me into what he calls 'the trophy room' and presents me with one of many photographs from a magnolia-coloured wall. It includes his four closest friends in football: Bill Shankly, Bob Paisley, Joe Fagan and Reuben Bennett.

'Every morning, I wake up and sit looking at that crowd,' he says, lightly grinning and pointing with thickset fingers. 'I remind myself that I'm the only one still here. It's very sad when you think that all that knowledge has been lost. But I also feel very fortunate to have been a part of it. They were a good bunch. I miss them.'

Although Moran had already served Liverpool for nearly 30 years by the start of the '80s, I decided to interview him because he is the only person still alive with genuine inside knowledge that can contribute towards explaining why the club sustained its culture of success for so long and the mindset behind the staff that helped make the decade become Liverpool's most dominant in terms of trophies.

After just a few minutes speaking to Moran, you can quickly sense the intrinsic qualities in an individual that, when placed in a collective, engineered Liverpool's greatness. His loyalty to those with whom he shared the Bootroom is admirable. His uncompromising attitude towards commitment is also evident.

'Football is about character and showing balls, see,' he says, directing a stern digit in my direction. 'The minimum you can ask is to give your best. With that and with the right people around you, you've got a chance.'

Just as Howard Gayle was a product of the environment he grew up in, so was Moran. Gayle had no option but to confront problems because he was on his own. Moran had no option but to work tirelessly and struggle through them like the rest of his family. Moran remembers the Second World War. He was five when the war began and eleven when it finished. Life was harsh.

'My father worked as a binman, and he transported rubbish around the borough by horse and cart. He tried hard, you know. I valued his effort. Whenever he came down our road, I'd go out and give him a hand. When the war started, he helped the Home Front. It was his job to ring the town siren from a nearby station to alert the residents when the bombs started dropping. We'd hide under the stairs. It was a squeeze with a family of our size.'

He continues retelling tales of his childhood using simple but effective language. I learn that he met his wife Joyce at school. They have been married for 55 years. Sadly, he is old enough to have lost a daughter and a son-in-law. They died within 18 months of each another.

And then comes his interest in football. It began when his eldest sister's husband took him to Goodison Park. 'Football never bothered me in that way [in terms of rivalry]. As a kid, I wouldn't say I had a preference. If anyone, Formby was my team because two of my brothers played for them as amateurs. One was a goalie and the other was a right-back. You'd only get 20–30 people watching. But you could hear everything that was being said. It made me realise from a very young age how important it was to not just communicate on the pitch but say the right things as well.'

Moran grew up in an era when Billy Liddell and Dave Hickson were the undisputed heroes of Merseyside football. This was a time when abilities, though, were not readily showcased to the masses. Supporters only knew of their genius if they watched live the matches in which they performed.

'Billy was the god and Dave wasn't a bad player too,' Moran says. 'I could see that from just a few games. But I have to be honest, I did not know much about the people that played football, because there was no TV and nowhere near as much coverage in the papers. I just knew how to play football.'

The path towards a professional career became clearer when Moran won a scholarship at Bootle Tech. He insists it was the most crucial moment of his life. 'It meant that I could play for Bootle Boys, and they were a bit better at the football than Crosby Boys.'

The decision to move his schooling just a few miles down the Mersey River displays Moran's determination to become a footballer. It is common for children now to make the opposite journey in search of a supposedly better education in a more salubrious area.

'I would have gone to the other end of the earth to become a footballer, but instead I just had to go to Bootle,' Moran says, lightly laughing away. 'School football was really competitive in my era. There was a real sense of pride in beating the districts around you. I got a fair amount of stick off friends in Crosby for playing for Bootle. So whenever we beat them, I made sure I gave it back to them.'

Everton and Liverpool scouts were always about, 'spying'. Aged 15, Moran was preparing to leave school and take up a job as a labourer when one of his performances for Bootle prompted a firm offer. 'A teacher took me to one side and told me that a man with a hat and a long coat wanted to speak to me. So I approached him and he said, "Everton want to sign you, son." I told him he was unlucky. "You're seven days late, mate. I signed for Liverpool a week ago."'

Moran was impressed by the Liverpool manager, Don Welsh.

'He was a big army bloke and into discipline. That suited me down to the ground. Within a few years, I did my national service, and I think that helped my football because it really hammered home how important it was to work hard and be focused. A lot of people my age didn't like national service, but I enjoyed it.

'I was also lucky that the year I joined Liverpool, the club bought training pitches [now Melwood] from SFX [Saint Francis Xavier School]. It was good because it meant I had somewhere to practise properly.'

Players would park their cars if they had them at Anfield and then travel to Melwood by minibus for daily sessions every day. That process only changed during pre-season, when the squad were tasked with running the three miles as part of their training.

'Some cheated, though,' Moran remembers sharply. 'I wasn't one of them, because I was afraid of getting caught, but you'd get people that would park a few streets away from Anfield, pick their car up and then park out of sight from Melwood. I suppose you could say it was funny, but it benefited nobody in the long run. There are no shortcuts to success in football.'

When Bill Shankly arrived as manager in 1959, attitudes towards training improved. In the seven years since Moran's debut, Liverpool had languished in the Second Division for five of them, with limited sign of progression.

'Bill saved the club,' Moran beams. 'After the first day of training under him, I knew he was going to be a success. He insisted on playing in the five-a-sides. His enthusiasm infected everybody else. He would never finish on the losing team. At first, the players thought it was funny, because he got so wound up. But after a while, we desperately wanted to beat him. These games ended up as Mexican stand-offs, because nobody liked losing. Shanks would go round kicking the young lads. He'd do anything to win. It rubbed off on everyone.'

Shankly surrounded himself with a staff that shared a similar mentality towards defeat. Paisley, Bennett, Fagan and eventually Moran himself would form the staff team. It instilled a simple culture of winning football matches.

'You saw Reuben – he was a goalkeeper and in his '50s. But he'd take part in the pre-season and never finish outside the top ten in the sprints. Joe was that way as well. I was always a bit porky, but I could shift as well, and Bill recognised that. He knew my attitude was right. He knew I wouldn't accept losing easily.'

A day before I met Moran, Liverpool were beaten 2–0 at home by West Bromwich Albion. He believes that one of Liverpool's current problems is acceptance. 'You hear some people argue that the team played well. If it was me – Christ, son, I'd be crying my eyes out. I know there are so many matches these days, you can't afford to get too down, but it doesn't seem to hurt some as much as it should.'

In 1966, after 379 games for Liverpool, Moran joined the coaching staff and continued playing in Fagan's reserve team for a further two years, helping the club's younger players. He admits that he was 'sometimes harsh' on his subjects.

'I enjoyed it. I was a tough player and reacted well to discipline. I was on the staff for a reason. Everybody was different, and I brought the discipline. Players need to be kept on their toes. In my first few years as a player, Liverpool were relegated. A few years before that, the club was top of the league and won the championship. If you settle and think everything's OK, you can get into trouble. Even during my playing days, I'd do extra training on the field near where I lived after getting home from Melwood. It used to drive the wife mad, but it was what I had to do. I'd try to be different from the fly-by-nights that came in and didn't do the extra work. When I was the coach, I asked for the same of the lads.

'It didn't bother me who they were; how much they'd won. If they weren't trying as they should be, I'd let them know. There was one player – I won't tell you his name – but he was an international defender and he was making dangerous passes out of defence. It was putting us under pressure. I told him in no uncertain terms that he needed to learn how to get rid at certain times. We wanted the team to keep the possession but not if it meant conceding a goal. I shouted at the lad for weeks until he stopped doing it.

'I'd bump into a lot of players that moved elsewhere and they'd come up to me and say, "Ronnie, you were a bastard to us. I wish I'd listened because I'm getting chased out of my [current] club for not working hard enough." There was a lot like that, even from Bill's day.'

Moran says his direct approach extended to matches. Afterwards, he would entertain opposing coaches and managers in the Bootroom in a beguiling manner, attempting to accrue information about their teams for future reference. But during games, Moran's voice was heard louder than anyone else in the dugout. If there was a problem, he would attempt to 'sort it'.

'You couldn't do it now, because there are so many cameras around Anfield,' he says. 'Every argument would be picked up on. But back then, there was a lot of activity between both benches. It's funny now when I hear people talk about "mind games", because we were the first to do that. There was nothing malicious about it, but you'd try to get whatever edge you could over the opposition. That stretched to the bench too. I remember arguing many times with Alex Ferguson when he became manager of United in the '80s. I like Fergie because he's a football man and there needs to be more of them. But when he first started at United, we'd be bickering all the way through games. It must have been the Celtic blood in us. We were two benches made up of Scots, Irish and Welshmen. There was bound to be a bit of conflict. Fergie gave as good as he got. All I can say is, I didn't teach him any swear words.'

Throughout this interview, Moran speaks about Ferguson with reverence. Despite the enduring enmity between Liverpool and the club that Ferguson represents, he continuously emphasises the idea that United have scaled the heights by following similar principles to those once held at Liverpool. When Ferguson decided to retire, he was in his third decade of success at Old Trafford. By the '80s, Liverpool had also been dominant for that period of time.

'You don't have to be a genius to realise that if you repeat something, you get better at it,' Moran continues. 'We'd tell the players to try to pass to the nearest red shirt in space. If that didn't happen, it was the nearest red shirt even if he was marked. And if that wasn't possible, look for something else. This wasn't rocket science. Over the years, the lads got to know the drill. And because there were five or six of us on the staff that thought the same way, when Bill retired it passed to Bob and the same from Bob to Joe and Joe to Kenny. Not much would change. It made it easier for the staff and easier for the players.'

There was a commonly held belief about the style of football Liverpool should try to execute. But there was no dogma. Liverpool could adapt accordingly when they needed to. That's why they were considered the most streetwise team in Europe.

'With football, it's all about getting the balance right between the team and the individual. You need to have a team where the individual can express himself. You need the clever ones, the ones with it up there. But you also need the ones that will do all the donkey work.'

Fundamentally, though, one character trait linked all of Liverpool's players.

'They mustn't like losing,' Moran reiterates. 'You can't have someone that comes up with excuses like injuries, either. I'd tell them to fuck off. After that, you had to love playing. I knew a few – even back then – that didn't give a bollocks what was going on. They didn't last long. You had to really care, like anything in life. If you care, you try harder and do better.'

Moran retired from Liverpool in 1998 following 46 consecutive years with the club. Until recently, he would spend Tuesdays and Fridays at Melwood, walking around the perimeter of the training pitch for his morning constitutional at the invitation of former player and assistant manager Sammy Lee. 'I'd never look at what was going on,' he says. 'It wouldn't be right, nosing into someone else's business.'

With that, it really dawns how privacy was arguably Liverpool's greatest strength. Moran has a knack of telling you something interesting but not the interesting thing you really want to know. At his age, the mind searches for an answer that sometimes it cannot offer. Yet I am also convinced that this is a tactic indoctrinated into him – not to reveal too much. At the end of our chat, when I've stopped making notes, he places his hand on my shoulder and says with an emphasis, 'I haven't let too much slip there, have I?'

Moran informs me that he has been offered book deals before, 'to tell stories about fights and girls'. But he did not feel comfortable complying with the idea. 'I bollocked it off after that was suggested,' he explains.

In keeping with Bootroom traditions, Moran never sought the limelight and never promoted himself above his colleagues or the team. It was the Liverpool way to deal with any problems internally. 'We were no different to Manchester United now,' he says. 'You see Fergie – he doesn't let many leaks out, does he?'

Like those that supposedly protected the Ark of the Covenant,

Moran will take many of Liverpool's most intimate secrets to his place of rest. But I leave him believing that perhaps it was Liverpool's simplicity that outsiders found most complex.

'Them lot there,' he says, pointing again at the photograph from the beginning of our meeting. 'They didn't want to lose. That's what football boils down to.'

BIBLIOGRAPHY

Aldridge, J., *Alright Aldo*, Sport Media, 2010

Barnes, J., *John Barnes: The Autobiography*, Headline, 1999

Barnes, T., Elias, R. and Walsh, P., *Cocky: The Rise and Fall of Curtis Warren, Britain's Biggest Drugs Baron*, Milo, 2001

Belchem, J. and Biggs, B., *Liverpool: City of Radicals*, Liverpool University Press, 2011

Canoville, P., *Black and Blue: How Racism, Drugs and Cancer Almost Destroyed Me*, Headline, 2008

Dalglish, K., *My Liverpool Home*, Hodder & Stoughton, 2010

Fowler, R., *Fowler: My Autobiography*, Macmillan, 2005

Frost, D. and North, P., *Militant Liverpool: A City on the Edge*, Liverpool University Press, 2013

Grobbelaar, B., *More than Somewhat*, HarperCollins, 1986

Hill, D., *Out of his Skin: The John Barnes Phenomenon*, WSC Books, 2001

Hughes, S., *Secret Diary of a Liverpool Scout*, Sport Media, 2009

Kuper, S., *The Football Men: Up Close with the Giants of the Modern Game*, Simon & Schuster, 2011

Mitten, A., *We're the Famous Man United*, Vision, 2006

Platt, M. and Fagan, A., *Joe Fagan: The Reluctant Champion*, Aurum, 2011

Reade, B., *43 Years With the Same Bird: A Liverpudlian Love Affair*, Macmillan, 2008

Souness, G., *The Management Years*, Andre Deutsch, 1999

Taaffe, P. and Mulhearn T., *Liverpool: A City that Dared to Fight*, Fortress, 1998

BIBLIOGRAPHY

Thompson, P., *Liverpool in the 1980s*, The History Press, 2006

Turner, A., *Rejoice! Rejoice!: Britain in the 1980s*, Aurum, 2010

Vinen, R., *Thatcher's Britain: The Politics and Social Upheaval of the 1980s*, Simon & Schuster, 2009

Wark, J., *Wark On: The Autobiography of John Wark*, Know the Score Books, 2009

ABOUT THE AUTHOR

Simon Hughes is a journalist and author. He writes for the *Daily Telegraph*, *Sunday Telegraph* and the *Independent*, as well as Liverpool Football Club's official magazine.

Red Machine won the Antonio Ghirelli prize for the Italian Soccer Foreign Book of the Year, 2014. His other titles include *Secret Diary of a Liverpool Scout* and *The Torres Story*.

Simon's latest book, *Men in White Suits: Liverpool in the 1990s, the Players' Stories* is the inside story behind the decline of Liverpool FC, as told by a host of influential characters associated with the team during this tumultuous period in the club's history.